THE OFFICIAL

ADOBE

PHOTOSHOP

HANDBOOK

THE OFFICIAL ADOBE PHOTOSHOP HANDBOOK

DAVID BIEDNY

BERT MONROY

BANTAM BOOKS

TORONTO · NEW YORK · LONDON · SYDNEY · AUCKLAND

THE OFFICIAL ADOBE PHOTOSHOP HANDBOOK
A Bantam Book/June 1991

Eye photo by J.M. Casey
Interior Design by Nancy Sugihara
This book was produced by Publishing Synthesis, Ltd., New York, N.Y.

*Throughout the book, tradenames and trademarks of some
companies and products have been used, and no such uses
are intended to convey endorsements of or other affiliations with the book.*

ISBN 0-553-34876-0

Published simultaneously in the United States and Canada

Bantam Books are published by Bantam Books, a division of Bantam Doubleday
Dell Publishing Group, Inc. Its trademark, consisting of the words "Bantam
Books" and the portrayal of a rooster, is Registered in U.S. Patent and Trademark
Office and in other countries. Marca Registrada, Bantam Books, 666 Fifth
Avenue, New York, New York 10103.

PRINTED IN THE UNITED STATES OF AMERICA

0 9 8 7 6 5 4

To Louis Biedny,

Zosia, Sean, and Erika

Foreword

Our goal with Adobe Photoshop was to create an image processing tool that allowed users with varied backgrounds and levels of experience to achieve results on the desktop that, until now, could be obtained only by professional, prepress technicians. In this, we have exceeded our expectations. Adobe Photoshop has succeeded in opening doors to artists, photographers, desktop publishers, and service bureaus, as well as to the advertising, multimedia, scientific, and medical professions.

Now we are reaping the rewards of having developed the program as we witness the extraordinary works being created by Adobe Photoshop users. They are using it in ways we never dreamed of, and are proving that the program's capabilities are extensive.

Therefore, we're extremely pleased to see many of these ideas and techniques for using the program consolidated in one book, *The Official Adobe Photoshop Handbook.*

In this book, David Biedny and Bert Monroy explore the myriad uses of Adobe Photoshop. They help the reader understand how to put some of the program's complex features into practical application. They also show the reader how to use some of the basic features more fully. As expert users of Adobe Photoshop, David and Bert offer knowledge, advice, tips, and techniques to help the beginning or advanced user take full advantage of the program.

If you do not yet own a copy of Adobe Photoshop, this book will give you an excellent idea of the program's power, and how you could use it in your work.

If you have already purchased Adobe Photoshop, this book will be an invaluable reference on how to use its features.

John Warnock, President and CEO, Adobe Systems

Preface

This book is not a replacement for the Adobe Photoshop reference manual.

That's right. The authors have come across droves of books that were minimanuals for the program they were written for—you didn't really need the original program documentation if you spent some time ingesting the whole book and taking notes. We suspect that someone is working on such a book for Photoshop.

Well, this isn't it.

While some of you might suspect that Adobe had some hand in this and tried to make sure that this book wouldn't end up being a Photoshop pirate's manual, the authors would like to go on record and say that Adobe had no direct control over the contents of this book. Instead, they cooperated with us in every possible fashion and gave us creative freedom and control over our work. In fact, even though this isn't the place for acknowledgments, we'd like to thank Steve Guttman at Adobe for being understanding and supportive of the charter of this book and the desires of the authors.

The manual that's included with Photoshop is one of the better pieces of documentation that we've ever seen for a Macintosh program: It describes, in extreme technical detail, every functional aspect of the program you do and don't want to know about. Our goal was to create a book that would share some of the techniques we've come up with over the years that we've been using in the program. We won't discuss every little detail of the program the way the Photoshop manual does, but we will show you some major features and capabilities that aren't anywhere in the program's documentation. We wanted to make a book that would complement the reference manual—while the manual tells you exactly what a feature is, we tell you what to do with it and how to use it with all of the other features of the program in order to end up with something that is more than just the sum of the parts. We take pains to make sure that you'll understand alpha channels, arguably the most potent and misunderstood of Photoshop's talents. We'll show you things about those alpha channels that the manual doesn't even hint at: how to create digital crossfades between images, selectively apply special-effects filters to areas of an image, make complex, layered composite images, make objects glow, create luscious textures, and much more.

Some of the features of the program are more useful than others for desktop publishers, while some of the filters are more appropriate for special animation effects than for corporate newsletter production. We'll look at many of the areas that Photoshop can be applied to: print production, fine arts, animation, and more.

Photoshop is a vast software universe, complete with silicon galaxies and black holes. Hang on for one wild rocket ride!

Book Organization

This book was written with the Photoshop artist in mind: While you can learn just about any program by methodically plowing through each and every command in sequence, in Photoshop, the tendency is to play with the features and discover how they work by making "happy accidents." Many of the techniques described in this book were discovered in this fashion, and we encourage you to do the same (as long as you keep backups of your master graphics files!). Use this book as a secondary reference manual, and as a Photoshop trick cookbook.

This book consists of 11 chapters and two appendices.

Chapter 1: Photoshop's main features, the speed issue, who will use Photoshop, system requirements.

Chapter 2: Step-by-step tutorials for novice Photoshop users. Basic aspects of file creation, using the standard selection and painting tools, processing controls, and production techniques.

Chapter 3: Setup and document management, opening, preferences, creating and saving files, display modes, graphic file formats.

Chapter 4: Tool overview, tool settings, choosing colors with the color picker and palette dialogs, creating text, using the paste controls.

Chapter 5: The Selection tools, masking, alpha channels.

Chapter 6: Image processing. Using filters, color correction and processing controls, dynamic effects.

Chapter 7: Advanced Techniques. Cookbook of special effects and advanced multichannel and alpha channel techniques.

Chapter 8: Output. Printing, halftones, integrating Photoshop with Illustrator, color separations.

Chapter 9: Creating animation with Photoshop. Video considerations and using Photoshop with Macromind Director.

Chapter 10: Color publishing and retouching case studies.

Chapter 11: Fine art case studies.

Appendix A: Graphics file formats.

Appendix B: Third party software and hardware peripherals for Photoshop.

While we have structured this book in a fashion that allows for random access, you might want to go through the book sequentially the first time around, especially if you're new to Photoshop. We would also suggest that you keep the Photoshop User manual handy for further reference.

Acknowledgments

First and foremost, we'd like to thank Tom Knoll and John Knoll for creating the ultimate Macintosh graphics program. Their vision, dedication, talent and personalities are all directly reflected in the amazing world known as Photoshop. If left to their own devices, it's quite possible that they may take over the world someday. Their families also deserve our thanks for letting them follow their intuitions. Thank you, gentlemen, for giving us the reason for writing this book. We can only hope that it does the program justice.

Special thanks and love to our ladies, Hellene Orenstein and Zosia Rostomian–Monroy, for their loving support, patience and presence. They deserve big hugs and kisses.

Our office associates were invaluable in their support and feedback: Thanks to Wippo "Ron" Meckler, a "Classic" Mac digital designer and artist and all around Jewish guy, for his wisdom, insights, and cool tricks. An NTSC–legal thanks to Christopher Cave, our favorite video maniac and harmonica player. A warm thanks to our assistants, Deborah Pashkoff, Karin Åberg and Sarah Getz. Special thanks to John F. Simon Jr. for access to his vast technical knowledge and stash of unsalted penguin butter.

Steve Guttman, Photoshop product manager with Adobe Systems, nurtured and backed us up all the way on this project. He made sure that we had the freedom to do what we needed (and wanted) to accomplish. This man performs admirably at a very difficult job. Special thanks to Russell Brown, Dan Campi, Scott Fredrickson and Wes Lem, the best guys we know at Adobe Systems. Additional special thanks to John Warnock and Charles Geshke for knowing a good program when they saw it.

Michael Roney is the best editor on the planet. His saintly patience, understanding and friendship made this project possible. He gave us breaks above and beyond the call of editorial duty. Whatta guy!

Thanks to Paul Beyer for his killer pages—we were lucky enough to get the best PostScript hacker in New York for our output. This guy knows too much. Thanks to Kevin O'Neill at Duggal for additional output assistance.

Special thanks to David "Sideburns" Schargel, Jon "Buhdda" Kahn, Chuck "Twinkle Fingers" Farnham, Ray "Stuffing . . . " Lau, Steve "LISPy" Mitchell, Joe "Deep Field" Pavone, Eric "More Cod," Lisa "TGIF" and UBU "cool cat" Reinfeld, Scott "A/D" Meyers, Tom "No Compressor" Kushwa, Jim "3D" Ludtke, David "Rendering . . . " Poole, David "In Control" Acosta, James "I'm not Stuart Gitlow" Erlich, Stuart "I'm not James Erlich" Gitlow, Stuart "4/4" Sharpe, Anthony "Don't you wish you were me" Albarello, Carol Ann "The Face" Kelly, Gary "Potato Farmer" Rottger, Ty "Steve Says . . . " Roberts, Bob "Dr. Macintosh" Levitus, Mary "So Cool" Abbajay, Roy "Alphas are Easy" Santiago and Michael "Verbum" Gosney. Warm thanks to Leo and Selma Orenstein, Oma Reinfeld, Irma Monroy, Diana and Richie Principe and Joey, Fay Biedny, Barry Biedny, Thea Grisgby, Mike Rinnart, Michael Hanes, Irving Berman, Lawrie Kaplan, Mike Miley, Carol Person, Tim Binkley, Lauretta Jones, the Wizards at ILM, Jackie Shapiro, Judy Van Wicklen, Paul Goodman, James M. Scrittorale, Rick Barry, Bill Whitford, Darryl and Benna Lovato, Marco Gonzalez, Marc and Devorah Canter, Holly Jo Klein and family, Jack Davis, Bren Anderson, Peter Mengaziol, Abner Dumoff, Gene Panhorst, Travis Rivers, Todd Rundgren, David Levine and Michelle Gray (great parties and Flowfazer™), Neil Cormia, Katrina Mistal, Huggy Bear, Terry Satterswaithe, Keith McGreggor, Jerry Harris, Mark and Tom, Liz Bond, Jahan Salehi, Paul Constantine, Eric Taub, Paul Hardwick, Bill "Emerson" Vellekoop, Rick Kutner, all of our students, and everyone else who helped along the way.

Contents

CHAPTER 2

The Tutorials 15

CHAPTER 3

Setup and Document Management 43

CHAPTER 4

Using the Tools 87

CHAPTER 6

Image Processing 155

CHAPTER 7

Advanced Photoshop Techniques 227

CHAPTER 10

Color Publishing and Retouching 307

CHAPTER 11

Fine Art 347

Adobe Photoshop 2.0: What's New

In June 1991 Adobe announced the first major upgrade to Photoshop—version 2.0. Some changes are minor in their effect, whereas others are major new features and functionality additions. This chapter was created while the 2.0 development was still underway, so we won't document the new features in extensive, step-by-step detail. If the descriptions of the new capabilities sound intriguing, we strongly recommend that you obtain the update. Contact Adobe Systems, Inc., concerning the pricing and availability of Photoshop 2.0.

How 2.0 Relates to Our Book

Many of the tutorials and exercises found in this book were written with Photoshop 1.0.X in mind. While none of the exercises have become obsolete, some will be easier to accomplish thanks to the new added functionality of Photoshop 2.0. What follows are some examples.

Alpha Channels

In all exercises utilizing alpha channels, the mechanism to overlay an alpha channel onto a color image is as follows: Make the desired alpha channel the currently visible channel by choosing it from the

Channels command in the Mode menu, and select the "Alpha to Selection" command in the Select menu (unless there was only one alpha channel in the document, in which case you could choose the "Alpha to Selection" command while viewing the full color, or RGB, image).

Photoshop 2.0 has been changed slightly: A document's alpha channels now appear in a hierarchical menu called "Load Channel," which has replaced the "Alpha to Selection" menu command (found in the Select menu). "Selection to Alpha" has been replaced with "Save Channel," which allows you to save a selection in any of the document's current alpha channels, or a new alpha channel. You no longer need to leave your current RGB, or grayscale display, to select alpha channels. You can also load any channel onto any channel (making interchannel editing and processes much more streamlined).

The Gradient Tool

In our Advanced Tips and Techniques (Chapter 7), we describe how to use the Gradient tool and Paste Controls to add color gradient shading to an image. In Photoshop 2.0 the gradient tool now has the familiar "Normal, Color Only, Lighten Only, and Darken Only"

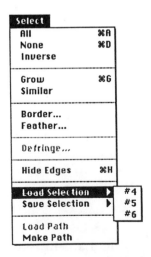

The Load and Save Channel commands in the Select menu

parameters found in some of Photoshop's other tools. In order to tint an image with a gradient, you'll now simply select the "Color Only" mode and apply the gradient tool to a selected area.

The Blur and Sharpen Tools

These have been reduced to one palette position. The parameters dialog (option-click or double click on tool) now has a button to select either blur or sharpen modes. The appropriate tool icon will be displayed in the tool palette.

New Overall Features

Interactive CMYK Changes

When working in CMYK display mode, you can now have a window showing a live RGB view, interactively displaying the changes made to individual CMYK channels. When using tools, the RGB display is updated immediately after you release the mouse (exactly like multiple windows in Photoshop 1.0.X) or after a filter or process has occurred.

Rasterization of EPS Files

Using either the new Place command or standard Open command, you can select EPS files and rasterize them into smooth, antialiased bitmaps. You can select to have an EPS file imported with its original size and aspect ratio or select new parameters. If you have an active Photoshop document, you can choose to Place the EPS image on top of the active document; the imported EPS image then comes into the document selected (exactly like Photoshop type). The antialiased edges of the placed image are retained as you move it around the background and deselect the image, making it part of the document. PostScript type imported as an EPS image is also antialiased.

Adobe recommends that you use files created with Illustrator, in either native or EPS format. Other EPS files, including those created in FreeHand, may not rasterize properly.

The rasterization feature will not work with EPS or Illustrator files that contain defined patterns, stroked text, or any kind of placed artwork.

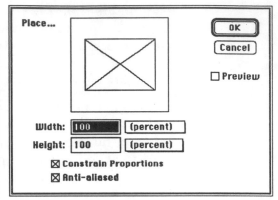

The EPS Import and Place dialogs

New Preference Controls

Preferences has been divided up into seven different hierarchical menus due to the large number of new controls. Most of the original parameters found in Photoshop 1.0.X's Preferences dialog are now located in the PS 2.0 General Preferences dialog. Among the new functions found in the modular preferences menus are:

- The ability to set the eyedropper to pick up either a single pixel's color (normal functionality found in Photoshop 1.0.X), or use two different pixel averaging techniques (3 x 3 or 5 x 5) to choose the average colors of an area. This is useful when choosing colors from a grainy area of a scanned image.

- Making the Mac beep when a processing function is done. The beep is very handy when you walk away from a lengthy filtering or color correction process and want to be notified audibly when processing is complete.

- The ability to have Photoshop 2.0 default to either the standard Apple color picker of the Photoshop color picker.

- Extensive controls for setting monitor gamma, screen color calibration, monitor temperature, and ink specifications. We strongly suggest that you refer to the new Photoshop documentation for complete discussions of these new calibration tools.

Other general notes regarding the new Preferences structure are:

- The Units and Clipboard controls have been separated into their own menus/dialogs. Each has a separate hierarchical menu under the Preferences command.

- Virtual memory is no longer linked to the location of the Photoshop preferences file. Photoshop can be set to use any available volume (one at a time) as the virtual memory disk, allowing you to keep a single Preferences file in one place with all of your filters and other plugins. It's very convenient.

- Color correction—Under Color Removal and Gray Component removal are both available, as well as visual curves for these parameters.

- A new Info window (selectable from the Window menu) interactively displays RGB and CMYK values for any tool's hotspot location, as well as the length and width of selections, angle and length of a line, and so on.

Pantone Color selection

Photoshop now has a Pantone color picker button in the standard Photoshop color picker window. You can choose a Pantone color visually or numerically. Any color selected in the standard color picker window is automatically matched to its nearest Pantone equivalent anytime you press the Pantone button.

Duotones

There is now an additional display mode for images. Photoshop 2.0 can create duotones as well as tritones and quadtones. You can set each plate's hue and gamma curve, giving precise control over individual color distribution.

Indexed Color Conversion

You now have much more control over converting images from RGB to indexed color mode.

- You can choose to have Photoshop use a specific custom target palette for it's RGB to Indexed conversion. You can either create the custom palette using the Edit Table command or use

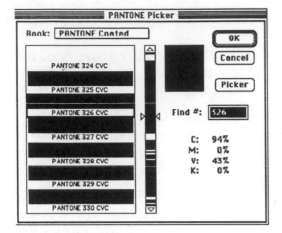

Pantone color picker dialog

palettes created in other graphics programs. Photoshop can dither an RGB image to take the best advantage of the custom palette.

- You can specify an exact number of colors to be in the target palette instead of just the overall bit depth.

Duotone settings dialog

```
┌─────────────────────────────────────────────┐
│  RGB Color to Indexed Color...      ┌───────┐ │
│  Resolution:                        │  OK   │ │
│                                     └───────┘ │
│     ○ 3 bits/pixel                  ┌───────┐ │
│     ○ 4 bits/pixel                  │Cancel │ │
│     ○ 5 bits/pixel                  └───────┘ │
│     ○ 6 bits/pixel                            │
│     ○ 7 bits/pixel                            │
│     ○ 8 bits/pixel                            │
│     ● Other: │ 73 │ colors                    │
│                                               │
│  Palette:           Dither:                   │
│     ○ Exact            ○ None                  │
│     ○ Uniform          ○ Pattern              │
│     ● Adaptive         ● Diffusion            │
│     ○ Custom...                               │
│     ○ Previous                                │
└─────────────────────────────────────────────┘
```

RGB to Indexed color dialog

- When converting batches of images, the last settings are remembered and can be applied by selecting Previous in the conversion dialog.

Improved Images Size and Canvas Size Dialogs

The Image Size and Canvas Size dialogs have been improved and are more user friendly. The option to automatically select screen and window sizes as the target size, however, have been removed. If you use these features regularly, you'll want to have Photoshop 1.0.X available.

New Stroke Command

This allows you to automatically create an outline on the edge of a selection. You can specify the width, opacity color, application mode (normal, color only, lighten only, or darken only), and the "location" of the stroke (outside of, inside of, or centered on the actual selection edge, very much like a programmable Border/Fringe which is now called "Border" in the Select menu).

Expanded Hue/Saturation Control

This control, found in the Adjust command in the Image menu, has been expanded.

- You can now have an idea of the effects of the Hue slider by watching the color swatch boxes at the top of the Hue/Saturation dialog. Normally, when using this control while in 24-bit display mode, there is no interactive screen updating.

- You can apply the hue, saturation, and brightness controls to the individual RGB and CMY component of an image by choosing the desired channel from the bottom of the Hue/Saturation dialog.

Enhanced Distort/Perspective Control

Now includes vertical as well as standard horizontal distortion.

CMYK Default Mode

When creating a new document, you can now choose to default to a CMYK display mode.

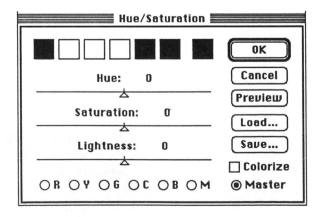

Hue/Saturation dialog

New Filters Menu

Filters now have their own menu and are separated into hierarchical menu categories—Stylize, Noise, Blur, Sharpen, Distort, and Other.

New Tool Features

Antialiased Button

The Fuzziness parameter in the magic wand and bucket, which is used to determine the antialiasing of the region edge, has been replaced with an "antialiased" button in the respective parameter dialogs. The optimum value for the antialiasing factor is automatically calculated and used when this control is on. You no longer have to experiment by plugging different numbers into the fuzziness field.

Tool Transparency Keys

You can continually set the transparency of any tool by using the numeric keys 1 through 0; 1 sets the tool to 10% opaque, 5 equals 50%, and so on.

New Pen Tool

The **Pen** tool is a new way to make precise irregular selections areas, which can be made into masks or friskets. It is similar to the pen tool in Adobe Illustrator.

- The Pen tool is used to create irregular, precise masks.

- When invoked, the Pen tool puts up its own menu. It's the only selection tool with its own menu.

- You can click and drag the Pen tool to create handles. As you create new handles, a spline is drawn from the last handle to the current one.

- You can change the angles of the lines coming into and out of a handle by pressing the command key. This temporarily turns the Pen into a cursor, which can be used to select and modify handles. By using the **Command-Control** keys, you can change just one of the incoming/outgoing line angles of each handle, leaving the others intact.

- You can add handles to an existing Pen path by pressing the **Command-Option** keys and moving the Pen right on top of any segment of the existing spline/line. The Pen cursor will display a [+], and when clicked on an existing path, a new handle appears.

- To close the path, bring the pen cursor back to the first handle. As you approach the handle, a small circle will appear to the right of the Pen cursor, indicating that you can close the path by clicking the mouse at that moment.

- You can save the path in an object format by choosing the **Save Path** command and giving the path a name. Be careful, because it's very easy to overwrite an existing path with a newly created path. (If you want to make a new path, make sure you choose **New...** from the Save Path hierarchical menu.) Paths are saved with specific documents.

- In order to make the finished Pen path a selection, choose the **Make Selection** command from the Path menu. You can also click the tool inside of the path to turn it into a selection. When you do this, the Path menu is replaced with the usual Photoshop menus.

- Multiple-saved Pen masks can be stacked into one mask layer by using the **Append Mask** command in the Path menu.

System 7.0 Features

32-bit Cleanliness

Photoshop 2.0 is fully "32-bit clean," which means that it takes advantage of 7.0's enhanced 32-bit memory addressing heavily RAM-populated Macs. When you are working with large color files under 7.0, you'll see improved screen redraw speeds and faster overall processing due to a lesser need for disk access.

Publish/Subscribe Support

There is now support of the Publish/Subscribe capabilities in System 7.0.

A Super Icon Feature

Probably the neatest new feature is the ability to save a miniature color version of the actual document image in the file icon on the desktop.

New Filters and Plugins

There is a wide variety of new plugin Acquisition modules and Filters, which are included with the Photoshop 2.0 package. Many are also available on public electronic networks.

HAM Export

HAM Export, an export module for Adobe Photoshop, writes images in Amiga HAM (Hold And Modify) format for Amiga computers. HAM Export supports RGB, indexed color, and grayscale images. Hold And Modify is an encoding scheme that packs almost the equivalent of 12 bits of image data into 6 bits/pixel. This format generally is not supported on the Macintosh. It is of use only to those who wish to transfer Macintosh images to an Amiga computer.

Adobe Photoshop can read Amiga HAM images, but it cannot write them without this plug-in.

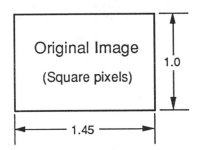

Officially, a HAM image can be one of two sizes: 320 x 200 and 320 x 400. Many paint and display programs can now deal with non-standard sized HAM images, so arbitrary sizes are allowed. These modes use nonsquare pixels, and the two standard sizes represent images with about a 1.45:1 aspect ratio. If it is important to you to maintain the proportions of your image, resize it 83%

vertical or 120% horizontal for noninterlaced images and 166% vertical or 60% horizontal for interlaced images. Since the Macintosh always uses square pixels, the image will appear distorted. The Amiga, however, will know how to display it correctly.

When you select this plugin, you will be presented with a standard file dialog prompting you for a name to save the file under. This plugin makes its best guess as to whether the image is supposed to be interlaced or not; but there is also a checkbox at the bottom that lets you manually override this setting.

ImageWriter Color

ImageWriter Color is a plugin export module for Photoshop that prints images in color on the ImageWriter II with a color ribbon.

Displace

Displace is a plug-in filter module for Photoshop that displaces one image with another.

Displace reads a color value from the displacement map and uses it to control how far the input image is displaced. A gray value of 128 is no displacement, 0 is maximum negative displacement, and 255 is maximum positive displacement.

When the displacement map is not the same size as the image being filtered (most of the time), you can adjust the map to fit the image. It can be resized, or it can be tiled (filled with a pattern).

The scale controls are used to control the magnitude of the displacement. When the scale factors are at 100%, the maximum

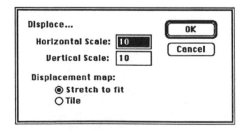

Displace filter dialog

displacement is 128 pixels (remember that middle gray is zero displacement).

What is a displacement map? It's any legal Photoshop file, except a bitmap. If the map has more than one channel, horizontal displacement will be read from the first channel, and vertical displacement will be read from the second channel. If a one channel map is used, all of the displacement will be along a diagonal defined by the horizontal and vertical scale ratio. On the other hand, if a two channel map is used, the displacement can be completely arbitrary, and any pixel can point to any other. For example, say you want to make an image sag in the middle, as if it was printed on a cloth that was held by the corners. First, make a new grayscale image, 256 pixels wide by about 100 high (this dimension is not important, but small maps are better than big ones for memory reasons). Set the foreground color to black and the background color to white. Make a linear graduated fill from left to right. Using the Arbitrary map, filter the image with a curve that looks somewhat like this:

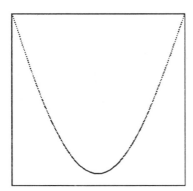

This is the shape of the distortion you're going to use. Save this image to disk. Open the image you wish to distort, and call up the displace filter. Set the horizontal scale to 0 and the vertical scale to about 50%. Set the method to "stretch to fit". When you hit "OK," you will be presented with a standard file dialog. Select a displacement map, then select the map you just made. When the filter finishes, the image will be distorted in a parabolic shape.

Displace requires enough memory to hold both the entire image to be filtered and the displacement map. If you try to filter an image bigger than the memory of your computer, or use a displacement map that is too big, Displace will fail with a "not enough memory" message.

Most of the example displacement maps require that the horizontal and vertical scale be set to 20% and the "tile" method be used for the effect to work properly. How do they work? Most of these maps are divided into regions that are all displaced from the same pixel, giving them a uniform color for that cell.

This is not an easy thing to understand. Experiment a little and perhaps you will gain insight into how it works. It is worth learning, because this filter can do amazing things.

Crystalize

Crystalize is a plugin filter that breaks up an image into a number of randomly shaped polygonal areas, each filled with solid color sampled from the image inside the area. You will be presented with a dialog where you can set the average cell size.

Pointelize

Pointelize creates an effect similar to a pointillist painting. It breaks an image up into a great number of randomly placed dots, with background color in the "canvas" area between them. You will be presented with a dialog where you can set the average dot size.

Radial Blur

Radial Blur simulates motion blur from a zooming or rotating camera.

The Zoom method blurs along the radial lines, simulating the effect of leaving a camera shutter open while zooming in on an

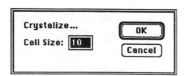

Crystalize filter dialog

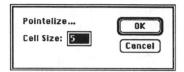

Pointelize filter dialog

image. This can be used to simulate the effect of an object moving toward or away from the camera. The Spin method blurs along concentric circular lines, simulating the effect of a camera rotating along the lens axis while the shutter is open. This can be used to make a stationary wheel appear to be spinning, for example. For this method, the amount indicates the number of degrees to rotate the image.

The Blur Center control lets you select the center of the blur effect. It's location within the bounding box of the selected area will be proportionately the same as in the control.

This filter is very computer intensive and does not execute quickly. Because of this, there is a Quality control that allows you to balance quality with execution speed. The draft mode is the fastest, but produces somewhat grainy results. The good and best settings will produce smoother results and differ in how very large blurs are

Radial Blur filter dialog

handled far from the center; so the differences only will be noticeable with large blurs on big areas. Since this effect is selection size independent, it is best to work with downsampled images in draft mode, undoing the effect until you are satisfied with the parameters, and then running the filter on the full-res version with a higher quality setting.

Polar Coordinates

Polar coordinates is a filter for converting images from rectangular to polar coordinates and vice versa.

This filter can be used to distort the effects of other filters in interesting ways. For example, if you convert an image from polar to rectangular coordinates, then filter the image with a mosaic filter, and then convert back from rectangular to polar, the mosaic effect is warped in a polar coordinate system.

You can also use this filter to create cylinder anamorphoses, a type of art that was popular in the 18th century. This art, created with the polar to rectangular transform, appears distorted and difficult to recognize unless viewed in the reflection of a mirrored cylinder.

Pict Resource

Pict Resource is a plugin acquisition module for reading Pict resources from a file. It can be used to read frames from a PICS file. This plugin requires 32-bit QuickDraw.

PCX Read/Write

This plugin gives Photoshop the ability to read and write PCX files. PCX is a common file format on IBM computers, established by Zsoft's PC Paintbrush software. PCX format supports up to 8 bits/pixel indexed color.

1

Welcome to Photoshop

If you have purchased this book, you are either (a) the proud new owner of a copy of Adobe Photoshop or (b) trying to find out more about the program before resolving the burning issue of whether to buy it or not. Either way, you'll soon find out that there has never been anything quite like Photoshop, at least, not anything that worked on any computer that normal mortals were likely to have access to or own. Photoshop brings the capabilities normally found in high-end paintbox systems down to the level of the Macintosh, with few compromises or strings attached. As the coauthors of this book, we can tell you this: We have had access to, experience with, and, to a large extent, design input into every major—and not so major—graphics program to run on the Apple Macintosh. We have never seen anything like Photoshop on the Macintosh. It will change the way you approach Macintosh graphics now and in the future.

After seven years, the Macintosh has become the standard model for the "graphics computer." Other manufacturers have begun to use the Macintosh as a model for designing other graphics-based machines, due in large part to the elegant interface that has always been a main characteristic of the "feel" of the Macintosh. Unlike other types of microcomputers, the Macintosh is always in graphics display mode (IBM machines have various graphics modes: Because

1

these machines are primarily character-based, the different graphics modes are used in order to have different resolutions/numbers of onscreen colors). This graphics heritage, coupled with the advent of PostScript in early 1985, helped create the world of desktop publishing, indisputably the saving grace of the Macintosh (many Macintosh industry experts agree that the combination of Adobe PostScript, the Apple LaserWriter, and Aldus PageMaker helped saved the Macintosh from an early Lisa-style death).

Over the last seven years, a variety of graphics programs have been developed for the Mac, from basic black-and-white classics like MacPaint (which was actually created to demonstrate and sell the graphics ability of the Macintosh when no other software existed for the machine), to advanced color graphics programs in both the bitmapped arena (PixelPaint, Studio/8, etc.) and the object world (non-PostScript programs such as MacDraw, PostScript programs such as Adobe Illustrator, FreeHand, etc.). The Macintosh II, with its color capabilities and faster processing times, has allowed the Mac graphics software market to grow at a substantial pace.

As desktop publishing became more of a mainstream application market, an interesting (and predictable) phenomenon began to occur: The high-end publishing world, while finding the new desktop-based tools to be affordable alternatives to the pricey hardware they were accustomed to using, ran into the inherent limitations of desktop technology. The color prepress world looked at this new wave of tools with restrained interest, for they were aware of the technical limitations of PostScript in addressing the issues of professional color calibration and reproduction, as well as the economic factors that limited the feasibility of these new tools replacing time-tested systems such as the Scitex and Crosfield color prepress systems.

Photoshop belongs to a new generation of Macintosh graphics programs—sophistication on a level previously associated with the high-end computer graphics world. The tools found in Photoshop have their counterparts in systems such as the Scitex (a high-end color publishing and separation system, used to produce those glossy four-color weekly news magazines), TIPS and RIO (PC-based color paintbox packages that are written around the TrueVision NuVista 32–bit graphics card), and other professional paintbox environments, such as the Quantel PaintBox and Images II systems. Photoshop has the ability to communicate with the high-end prepress world—Pixar and Scitex CT formats are directly supported as an output option in Photoshop. Macintosh screen resolution, once a limiting factor in a Mac-based paint program, is no longer a restraint: Photoshop has the ability to work in virtually any resolution the user desires.

> **NOTE:** Many of the painting tools found in Photoshop differ substantially from painting tools found in other Macintosh graphics software.

In many ways, Photoshop doesn't have the same "feel" as other Macintosh color bitmapped programs: Many of the features found in Photoshop have their roots in high-end paintbox systems, such as the Quantel PaintBox and Images II graphics system. If you're used to using color bitmapped programs such as PixelPaint and Studio/8, you'll find that some of Photoshop's methodologies will take some getting used to—the way you use standard selection tools such as the Lasso and Marquee is distinctly different from anything you're likely to be familiar with from other color paint programs. Photoshop is a combination of raw power and a streamlined, but complete, Macintosh interface. This approach lends to the power of the program; you could compare it to a car with either a manual or automatic transmission—the same engine performs more efficiently with a manual transmission, while the automatic sacrifices performance for ease of use. The payoff, of course, is in the substantial leap of power you'll get when using Photoshop. This is *not* just another color paint program.

The Speed Issue

There's an old computer adage many of you might be familiar with: "You can never have enough processing speed or RAM." Macintosh owners are especially sensitive to the realities of the limitations of the current generation of hardware—ask any Macintosh owner if they think their computer is fast enough, and listen to their response. You may as well be asking them if they think they have too much money in their bank accounts.

As you work with Photoshop and begin to explore some of its more powerful capabilities, you will find that some of the program's operations aren't as fast as you might like them to be: If you load a 3 x 5–inch,

300–DPI color scan into your trusty 4–megabyte Macintosh II, and you choose to color separate the image by switching into CMYK display mode, you might find yourself tapping your fingers on your desktop (the real one, that is) and grumbling about "wanting it done before sometime tomorrow." Some of the filters take time (and in some cases, with large files, considerable time) to complete their processing, some of the dynamic effects (such as free rotate and distort) may seem to take ages to do their thing, and in general you might question just how slow Photoshop appears to be. Before you do that, consider the realities of your circumstance: You are using a program that truly pushes the envelope of the Mac's graphic power right to the edge. The Macintosh is, after all, a microcomputer, and considering that Photoshop does things that many people thought would never be possible on a Macintosh, the truth is that it's pretty fast.

Consider this: As you try out Photoshop's airbrush tool on a Macintosh II with an 8–bit (256–color) display, look carefully at the paint flow deposited by the tool. The airbrush is creating a smooth, transparent flow of paint with a full 24 bits of data (16.7 million colors available), and converting it into an 8–bit (256–color) optimized image in real time—as you use the tool. This is no easy task, both from a programming point of view and in terms of the inherent capabilities of the Macintosh (considering that, until recently, no Macintosh-based graphics program has ever been able to deliver a true, paintbox-like color airbrush tool as nice and smooth as the one found in Photoshop). The first time you use the paintbrush tool, you might be annoyed to find that Photoshop has some trouble keeping up with brisk, sweeping mouse motions; this lag is also noticeable in some of the other painting tools. This is the kind of thing that a magazine reviewer might decide to single out and criticize in a review of the product; and while it's a fact, we would like to point out that most artists and illustrators don't spend a major amount of time engaged in seeing how fast they can move a brush tool across a screen (although artists who base their styles on sweeping brush strokes might take exception to this statement). In our opinion, the power of the tools and the beautiful results they yield more than make up for the trade-off of absolute response speed.

▼ **Tip:** When using the painting tools, such as the airbrush, paintbrush, and stamp tools, experiment with moving the mouse in a slower, more stable, and controlled manner than you would typically utilize for a normal 8–bit color painting program.

Main Features

Photoshop is capable of feats that put it into a class all its own:

Variable Resolution

Photoshop can import graphics files scanned or created at virtually any resolution; unlike most Macintosh color bitmapped programs, which are limited to the resolution of the standard Macintosh screen (72 DPI), Photoshop's tools work at all resolutions. Photoshop can also handle any resolution output format, ensuring compatibility with output devices available today and into the future.

Variety of File Formats

Photoshop can open and save more graphics formats that any other Macintosh graphics package. Besides allowing you to work with almost all of the graphics formats found in the Macintosh world, Photoshop also supports formats found in the Amiga, IBM PC, and higher-end environments. The ability to support Scitex and Targa formats opens a plethora of possibilities in terms of output options and integration with high-end prepress systems. In fact, Photoshop can handle more formats than any other microcomputer-based graphics program we've seen or used. Many of the limitations of the clipboard and scrapbook in converting different bitmapped graphic-image file formats have been resolved in Photoshop.

Masks and Layers

One of the major limitations of Mac bitmapped programs is that there has been no way to properly maintain layers, or levels, normally associated with illustration programs and object-oriented design software. The multichannel aspects of Photoshop allow you to have up to 16 layers (each layer can contain 8 bits of information). Normally, when working with a 24-bit color image (which takes up three of the 16 channels for the red, green, and blue components which make up the 24-bit image), you can have up to 13 alpha channels saved along with the image file (when saved in Photoshop format). Each alpha channel contains an 8-bit image mask, which can be created from any color or object in the RGB 24-bit color image.

The term "alpha channel" has its roots in the world of video: the next time that you watch television, take note (especially during commercials) of graphics or titles which appear to be suspended over live video, either as opaque images or letting some of the live video show through. This is accomplished with video alpha channels, live masks which are implemented in the hardware of the special effects devices used in video production. The alpha channels in Photoshop are essentially the same, except that they're made to work with static, still images.

> NOTE: While working with 24-bit color images, the alpha channels contain 8 bits of information. Alpha channels aren't color; they only contain grayscale information. When you copy something into the alpha channel, Photoshop automatically strips color/hue information from the pasted image, leaving a precise anti-aliased mask that will perfectly match the color image.

By using the alpha channels, you can create a bitmapped image with specific portions of the image—colors or objects in any combination—saved as separate layers. You can process any of the alpha channels independently, with all of the program's tools and filters.

▼ **Tip:** Alpha channels aren't free: they occupy memory. In a 24-bit color image, each alpha channel is 1/3 of the size of the overall color file size. The more channels you make in a file, the bigger the file gets for disk storage.

Remapping to Any Color Palette (RGB-to-Indexed Color Conversion)

One of the biggest challenges facing Macintosh multimedia artists and animators is getting the most out of the limitation of 256 colors on the screen at any one time. Photoshop can convert a 24-bit color scan into a 256-color image with the highest possible onscreen quality. It can make optimum use of the standard Mac II system palette, or create a custom palette based on the colors it finds in the 24-bit color file. Users can choose from multiple dithering schemes, or choose to convert to less than 256 colors (if you want the best possible quality in displaying a color image on a 4-bit, 16-color Mac graphics cards, Photoshop can do it).

No Screen Redraw

A unique feature of Photoshop is that you usually can open menus and access the program's tools while the screen is being redrawn without having to wait for the redraw to finish. When working with large, high-resolution images, this time saving can be quite substantial. We have never seen another Macintosh graphics program with this capability, and we suspect that you'll quickly grow used to it and wonder why other Macintosh programs don't work in a similar fashion.

DirectSetEntries on Real-Time Color Controllers

Many of the currently available 24-bit color display boards (such as those in the RasterOps and SuperMac lines) offer hardware support for DirectSetEntries; this allows color and brightness changes to occur in real time. Photoshop's color correction and processing controls work in real time with these display boards, allowing you to see changes on the screen interactively with the controls. As you drag a color correction slider, the screen is updated instantly.

Support for Multiple Open Documents

Photoshop is one of the first high-resolution Macintosh graphics programs to support multiple open documents. Full editing functions (cut, copy, and paste) are supported between documents. Undo is specific to each document; if you make a change in an image file—access another image file and manipulate it—chances are that you will be able to undo the last action applied to the first file. This doesn't always work (it depends on the size of the images in question, as well as the available amount of RAM); but when it does, it's wonderful.

Color QuickDraw Anywhere

To our knowledge, Photoshop is the *first* color Macintosh program capable of handling full 24-bit color images on a black-and-white Macintosh (the Macintosh Plus and SE). Even though the ROMs of these machines do not include color QuickDraw, you can work with color files and save your work, which can then be viewed on a color Mac at a later time. If you have a limited number of color Macintoshes in a production environment, and you need to process large numbers of color scans (for example, cropping 300 color scans to a predetermined size), Photoshop and a Mac Plus with two to four megabytes of RAM can be used instead of a costly Macintosh II. In fact, this capability extends to processing 24-bit color files—Photoshop is not reliant upon 32-bit QuickDraw for any of its functions, including working with 24-bit images. Imagine opening a 24-bit color file on a Mac SE, adjusting the brightness, and saving the changes back to the 24-bit file, without 32-bit QuickDraw anywhere nearby. Quite a trick!

Virtual Memory

Photoshop doesn't rely on gobs of RAM memory in order to work with large images—by using a hard disk to "emulate" RAM memory, you can manipulate images much larger than the available RAM in your computer.

▼ **Tip:** Photoshop likes hard-disk space. Lots of it. Make sure that you have at least a few megabytes of free space on your hard disk. The more space you can spare, the better.

This feature is built into Apple's System 7.0; however, Photoshop gives you these capabilities today, without System 7.0. If for some reason you decide not to upgrade to System 7.0, you'll still have virtual memory capabilities when using Photoshop.

Virtual 24-Bit Working Environment

When you are working in Photoshop's native RGB mode, everything you do—a stroke with the paintbrush, a spray of the airbrush—is calculated in 24-bit "space." Even if you are running the program on an 8-bit Mac II, all operations and output are 24-bit. The first time you use the paintbrush, airbrush, or line tool, you'll be amazed at the smoothness of the edges of the strokes. Anti-aliasing, a technique used to enhance the "softness" of hard edges, is built into all of Photoshop's tools (with the exception of the Pencil tool).

Anti-Aliased Typefaces

When creating text in Photoshop, you can specify that the type appear on the screen with anti-aliasing. Anti-aliasing is a process by which harsh edges can be made to appear very smooth on the screen by the use of lighter and darker shades of an object's color. Essentially, the edges of an object are blended with the background to simulate a smooth transition between the foreground and background objects. Photoshop supports anti-aliasing through two methods:

1. Any screen face with larger sizes installed in the system can be drawn on the screen with anti-aliased edges; for example, if you have a screen face in sizes 12, 24, and 48 fonts installed in your system, you can create smooth 12- and 24-point sizes on the screen. Photoshop accomplishes this by using the larger installed sizes to create optimized versions of the smaller faces. This is a trick long employed by ImageWriter owners to maximize that printer's output quality.

2. If you are using ATM (Adobe Type Manager), you can create smooth type of any size and color from the Adobe printer fonts in your system folder. ATM is a program that allows you to have smooth, optimized screen representations of any Adobe typeface in most programs; when combined with Photoshop, these faces are fully anti-aliased. Photoshop is the first Macintosh program that offers this powerful method for creating beautiful onscreen type.

Sophisticated Color Correction Control

Photoshop gives you absolute control over every aspect of an image—not only will you have the standard brightness and contrast controls found in grayscale programs such as Letraset's ImageStudio and Silicon Beach's Digital Darkroom, but you'll also have control over each individual color component in the image in ways you've always wanted (and, in some ways, never imagined). All color correction and enhancements features can be applied to entire images or to specific portions of an image.

Color Separations

Photoshop can fully color-separate a color image, breaking it down into its four primary components—cyan, magenta, yellow, and black layers—which a printer uses to create four-color process printing plates. While most programs with this capability separate the file only at printing time, Photoshop does the separation in software, and displays the separated layers *onscreen.* This allows you to preview the effects of the separation process and manipulate the individual plates before sending them to the output device. Using the Desktop Color Separation format, you can export images to Adobe Illustrator or Quark Xpress to be separated on pages with full text and illustration art in place.

Wide Variety of Image-Processing Features

The image manipulation and enhancement features found in Photoshop stand alone in the Macintosh world—the variety of filters, image processing tools, and controls over every aspect of an image can be almost overwhelming. Besides the built-in filters, Photoshop accepts "drop-in" filter modules which, when placed in the same folder as the program, appear in the standard filter menu. Many Image controls—such as the color correction, brightness and contrast, posterization, and hue/saturation—work in "real time" on 8 and 24–bit displays: As you change the settings, the screen display responds by displaying the changes instantaneously.

Compatibility with Object-Oriented Illustration Programs

When you open an EPS or object-oriented PICT file, Photoshop extracts the screen representation and delivers it as a 72–DPI bitmapped image. You can use the resample feature in Photoshop to bump up the resolution with a reasonable degree of success.

Who Will Use Photoshop?

The audience for Photoshop is a large one, indeed.

- Desktop Publishing and Corporate Communications: Desktop publishers will find Photoshop to be an invaluable production tool for enhancing and manipulating grayscale scanned images.

When you decide that you want to enter the world of color printing, you won't need a separate program to handle color.

- Service Bureaus: file conversion capabilities. Besides output, these establishments will find themselves offering services far beyond their typesetting roots. One major new service is color separations, providing the film for engravers. This has always been a costly process; a service bureau can now handle it at a fraction of the traditional cost.

- Advertising: The first major use of Photoshop in this industry is the creation of comps. This is currently handled by hand at an enormous cost in time, money, and legibility. For better results, high-end systems are employed at an even higher cost. Photoshop will put that capability in the hands of the art director and the board artist. The production department will have more control over the final production phases, thus reducing costly and timely redos.

- Multimedia and Animation: The labor-intensive process of creating visuals for animation is greatly simplified. Some of the special-effects filters, when animated, are simply mind-boggling. The ATM-based anti-aliased text is unequalled for smooth onscreen type for use in animated presentations.

- Fine Arts: The vast array of tools and special effects will open the door to unseen corridors of the imagination. The filters alone provide endless hours of experimentation to create striking and exotic visual fantasies. Photographs can be manipulated to create special effects never before possible with a microcomputer. Artists who complain of the digital look of computer imagery from paint programs can now create images of superb clarity and complexity.

- Scientific and Medical applications: Many of the image processing features in Photoshop (such as the convolution, high-pass and sharpening filters, multichannel mathematics, and the ability to read raw multiple-channel data files from sources such as satellite data) will appeal to professionals working in many scientific fields.

System Requirements

To properly use Photoshop, you'll want to have a minimum configuration with

- Macintosh II/IIX/IICX/IICI.

- At least 2 megabytes of RAM; 4–8 megabytes are optimum.

- 8–bit video display; 24–bit display board for maximum onscreen previewing accuracy.

- At least 2–10 megabytes of free hard-disk space; more if you plan on processing large, high-resolution (150+ DPI) color scans or multiple scans simultaneously.

▼ **Tip:** Photoshop will work perfectly well on a black and white Macintosh Plus or SE (you'll want at least 2 to 4 megabytes of RAM and as much disk space as you can spare). Under these circumstances, Photoshop substitutes onscreen color with dithered black and white patterns. All of the program's functions work on these machines, including the color effects and controls.

A primary consideration when using Photoshop is hard-disk space and speed: Because of the virtual memory capability, Photoshop is constantly writing to and reading from the disk drive. Faster hard disks (such as drives based on the CDC Wren/Imprimis series of mechanisms) will generally improve the overall speed of the program.

▼ **Tip:** The location of the Photoshop Preferences file determines which drive will be used as the "virtual" drive. Make sure the Preferences file is on your largest, fastest drive.

We've found that a removable hard-disk system (such as a Syquest-based or Bernoulli cartridge drive) is a must for archiving large numbers of scanned images. Actually, considering that a 3 x 5–inch 300–DPI scan is more than a few megabytes in size, you might find that a removable cartridge drive is a necessity, not a luxury. The Syquest technology has gained a good deal of support in the Macintosh world: A number of third-party companies sell Syquest-based cartridge drives. Each company buys the drive mechanisms directly from Syquest, so the drives are all essentially made from the same guts, the only differences being the power supplies and supporting software. In most cases, a Syquest drive formatted on one drive can be read and written to on any other Syquest drive, regardless of the brand name on the drive. The trick is in the formatting software: While this is one of the great debates of the Macintosh world, we'd like to say that we've found the MicroTech and PLI (Peripheral Land Inc.) formatter software the most preferable. Unfortunately, when you buy a drive, you get the formatting software from the vendor, so you end up with whatever they give you. Companies such as MicroTech and PLI don't sell their formatter software separately, so you might want to consider getting their Syquest drives. We have worked with drives from both companies and have been quite pleased with their products.

We've also had a great deal of success in using some of the currently available read-write magneto-optical cartridge technology. A number of third-party suppliers are packaging mechanisms manufactured by Sony, Ricoh, and Canon. We've had direct experience with the Sony-based drives, and we are very happy with their speed and reliability. The Sony cartridges are formatted in a standard fashion from drive to drive, which allows them to be read from and written to by any brand drive using the the Sony drive mechanism. While the seek and transfer rates of this technology are not up to par with many standard fixed hard disks, the sheer amount of storage (600+ megabytes) and convenience more than make up for the reduced speed performance.

RAM memory, while not quite as crucial as hard-disk space, is still quite influential on the speed performance of the program. While we have had complete success manipulating large (5+ megabytes) image files on a 4-megabyte Macintosh II, we strongly recommend using as much RAM as you can afford. If you try running Photoshop on a one-megabyte Mac, you'll find that many of the tools don't work, and that the program will invariably run out of memory and force you to quit. If there was ever a program to motivate you to get more memory for your Mac, Photoshop is it.

Obviously, to take full advantage of the 24–bit functions of Photoshop, a 24–bit display card is the most preferable option for driving your monitor. In fact, there is very little difference in speed when using the program on 8– or 24–bit display systems. The powerful screen dithering capabilities of the program make it completely usable on a standard 8-bit graphics display; we used the program for over a year in this mode and were quite happy with the results. If you plan on using Photoshop for crucially accurate color-photo retouching, you'll want a 24-bit display card. Photoshop also works well with 8-bit grayscale display systems.

2

The Tutorials

In this chapter we'll take you through some very straightforward and basic practice sessions; you'll learn how to use some of the tools and features of the program by creating some basic graphics from scratch (it's unfortunate that we couldn't include some scanned images with this book for you to start working with, which is why we're having you start by creating some images entirely from scratch with the program's tools). For advanced examples utilizing scanned images, see chapters 10 and 11.

Tutorial 1—The Basics

To give you a basic understanding of the way the paintbrush and type tools operate, this tutorial will allow you to create a simple logo.

- Double-click on the Photoshop program icon to launch it.

NOTE: In any Photoshop working session, including this one, you're going to need plenty of free disk space for the program's graphic operations. Most sessions will require at least 5 MB *plus* three times the expected file size of your document. For the following exercises, 5 MB should be sufficient.

15

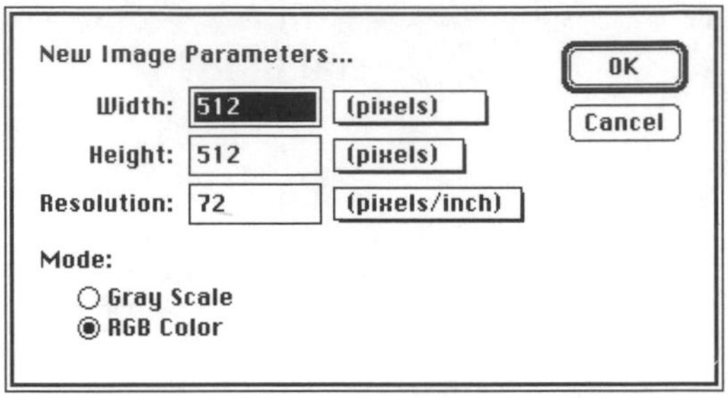

```
New Image Parameters...
    Width:  512        (pixels)          ┌─── OK ───┐
   Height:  512        (pixels)          │  Cancel  │
Resolution:  72        (pixels/inch)
Mode:
      ○ Gray Scale
      ◉ RGB Color
```

Figure 2–1   New Image Parameters dialog

- The program will open up displaying the menu. Under the File menu, select New.

Before a new image window opens, the New Image Parameters dialog appears (Figure 2–1). This dialog lets you determine the width and height of the image window in various units of measurement, including the default setting of pixels (the normal default is 512 x 512 pixels). You also specify the Resolution of the image; we'll leave it at 72 DPI (Dots-Per-Inch), which is the default setting. Finally, you can select a display mode: Gray Scale (which will give you 256 gray levels) or RGB (red, green, and blue; this is the normal Photoshop working mode, which gives you access to 24–bit graphics—16.8 million colors).

- For this tutorial, you will leave the settings at 512 x 512, RGB Color. Click OK.

- A blank window opens.

- At the bottom of the tool box there are three icons.

These icons control the way the image window is displayed on the screen. The first choice on the left is the standard stacked window with scroll bars visible. The middle choice is full screen with menu. The third choice is full screen with the menu hidden.

- Choose the middle icon for full screen with menu.
- Choose the magnifying glass tool and click once in the center of the white work area to zoom in. This will give you a clearer view of your work.
- Select the Type tool (by clicking once on the toolbox tool with the T).
- Bringing the cursor over to the work window, you will notice that it changes to the text entry I-beam cursor.
- Click once within the work window.

The Text Tool window will appear (Figure 2–2).

The top field displays the currently selected font. Click on this field and hold the mouse button down; the list of available fonts will be displayed. For the cleanest-looking type, it is necessary to have ATM (Adobe Type Manager) installed on your machine and to select Adobe fonts. If this is not the case, the type will probably have jaggies or stair-stepping.

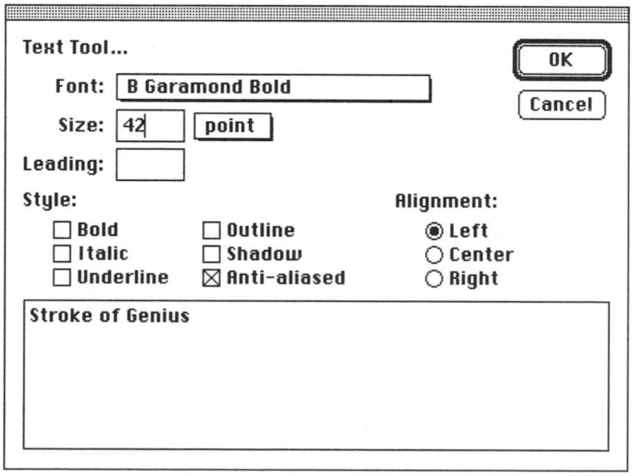

Text Tool...

Font: `B Garamond Bold`   [OK]   [Cancel]

Size: `42` [point]

Leading: [ ]

Style:
☐ Bold ☐ Outline
☐ Italic ☐ Shadow
☐ Underline ☒ Anti-aliased

Alignment:
◉ Left
○ Center
○ Right

Stroke of Genius

Figure 2–2   Text Tool window

- For this exercise, select Garamond Bold. If you do not have Garamond, substitute some other Adobe font.

- The next entry field is for entering the point size. Enter 42.

- Leading is the next choice; leave it blank—you are entering only one line of text. Leading determines the space between lines of text.

- Next, you have the Style selections. Choose anti-aliased. This will give the letters a smooth edge.

- Text alignment will remain at the default, which is left.

- Click in the text entry box (lowest part of text dialog) and notice the flashing cursor.

- Type in Stroke of Genius. Click OK.

- The type is displayed on the screen. If you want to reposition the text, placing the cursor over the text will convert the cursor to an arrow. With the arrow click and drag the mouse to move the text to a more desirable position.

- Click elsewhere on the window and the type will be deselected.

- With the type tool, click just below the Stroke of Genius.

- The Text Tool window appears again. This time use a Garamond Bold Italic, 24 points and anti-aliased.

- In the entry box, delete Stroke of Genius, then type Art Supplies (Figure 2–3). Click OK.

- Position the new text so that it is off-center to the right, as in the illustration at the end of this tutorial. Deselect.

- At the bottom of the tool box, you will find a small black box within a white square.

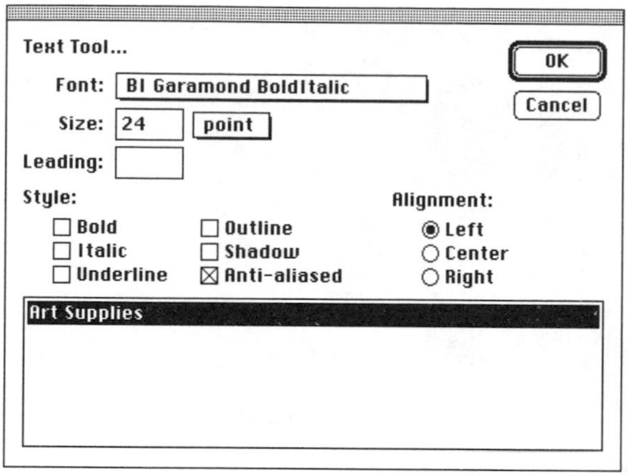

Figure 2–3   Text Tool window

This box represents the Foreground color. This is the color that will be used when you use any of the tools. The default for the foreground is black. Since you did not change this, the type was black. Had you specified a different color (by clicking on the box), the type would have been that color.

The white box surrounding the foreground color represents the background color. The default is white. This color is used both as the background, when using the eraser tool, and as an ending color when creating color blends, or gradients.

- Now you will change the foreground color to add a graphic touch to the logo. Click once on the small black box at the bottom of the tool box.

This brings up the Select Foreground Color window (Figure 2–4). The main box shows a ramp from white to black of the red hue seen at the upper right-hand corner of the box.

- Click on the upper right-hand corner of the box.

This selects a red consisting of approximately 0% Cyan, 97% Magenta, 93% Yellow, and 0% Black. (This may vary slightly, depending on where you clicked in the box. If you like, you can manually

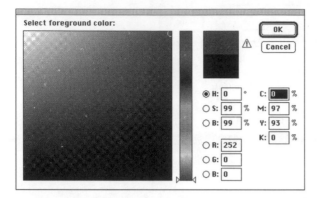

Figure 2–4   Select Foreground Color window

type in the color specifications to match our example.) Note that the CMYK values are displayed on the right side of the window as well as the RGB and HSB values. The bar to the right of the color box shows a rainbow of colors. Clicking on any of the tones in the rainbow will display the ramp for that color. The two boxes, which now should be red and black, show the new modified color on top and the original color in the bottom box.

- Click OK.

- Note that the small black box below the tools has been replaced by a red one. Red is now the current foreground color.

- It is now time to create the graphic device for your logo. Double-click on the Paint Brush tool.

- The Paint Brush Options dialog pops up (Figure 2–5).

- Select the sixth shape from the left in the top row. All the other settings will remain as is.

- Click OK. You now have a specifically sized brush with red paint on it.

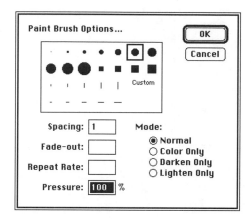

Figure 2-5 The Paint Brush Options dialog

• Paint a stroke under the word Stroke in the direction shown in Figure 2-6 and, as shown, double back to create a stroke that is thicker at one end.

Figure 2-6 Path of the Paint Brush stroke

There you have it, a logo.

Tutorial 2—A Complicated Creation

In this tutorial, you will create a complicated sign for a diner, such as the one in this book's first color section. You will use selection tools, gradients, and more.

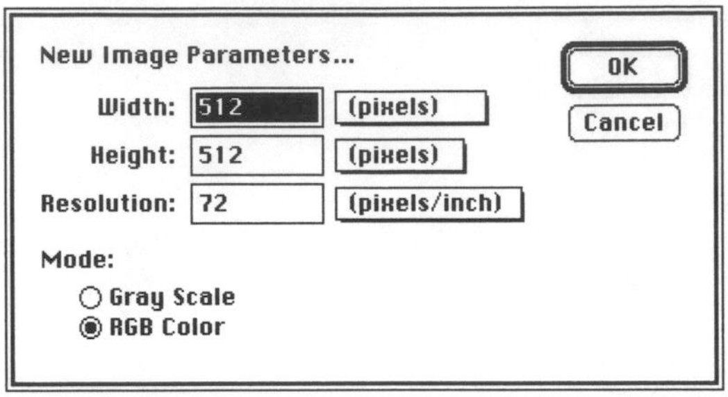

New Image Parameters...
OK
Cancel
Width: 512 (pixels)
Height: 512 (pixels)
Resolution: 72 (pixels/inch)
Mode:
Gray Scale
RGB Color

Figure 2-7 New Image Parameters dialog

- Start with a new file: Select New from the File menu. The New Image Parameters dialog appears (Figure 2-7). Change the default settings to 640 x 480, 72 DPI, RGB. Click OK.
- Choose a full screen with menu (the middle icon at the bottom of the toolbox). Then use the magnifying glass tool to make your working area larger, as you did in the first tutorial.
- Click in the Foreground color box (small colored box at the bottom of the tool palette). This action will bring up the Foreground color window (Figure 2-8).
- In the color window, a large box displays the color ramp for the currently selected hue. The default is in the red hue. To the

Select foreground color:
OK
Cancel
H: 0 °
S: 0 %
B: 59 %
R: 150
G: 150
B: 150
C: 43 %
M: 29 %
Y: 29 %
K: 5 %

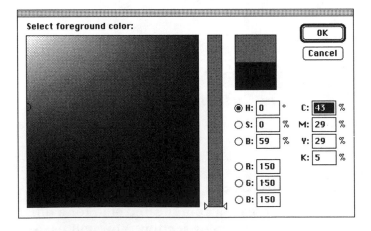

Figure 2-8 Foreground color window

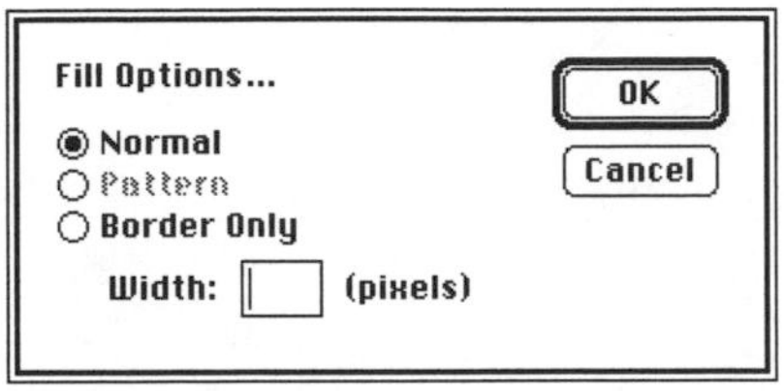

Figure 2–9   Fill Options dialog

right of this color box are the numerical value display and input boxes. Clicking within the color box on the shade of the color you wish to attain will select that shade.

- Click about halfway down along the left side of the large color swatch to select one of the gray tones. Or you can directly type in 43% Cyan, 29% Magenta, 29% Yellow, and 5% Black. Click OK.

- Select the Elliptical Selection tool by clicking on it once.

- Create a circular selection about two inches in diameter in the lower right-hand quadrant of the screen.

- Under the Edit menu, select Fill. The Fill Options dialog (Figure 2–9) will appear. For the purpose of this exercise you need a gray circle, so Normal should be selected. Click OK.

This will fill the circular selection with the gray.

- Deselect by clicking elsewhere on the screen.

- Make a second circular selection the same size as the first but slightly to the upper left of the gray circle, as shown in Figure 2–10.

- With the selection made, hit the delete or backspace key on your keyboard. This will turn the gray circle into a crescent moon. Click elsewhere on the screen to deselect.

- Save your work. Go to the File menu and select Save As... to name your file. Name it "Diner-1." At the bottom of the window are format choices that can be made. Photoshop will be the format for this exercise. For further information on the various formats, refer to Chapter 3 and Appendix A.

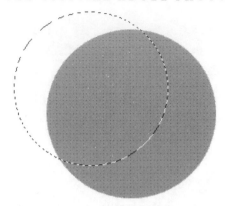

Figure 2–10 Second circular selection

- Click in the Foreground color box to bring up the Select Foreground color dialog box. In the color bar to the right of the main color window, click on the yellow to bring the yellow into the main color window. (If the bar only shows gray, click on the upper-right area of the main color window, and color will appear in the bar.) Select a bright yellow (Figure 2–11). Or you can enter 9% Cyan, 0% Magenta, 92% Yellow, and 0% Black. Click OK.

- Select the Magic Wand. With the wand, click within the gray moon. This will select the entire moon shape. The wand, when

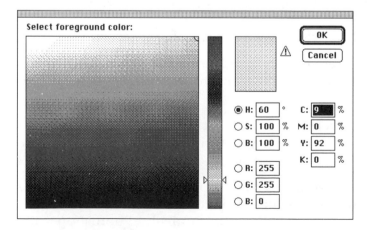

Figure 2–11 Color selection

clicked on a color, will seek out the edges of that color and select the entire region of that color. For more information on the magic wand, refer to Chapter 5.

Passing the Magic Wand cursor over the selected object (as with all the selection tools), turns the wand cursor into an arrow cursor. With this arrow cursor, the object can be moved around on the screen. If you hold down the option key before you move the object, you make a copy of it.

- Holding down the option key, click and drag a copy of the moon over to the left, or to the right, so that there are two crescent moons at the bottom of the work area. Make sure you leave enough space around the original to create a box around it.

- Select the moon on the left. Under the Edit menu, select Fill. This time the moon gets filled with the yellow you created (Figure 2–12).

- Select the Pickup Dropper tool.

- With the dropper, click on the gray moon to select that color. Notice the foreground color box has replaced the yellow with the gray.

Figure 2–12   Using Fill

- Select the Marquee or rectangle selection tool.

- Scroll down to give yourself some work space.

- Make a rectangular selection about 3 x 5 inches, leaving a few inches between the rectangle and the top of the work area.

- Go to the Edit menu and select Fill to fill the box with gray.

- With the gray box still selected, hit Command-C or select Copy from the Edit menu to put a copy of the rectangle into the clipboard.

- Select the Magic Wand tool and click on the gray moon.

- Move the moon so that the bottom third is over the top of the rectangle just off-center to the right.

- Save your work.

- For this next step, you will need more working room.

- Select New from the File menu. Notice that the default size reflects the size of the gray rectangle in the clipboard. Click OK.

- When the new window appears, press Command-V or select Paste from the Edit menu.

- The gray rectangle appears. Do not deselect it.

- Click in the Foreground color box, then click in the upper-right corner of the main color box. In the color bar to the right of the main color window, click on the warm red at the bottom to bring the red into the main color window. Click in the upper right-hand corner for a bright red (Figure 2–13). Or you can enter 0% cyan, 96% magenta, 92% yellow, and 0% black. Click OK.

- Now click on the Background color box. That is the white box surrounding the small box, which should now be red. Click along the right-hand wall of the color box just below the half-way point to create a dark red (Figure 2–14). Or you can enter 32% cyan, 100% magenta, 100% yellow, and 45% black. Click OK.

- Select the Blend tool.

NOTE: The first click of the mouse will use the Foreground color. The final release of the mouse button will end the blend with the Background color. This is the way the blended fill direction is determined.

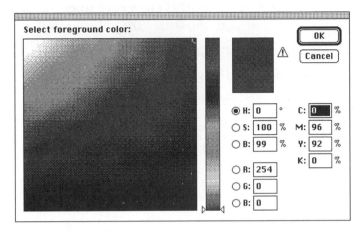

Figure 2–13   Choosing bright red

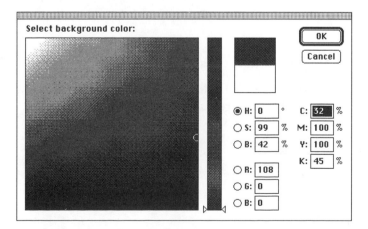

Figure 2–14   Choosing dark red

- Click and drag from the bottom of the gray rectangle to the top. Notice that when you drag the mouse, a line will follow the cursor. This will create a blend of the dark red at the top to the bright red at the bottom. Do not deselect it.

- Hit Command-C or select Copy from the Edit menu to put a copy into the Clipboard.

- Go to the Window in the menu. You'll notice that at the bottom of this menu, there is a list of the currently open documents. Select the first file that you know has the moons in it.

- Select the Marquee or rectangle selection tool.

- Make a selection around the gray moon and rectangle.

- Under the Image menu, you will find a hierarchical menu called Filters. Place the cursor over that choice and an additional hierarchical menu will pop down that displays the filters. Go down the list and select Gaussian Blur.

A dialog will appear asking for the radius. Type in 5 (Figure 2–15). For a more detailed description of this and other filters, refer to Chapter 6.

- Click OK. This softens the edges of the gray box and moon to make it into a soft shadow.

- Press Command-V or select Paste from the Edit menu.

The red rectangle that was in the clipboard should appear. Place it over the gray rectangle off to the upper left, as shown in Figure 2–16.

- Select the Magic Wand tool, and click on the yellow moon.

- Place it over the red rectangle in the same position as was the gray moon over the gray rectangle.

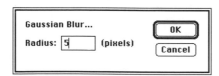

Figure 2–15   Pop-up dialog for radius entry

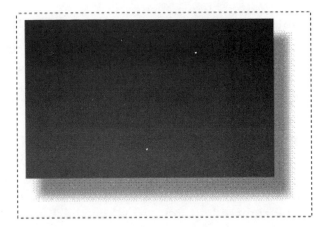

Figure 2–16   Placing an object over another

- Now you will create the name. Select the Type tool.
- Click in the Foreground color box. In the color bar to the right of the main color window, click on the warm red at the bottom to bring the red into the main color window. Click along the right-hand side wall about halfway down for a dark red (Figure 2–17). Or you can enter 45% cyan, 100% magenta, 100% yellow, and 0% black. Click OK.

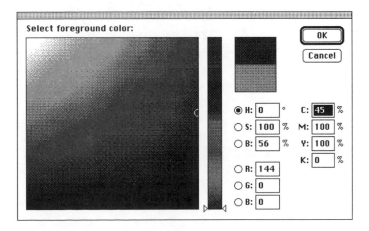

Figure 2–17   Choosing a dark red

- Click the type tool in the bottom portion of the rectangle.

- When the Text Tool box appears, select Goudy Bold or any Adobe font you have installed. Enter 65 points in the size field. In the Style portion, select Bold and Anti-aliased. Type the word DINER in the text entry box as shown in Figure 2-18. Click OK.

- The word DINER will now appear over the red box. Place the cursor over the type and it will transform into the arrow. With the arrow, click and drag the type into position at the lower right of the red box so that it is about a quarter of an inch from the bottom and the right side. Click elsewhere in the window to deselect it.

- Save your work.

- Click in the Foreground color box. In the color bar to the right of the main color window, click on the light blue to bring the blues into the main color window. Click just to the left of the upper right-hand corner for a bright blue shade. Or you can enter 87% cyan, 26% magenta, 12% yellow, and 0% black. Click OK.

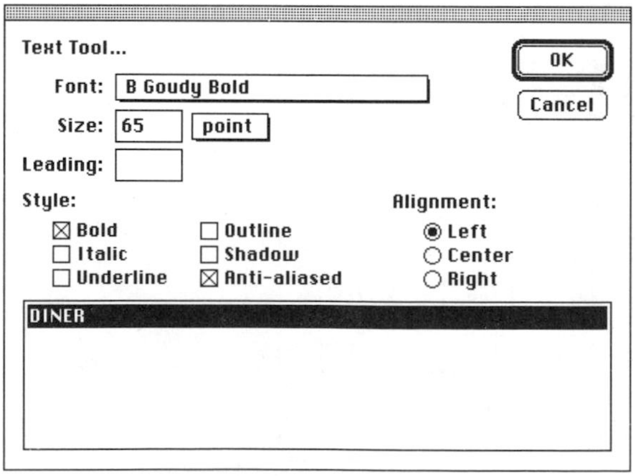

Text Tool...

Font: B Goudy Bold	**OK**
Size: 65 point	**Cancel**
Leading:	

Style: **Alignment:**

☒ Bold   ☐ Outline   ● Left
☐ Italic   ☐ Shadow   ○ Center
☐ Underline   ☒ Anti-aliased   ○ Right

DINER

Figure 2-18   Text entry box

- Click the type tool again in the bottom portion of the sign. You want to duplicate the same text, so just click OK. The Text Tool window remembers the last information entered.

- The word DINER appears again, but this time in blue. Place the blue text just above the red text and just slightly to the upper left, to give the impression that the blue type is casting a shadow. Deselect.

- Click in the Foreground color box. In the color bar to the right of the main color window, click on the warm red at the bottom to bring the red into the main color window. Click along the right-hand side wall about half-way down for a dark red. Or you can enter 45% cyan, 100% magenta, 100% yellow, and 0% black. Click OK.

- Now click in the Background color box. That is the larger box surrounding the small box, which should now be red. Click along the right-hand wall of the color box just below the half-way point to create a darker red. Or you can enter 9% cyan, 100% magenta, 100% yellow, and 69% black. Click OK.

- With the type tool, click above the word DINER — all the way to the left.

- In the dialog box, replace DINER with MOONDANCE. All other parameters should remain the same. Click OK.

- The type comes in selected. Do not deselect.

- Under the Image menu, in the Effects hierarchical menu, select the Stretch command.

- Four handles (small white boxes) will appear at the four corners of the type. Click and drag the top ones to elongate the type (refer to the finished image in the color section). Do not deselect.

- Select the Blend tool. Click and drag from the bottom of MOONDANCE to the top. This will give you a graduated shadow over the gradient of the red box. Deselect.

- Select the Eye Dropper tool and click over the blue word DINER to select that blue in the foreground again.

- With the type tool, click just to the upper left of MOON-DANCE. Click OK in the Type Tool window. MOONDANCE appears in blue.

- Follow the same stretch function as you did with the shadow. Make sure the word MOONDANCE is slightly to the upper left of its shadow as you did with the word DINER. Deselect.

- Lean back and view the results. Compare your results with those shown in the color pages.

Tutorial 3—Neon Type

The type tool opens the door for a myriad of special effects. In this exercise we will create an illustration with type. A neon sign will be our subject. It is not necessary to be an illustrator to achieve this result. To get this effect for your own choice of words or logos requires the same technique shown here. A trip to your local diner or any place with an outdoor neon sign will give you an idea of how the sign is constructed: The neon tubing or the lighted portion of a sign is usually encased in a shape of the letter, which is brightly colored for daytime viewing.

Before getting started, there is one system requirement — that ATM (Adobe Type Manager) is installed and *the desired Adobe typeface printer font/fonts are in your system folder.* This will allow you to get a clean representation of type at any desired size on the screen.

- If you're proceeding from the last tutorial, first reset the background color to white. Click on the background color box and reset color parameters to 0% for cyan, magenta, yellow, and black.

- Then, open up a new work area as we did in the last two tutorials.

- Select a color for a background of the sign; this is the base upon which the sign is mounted.

- Click on the Foreground color box. This brings up the select foreground color box (Figure 2-19). For the purpose of this exercise, pick a bright blue. Click on the narrow color bar to the right of the main color box to the position shown in Figure

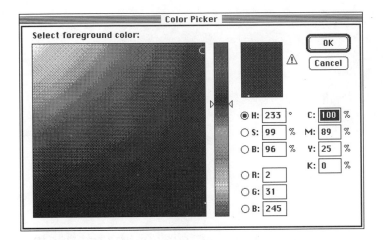

Figure 2–19 Foreground Color window

2-19, or enter the values for CMYK which are also visible in Figure 2-19. Click OK.

- Using the rectangular Marquee selection tool and depressing the Shift key for constraining, select the area to hold the sign's shape. This area should be about two inches square.

- Apply a blue fill to the shape by making the Fill choice from the Edit menu. A dialog will appear (Figure 2-20), displaying Fill options. Select Normal, then click OK. Once the shape is filled with the blue shading (Figure 2-21), deselect the shape by clicking elsewhere in the window.

- Select the type tool and click on the foreground color icon. Choose the type color by following the same color selection

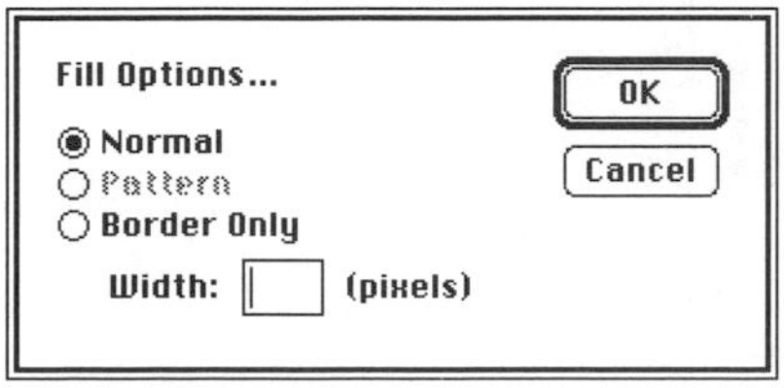

Figure 2–20 Fill Options window

Figure 2–21   Filled shape

procedure as before. This time, click on the red portion of the color bar to the right of the current Hue window. This will cause the current Hue window to display the gradients in red (Figure 2–22. Select a bright red from the upper right corner of the box. Click OK.

- With the type tool selected, click within the filled rectangle. The type entry box will appear. Select an Adobe font, make it 150 points high, and click on the Bold and Anti-aliased choices. The font used in the examples is Futura. Type "AI" into the text field (Figure 2–23). Click OK.

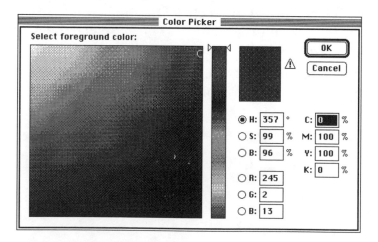

Figure 2–22   Current Hue window

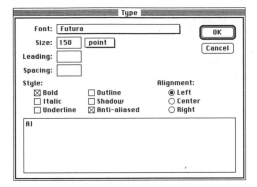

Figure 2-23 Text entry box

- When the type appears in the working window, you will notice that it comes in selected. Since it is selected, it can serve as a mask, making it easy to add depth and detail. (Note: If you are using ATM and the type still appears jagged, it is because the font you're using is not in your System folder.)

- Go back into the foreground color selector and choose a much darker version of the same red.

- Double click on the Airbrush tool to bring up its controls (Figure 2-24). Select the largest circle and click OK.

- Spray a tone along the top of the letters. The mask will keep the edges clean. Apply a tone to the right side of the letters (Figure 2-25) Note: In the case of the letter A, the edge below the opening and the left side should also be tinted.

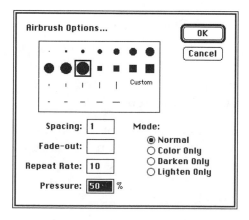

Figure 2-24 Airbrush controls

Figure 2-25   Using the Airbrush

- To add further depth to the sign, go to the Magic Wand selection tool and click on the blue of the background. Holding the shift key for multiple selections, click on the hole of the letter A. This makes a mask of the blue shading.

- Click on the foreground color to bring up the color selection box. Select a dark gray. Click OK.

- Select the airbrush tool. Spray a tone along the outside edges of the letters, along the top and left sides, and the upper interior hole of the A. By holding down the shift key, you simply click from corner to corner and the stroke will be constrained to a straight line between subsequent mouse clicks. This feature is especially helpful for unsteady hands.

- Now we'll create the neon tubing. Using the Eye Dropper tool, click on the blue background to select that color. When we apply the appropriate filter for the neon effect, this color will be transformed into a bright yellow neon.

- With the type tool, double click on any clear area in the window other than over the sign. Notice that when the text window appears, the previous text with its attributes is still registered. Change the size to 142 points and deselect the Bold style; click OK. The result should look like Figure 2-26.

- Certain letters, such as the A in this case, have a top which comes to a point (Figure 2-26). Using the eraser tool, take off

Figure 2–26   Changes made in Text window

a small portion of the top. This will make the neon tubing more realistic. Since it will be necessary to distort the A to make it fit, cut off a small bit of the top and bottom (Figure 2–27).

- Using the rectangular Marquee selection tool, select the AI.
- Select Find Edges from the Filters list in the Image menu. This will outline the type, thus creating the neon tubing effect (Figure 2–28).
- With the Magic Wand tool, deselect all the black areas by holding down the command key while clicking in the black areas. Using the command key, you can "subtract" from the active selection area using any of the selection tools (Lasso, rectangular and circular selection Marquees, and the Magic Wand). Also, be sure to deselect the black areas within the letters. This will leave only the color of the neon tube selected.

Figure 2–27   Top and bottom of A cut off

Figure 2–28 Neon tubing effect

- With the airbrush or paintbrush you can add additional tones to the neon tubing. Since it is currently selected, it acts as a mask. With the foreground color set to white, just dab a few highlights onto the tube with the airbrush or paintbrush.

- Since the neon letters are smaller than the red letters that are the neon casing, they must be placed separately. Most letters, like the T or the I, in this case, fit perfectly within the case. Others, like our A, require some adjustment.

- Using the Marquee, select the A and copy it over the red A on the sign. Do not deselect it.

- Go to the Paste controls found under the Edit menu. In this window we can eliminate the black shading of the pasted object. Drag the left control of the Floating Selection slider over to the right until you see the number "50" in the numerical indicator located on top of the slider control (Figure 2–29). Click OK.

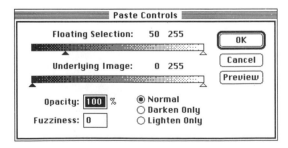

Figure 2–29 Floating Selection slider

- Do not deselect the type. Maneuver the letter until it fits within the case letter. You can use the cursor keys on your keyboard to nudge the selection a pixel at a time in any direction.

- The A will still need some modification. Under the Image menu, you will find the Effects command containing additional choices: select Stretch/Shrink. Choosing it will add four handles to the corners of the selection. Placing the cursor over any of the handles will convert the cursor to an arrow. Clicking and dragging the handles will allow you to manipulate the letter until it fits perfectly. Once it fits, copy it into the clipboard.

- To get the full effect of a neon sign, it is necessary to create a glow around the tubing. Go to the foreground color selector again, and this time pick a pure white. Click OK.

- Double-click on the airbrush tool, and this time pick the second largest circle (Figure 2–30). Click OK.

- Click on any corner of the letter A and then, holding down the shift key, follow the edges by clicking from corner to corner. Release the shift key, then start again within the interior opening. It should look like Figure 2–31.

- Paste down the A, which is still in the clipboard. Use the Paste control (as previously discussed) to eliminate the black and place it over the first tube, which has the glow.

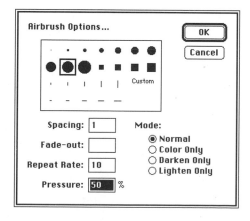

Figure 2–30   Airbrush tool selection

Figure 2–31   Glow on edges

- Follow the same procedure for the letter I. It will fit without any modification.

- The sign needs a frame. Choose the rectangular Marquee selection tool. Then, create a square selection about a quarter of an inch larger than the original blue square. Go into the color selector and pick a light gray. Go into the background color selector and pick a dark gray. Now select the blend tool and click and drag from the upper left corner to the lower right corner. This will produce a blend of grays. With the airbrush, spray some additional highlights along the edges (Figure 2–32).

- Using the Marquee selection tool, select the blue box with the neon in it and drag it over the gray square. You now have a neon sign (Figure 2–33).

If desired, the entire sign can be further modified: perspective, distortion, skewing or whatever you wish. Wear and tear and addi-

Figure 2–32   Creating highlights

Figure 2-33   Finished neon sign

tional details can be added by selecting the blue background with the Magic Wand tool and spraying tints with the airbrush.

You now have some practical working experience in Photoshop. For examples using scanned images, refer to the chapters discussing the use of Photoshop for advertising and fine arts.

3

Setup and Document Management

Introduction

As you've probably already discovered, Photoshop is chock-full of menus, dialogs, and controls for the exhaustive selection of tools and features. Navigating through the maze can take some time and requires a certain degree of patience.

This chapter is a general overview of some of the more important concepts of Photoshop, including the display modes, program preferences, and the process involved in creating and saving files. The most important thing is to remember not to be overwhelmed by the sheer number of options in the program: If approached methodically, the program has a very logical organization and way of working.

General Organization

When you first start using Photoshop, your first impression will probably be that you are in one of the most complicated graphics programs you've ever seen. That is probably true: We don't often see graphics programs quite this dense (though programs such as Studio/8 and MacroMind Director certainly come close). This is the price one pays for power.

43

Some software, such as MacroMind Director and Microsoft Word, have Short/Full or Beginner/Expert modes; these modes toggle certain features that the beginner might find confusing or intimidating. Once familiar with the basic operations of a program, you can then turn on the full, or expert, menus to access all of the features of the software. One of the negative points of Photoshop is that it doesn't offer a similar set of modes; all of the program's features are always there, whether you need them or not. This is something that takes some getting used to. After you spend some time with Photoshop, you'll find that it's more straightforward that you might have imagined.

The Menus

The menus in Photoshop are

File: Contains all of the pertinent file functions (New, Open, Save), as well as menus for any external drivers (such as JPEG compression routines, scanner drivers, etc.) and printing functions.

Edit: Basic editing functions (Cut, Copy, and Paste); Special Paste modes; Fill and Crop commands; Brush and Pattern define; and Preferences.

Mode: Display modes, indexed color tables, channel controls.

Image: Image processing, filters, multichannel effects, dynamic effects, resizing and resampling, and trap controls.

Select: Special features which apply to the selection tools plus the creation of alpha channels.

Windows: Windows and zoom control, control display toggles, histogram.

For a full discussion of the menu items, see Chapters 4, 5, and 6.

Screen Display Management

At the bottom of the main tool palette you'll find three small icons that control the screen display mode (Figure 3–1).

The default mode is the left-hand icon, which displays the menu bar and all open document windows. When you click on the middle

Figure 3-1   Screen display mode icons on tool palette

icon, the current active document fills the screen and the menu bar remains visible. When you click on the icon to the absolute right, the menu bar disappears, expanding the current active document to fill the whole screen.

▼ **Tip:** You can temporarily make the tool palette invisible by pressing the Tab key on your keyboard; this toggles the tool palette on and off. Also, when in the full-screen mode with menu bar, you can switch the active document by opening the Window menu, and choosing another open document from the list of open files at the bottom of the Window menu. This also works with the colors and brush palettes.

You can zoom into and out from an image by using the magnifier tool in the main tool palette; simply click the magnifier where you want to zoom in, and press the Option key to use the magnifier to zoom out, or away. You know whether you're zooming in or out because the magnifier icon will contain a "+" character when zooming in and a "−" character when zooming out. When the character disappears from inside the zoom tool, you know that you're as far as you can go. The maximum magnification and reduction ratios are 16:1 (1600%) and 1:16.

Zoom controls are also located in the Window menu. See Figure 3-2. You can use these instead of the magnifier tool, and they have keyboard equivalents [Commmand-+ for magnification, Command-− (minus) for reduction], allowing you to zoom through the keyboard instead of the magnifier tool. There is also a Zoom Factor dialog allowing you to "jump" directly to a magnification or reduction view by specifying the zoom factor in the dialog. The default factor is 2, so that as you zoom in or out, you double the percentage of each subsequent view (1:1. 2:1, 4:1, 8:1, etc.). If you specify a different factor, such as 3, you'll triple each magnification, but if you

Figure 3–2 Zoom Factor dialog

hold the option key and reduce, you'll jump back to the default factor of 2.

The current magnification ratio is displayed in the title bar of a document's window: as you zoom in and out of a document, the ratio is updated in the title bar (Figures 3-3, 3-4, 3-5).

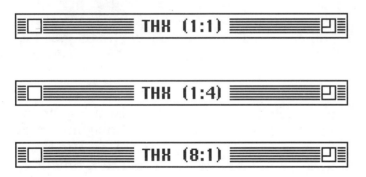

Figures 3–3, 3–4, 3–5 Title bar showing 1:1 (actual size), 1:4 (400% reduction), and 8:1 (800% magnification)

▼ **Tip:** If you are working on a document and wish to create multiple views of the image, you can choose the New Window command from the Window menu. This is useful for creating multiple simultaneous magnification views of a working document: If you paint in one view, the other views are updated immediately after you release the mouse button.

Document Size Indicator

In the lower left corner of a document window is a numerical readout of the size of the document, in kilobytes (Figure 3-6).

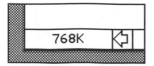

Figure 3-6 Size Indicator is in left corner of a document window.

Most of the time, this is the size of the document as saved on disk. We've found that in certain cases, such as 24-bit PICT files, the disk size is smaller than the size that appears in the size indicator.

▼ **Tip:** In the case of 24-bit PICTs, a 640 x 480 image might take up 379K on disk, but when opened into Photoshop, the size indicator displays a size of 900K (the size of a 640 x 480 RGB image). If you manipulate the image without resizing it, and save it back to disk as a 24-bit PICT, the size will be reduced back to the original incoming PICT file size.

Previewing Page Size

If you click on the size indicator number, a Page Preview window pops up and displays a dummy of a full page (as specified in the Page Setup dialog). It shows a bounding box of the the total area occupied by the image/images in the document. Even if you have two separate elements on two extreme sides of the document, the bounding box is drawn based on the combined rectangular area of the two images (Figures 3-7, 3-8, 3-9).

▼ **Tip:** Anything selected in the Page Setup dialog is reflected in the miniature page view, including crop and registration marks, calibration bars, negative output, and emulsion type (Figure 3-10).

If your image is bigger than the current page size, you'll notice that the bounding box extends off the edge of the page. Be careful: One of the things that Photoshop can't do is to tile an image for multiple-page registered output, a capability found in many page layout programs. You'll have to take Photoshop images into Page-Maker or Quark XPress for such an operation.

Figures 3–7, 3–8, and 3–9 The Page Preview pop-up display: standard letter size, tabloid, and #10 envelope displays

Other Size Parameters

If you press the Option key while clicking on the size indicator, the Page Preview display is replaced by a numerical readout, which includes information of the resolution, size, and number of channels in the image (Figure 3–11).

The size of the image is displayed in both pixels and any other units selected in the Size/Rulers dialog found in the Page Setup dialog. You can select different display units for the horizontal and vertical size readouts in the numerical readout.

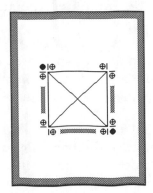

Figure 3–10 Page Preview with crop marks, registration marks, and calibration bars turned on in Page Setup.

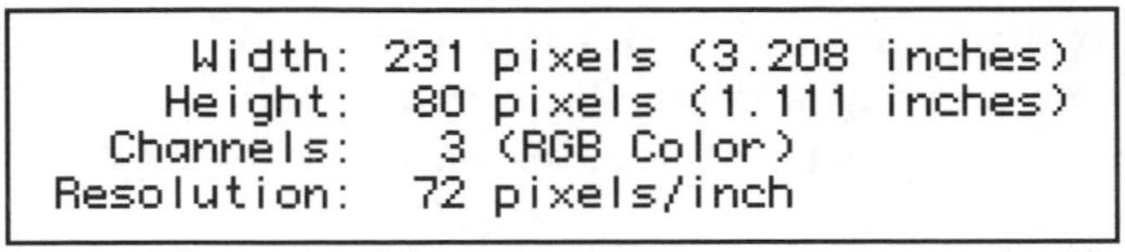

```
    Width: 231 pixels (3.208 inches)
   Height:  80 pixels (1.111 inches)
 Channels:   3 (RGB Color)
Resolution:  72 pixels/inch
```

Figure 3-11 This numerical readout dialog appears if you press the Option key when clicking on the size indicator.

Rulers

You can turn Photoshop's onscreen rulers on by choosing the Rulers command in the Window menu. The measurement units used in the rulers display are set with the Size/Rulers button in the Page Setup command in the File menu. You can set the units individually for the vertical and horizontal rulers: The available units are inches, centimeters, picas, and points (and in the case of the width, columns, discussed in this chapter under Preferences).

You can also change the ruler's origin points by clicking in the upper left-hand corner where the two rulers meet (Figure 3-12). This control works exactly as its equivalent in many other Macintosh design programs: Click the pointer in this area, drag to the new desired zero origin location, and release the mouse button.

Setting Preferences

Photoshop remembers a variety of your default settings by creating a Preferences file. When you run a fresh copy of the Photoshop application, you will be asked to save a Prefs file before serializing

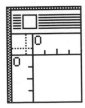

Figure 3-12 The Ruler's zero origin setting area

the program with your name. If there are multiple Photoshop preferences files floating around, Photoshop will use the preferences file located in the same folder as the main application.

▼ **Tip:** As mentioned in Chapter 1, Photoshop uses a virtual memory scheme to work with images that are larger than available RAM. The location of the Photoshop Preferences file is the location used for the virtual memory drive. With this in mind, make sure to place Photoshop and its preferences file on a drive with ample hard-drive space. Even though you can keep the main application and preferences file in two different places, we've found it most convenient to keep the two together. You should make sure that any external filters, custom acquisition or export modules are in the same folder as the Preferences file.

If you look in the Edit menu, you will see the Preferences dialog (Figure 3-13). In the Preferences dialog, you can adjust controls that affect the behavior of various aspects of the program.

Colored Separations

When you view individual RGB or CMYK channels on the screen, you may choose to have them represented as grayshades or in the actual color of the channel. For example, when looking at the red, green, and blue channels of a 24-bit color image, you can view the

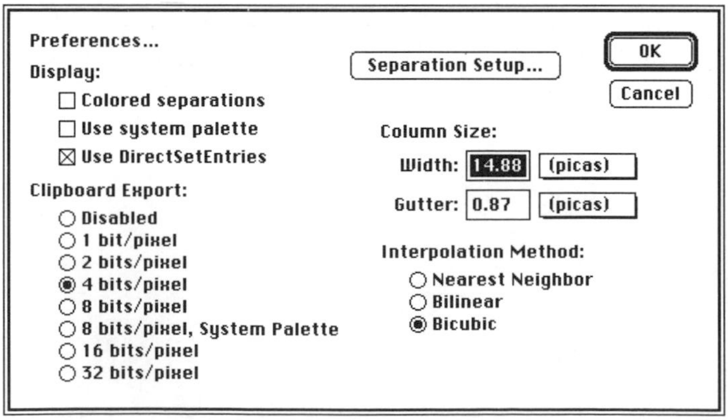

Figure 3-13 Preferences dialog

channels in their actual colors—the red channel displayed in shades of red, for example. This is important because it's sometimes difficult to view a channel in its actual color—yellow is a perfect example. Viewing channels without colors enabled allows you to precisely view the color saturation of a given channel of an image.

If you're using a grayscale monitor or black-and-white system, this setting will have no effect on your display.

Use System Palette

When working with Photoshop on an 8-bit Mac II, you can choose to force the display to always use the standard Macintosh II system palette to display all visible windows. This is important when running Photoshop on an 8-bit video display. When working with multiple 24-bit Photoshop files, each time you select a different document window, you will notice that the colors in each of the other document windows "go crazy" for a few moments—this happens because Photoshop is calculating an optimized 256-color palette to best represent the 24-bit data in the active document, and makes that palette the active palette. When this happens, the colors in the other open documents are remapped to the colors in the current palette, resulting in a fun but useless color effects show. By activating "Use System palette," you are effectively forcing Photoshop to use the standard Apple 256-color default palette to represent all of the open documents. The result is that you will have a much less accurate 8-bit representation of an image's 24-bit data with much heavier dithering artifacts.

Use this option if you plan to work with multiple PICT files at one time. If you've opened up various PICT files from programs such as Studio/8 or PixelPaint (or any program that can create and save images with custom 256-color palettes), you will notice that as you click on each different window, the colors in the other windows will redraw, and much of the time they will look very odd. This is because the custom color palette for the currently selected window overrides all other palettes. This redrawing becomes more noticeable depending on how many documents are open at once, and on the resolution of the images. The big problem you'll run into here is that if your open documents are high-resolution images, screen redraw might become quite bothersome (the higher the resolution of an image, the longer it takes to redraw the image on the screen).

With the "Use System Palette" toggle selected, the annoying color redraw will be disabled. To do this, Photoshop automatically uses an optimized dither (the same one used when converting an RGB image to a system palette pattern dither through the RGB to indexed color conversion command), to display multiple windows with indexed images with different palettes.

This control will have no effect if you are running Photoshop in 24-bit display mode with a 24-bit video card. In this case, many different 256-color palettes can be handled simultaneously without palette remapping.

▼ **Tip:** One way to know that a custom palette is being used by the foreground window is to check the little colored apple used by the desk accessory menu: If its colors aren't the normal rainbow, a custom palette is being used, and the normal rainbow colors are being replaced by the custom colors in the active palette.

Interpolation Methods

All of the dynamic effects in Photoshop, including resizing (both the interactive resizing controls and the Resize command in the Image menu), distortion, perspective, and rotation commands are tied into the interpolation settings. The quality and speed performance of these features are directly affected by the interpolation mode selected in the Preferences dialog.

Nearest Neighbor is the fastest of the methods, yielding the lowest quality. If you use this when distorting or resizing an image, you'll immediately notice that the image is recalculated with a large amount of distortion.

Bilinear is a medium quality method, with the quality residing somewhere between nearest neighbor and bicubic.

Bicubic is the slowest of the methods, but gives you the highest quality results. This method is the default setting when you run the program.

Here are three examples, using the Distort command, of the differences in quality when using the three modes (Figures 3-14, 3-15, and 3-16).

Figure 3–14 Nearest Neighbor   **Figure 3–15** Bilinear

Figure 3–16 Bicubic

Clipboard Export

When you use the copy and cut commands in the Edit menu and paste the contents of the clipboard into a scrapbook desk accessory, or leave Photoshop all together, you can filter the amount of data actually exported from Photoshop. For example, if you plan on moving the copied image into a program that only works properly with the standard Macintosh II system palette, choosing the 8-bits/pixel System Palette forces the clipboard to be dithered into the system palette whenever you open a scrapbook desk accessory. If you were moving images into another paint program that worked with full 24-bit color, you would select the 32-bits/pixel option.

▼ **Tip:** Every time you open a desk accessory while in Photoshop, or switch to another program if running MultiFinder, the clipboard is processed according the clipboard export option you've selected. If you have a large image on the clipboard, this conversion process can become quite annoying, as it makes you wait until the conversion is done before proceeding. If you need to access a peripheral desk accessory while in Photoshop—for example, choosing different printers for grayscale/color output while working, or the notepad to look up a phone number—you'll want to empty the contents of the clipboard before opening the desk accessory. Simply select a minuscule portion of the active document and copy or cut it; it will convert much more rapidly than a large copied/cut portion of an image.

Separation Setup

This button takes you to the controls that affect color separation variables; see Chapter 8, "Output," for a full discussion of this feature.

Column Size

The Column size and gutter controls allow you to "simulate" multiple-column layouts within Photoshop; this is especially useful when you are creating comp layouts without the need to use a page layout program. By setting a fixed column and gutter size that corresponds to the related settings in your page layout program, you can crop images with the assurance that the ratio of the cropped image will match the column specifications in the receiving page layout program. You can specify columns as a measurement unit in the cropping tool control dialog when resampling an image and when setting up output size in the size/rulers dialog in the Page Setup command.

Columns and gutters can be specified in units of inches, centimeters, points, or picas.

Display Formats and Modes

One of the most basic concepts in Photoshop is that of the display modes available from Photoshop's Mode menu. Different display modes are used to represent different types of images on the screen, and to allow you to change the image on the screen in various ways (such as the CMYK mode, used to convert images for prepress output).

You will use the different display modes when

- Editing grayscale images.

- Working with color images and creating color separations.

- Preparing images for optimized screen display quality.

- Creating and using masks with color and grayscale images.

- Working in the fully featured native Photoshop format.

Before we discuss the various display modes, it's important to understand some basic concepts regarding how Photoshop deals with its world.

- In Photoshop, every pixel of a grayscale image has a brightness value ranging between 0 and 255; 0 is black, 255 is white, and the values in between correspond to the grayscale spectrum.

- Every pixel of a color image consists of a mix of red, green, and blue tones; a pixel with a value of 0 for each of the RGB tones is black, while 255 for each of the RGB values results in a white pixel. A pixel with a red value of 255 and blue and green values of 0 is red, while values of 255 for both red and blue and 0 for green result in a magenta shade.

- When working with color images, you should always try to use the native Photoshop format for saving images. Regardless of the video card in your machine or the model Macintosh being used, the image will always retain the full color information it started with, whether imported into Photoshop as a 256–color indexed image or a 24–bit scan file.

▼ **Tip:** Not all of the filters and image-processing features in Photoshop work with all of the display modes. The only mode in which all of the program's features work is the RGB mode. If you want to process imported PICT files through most of Photoshop's special effects, you'll need to convert the indexed image to RGB, manipulate the image, and convert it back to PICT format for exporting. When working with grayscale images, the only features that will not work are those specifically relating to color (for example, the Hue/Saturation and color correction controls are disabled when you are working with grayscale images).

The Display Modes

Bitmap

Black-and-white bitmaps are the most fundamental form of Mac graphics—you'll need black-and-white bitmaps any time that you work with HyperCard. The Bitmap display mode is a simple black-and-white 2–bit display: All color and grayscale information is removed from the image when it is converted to bitmap mode. To convert a color image to bitmap mode, you must first convert it to a grayscale image, which simply removes the hue information from the pixels in the image, leaving the saturation and brightness values intact.

Normal MacPaint bitmap images are limited to 72 DPI, while the bitmap display mode in Photoshop allows you to have higher-resolution black-and-white images; when converting a color or grayscale image to bitmap mode within Photoshop, you can choose the input and output resolutions used for the conversion process (Figure 3–17). The different settings result in various image sizes and dot densities.

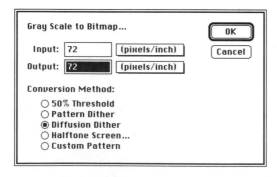

Figure 3–17 Grayscale to bitmap conversion dialog

To convert an image to bitmap mode:

- Open a 72–DPI grayscale screen image.

- Click on the size indicator in the lower left-hand corner of the image window. Take note of the actual size of the image.

- Select the bitmap display mode from the Mode menu.

- Specify 150 pixels/inch as the output resolution.

- Using either the Pattern or Diffusion conversion method (see below), press the OK button.

- Note that the image seems to have been magnified in its window; in reality, the image is the same size, but at a higher pixel density. Click on the size indicator in the lower left-hand side of the image window, and observe that the image is the same size as the original grayscale image.

The default settings in the Input and Output fields correspond to the resolution of the image being converted. You can specify units to be either pixels/inch or pixels/centimeter by clicking on the pop-up menus on the left-hand side of the units fields.

▼ **Tip:** With the bitmap conversion mode, you have full control over the characteristics of the halftone dots used to draw the image to the screen, as well as special dithering modes for optimized screen display of the bitmapped image. This mode is good for creating images with a "jaggy" or aliased look, which is sometimes desirable as a design effect. It is also good if you wish to process an image through a custom halftone and then convert the halftoned image back into RGB mode for special effects.

When converting a grayscale image (Figure 3–18) to bitmap mode, you can apply one of five types of dithering or halftone screens to the image:

- **50% Threshold:** This converts the image into a high-contrast, nontextured bitmap. When analyzing the grayscale image, pixels with a value of 128 or higher are converted to white, and those with values of 127 or lower are converted to black (Figure 3–19).

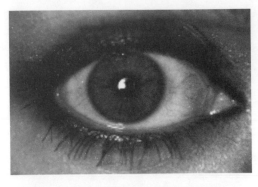
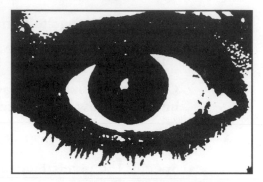

Figure 3–18   Original grayscale image   **Figure 3–19**   50% Threshold

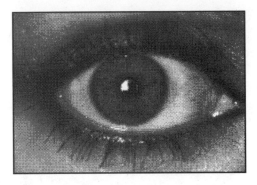
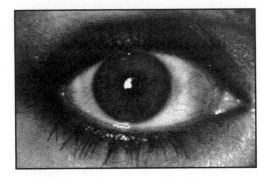

Figure 3–20   Pattern dither   **Figure 3–21**   Diffusion dither

- **Pattern Dither:** This conversion method "clumps" the grayscale values into geometric groups of black-and-white dots (Figure 3–20).

- **Diffusion Dither:** This is one of the most visually pleasing conversion modes; the look is reminiscent of the grainy look of early Macintosh scanned images produced with the Koala MacVision digitizer. When the bitmap conversion mode is used to prepare images for viewing on a black-and-white screen, this is usually the preferable conversion option (Figure 3–21).

- **Halftone Screen:** This conversion method allows you to process an image through a variety of halftone screens; while this technique is usually used when printing an image, this conversion method allows you to create printed halftone effects on the Mac screen (a very helpful visual effect) as well as to pre-halftone an image for optimized printing on a non-Post-Script printer. Using this technique, you can print custom halftones on any non-PostScript printer, something which has been quite impossible until the arrival of Photoshop.

When choosing this conversion method, you are presented with a dialog box containing the halftone options (Figure 3-22).

You may enter specific frequencies (also called linescreens) as well as the rotation angle of the dotscreen. Different screen frequencies are used depending on the final output applications—for example, when preparing an image for output to a 300-DPI non-PostScript printer, a frequency value between 60 and 80 lines/inch and an angle value of 45 degrees will produce the best results. There are also five types of dot shapes, each producing a different effect. (See Figures 3-23 through 3-30). Note that you can save specific combinations of settings on disk for use with other images.

- Custom Pattern: This option is used when you have predefined an area of an image as a pattern. Normally, this is done to create a custom fill or painting pattern for use with the painting tools (see Chapter 4, "Using the Tools"). When used in conjunction with the bitmap conversion mode, you can create gorgeous custom mezzotint effects that cannot be produced with *any* other Macintosh graphics program. This conversion option is

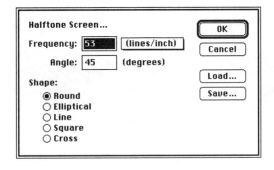

Figure 3-22 Halftone conversion dialog

Figure 3–23
Normal grayscale image

Figure 3–24
Frequency: 50
Angle: 45
Shape: Round

Figure 3–25
Frequency: 15
Angle: 45
Shape: Round

Figure 3–26
Frequency: 15
Angle: 45
Shape: Line

Figure 3–27
Frequency: 15
Angle: 45
Shape: Square

Figure 3–28
Frequency: 15
Angle: 45
Shape: Cross

Figure 3–29
Frequency: 25
Angle: 90
Shape: Round

Figure 3–30
Frequency: 25
Angle: 135
Shape: Line

discussed in detail in "Advanced Photoshop Techniques," Chapter 7.

▼ **Tip:** The Custom pattern conversion option is only available if you have defined a custom pattern during the current work session. See "Advanced Photoshop Techniques," Chapter 7, for details.

When you convert a bitmap image into grayscale mode, you have the option of specifying the size ratio to be used in the conversion process (Figure 3-31). Essentially, this controls the actual size of the resulting image; when the default setting of 1 is used, the resulting image is the same size as the original bitmap image. If you enter a value of 2, the resulting image will be scaled down 50% with respect to the size of the bitmap image.

▼ **Tip:** By using this feature, you can convert a 1-bit black-and-white scanned picture into an enhanced grayscale image by scanning at multiples of the desired size, and using the multiple as the size ratio when converting the black-and-white image into grayscale mode. Photoshop averages the groups of black-and-white pixels and creates "artificial" grayscale dots.

Grayscale

The grayscale mode uses up to 256 shades of gray for each dot in the image. When RGB or color images are converted to grayscale, all hue information is removed from the image, leaving the brightness and saturation values intact. Grayscale images are typically obtained by using black-and-white and grayscale scanners to create TIFF files (most common situation).

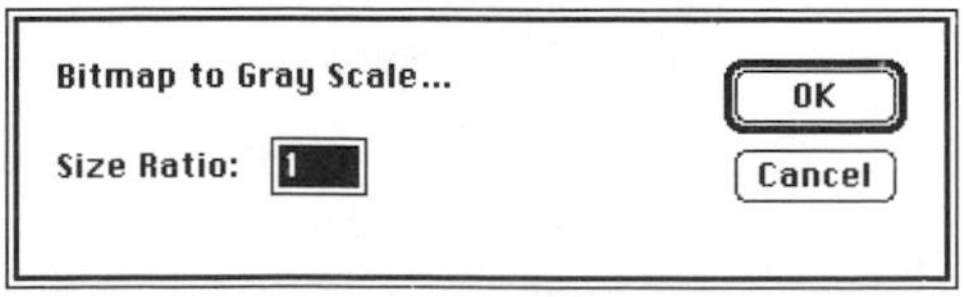

Figure 3-31 Bitmap to grayscale conversion dialog

▼ **Tip:** You can use the grayscale mode to slightly enhance the apparent quality of 4-bit, 16-gray scans by opening a 4-bit TIFF file, converting it to full grayscale mode, and applying a single pass of the Blur filter.

The painting tools and filters work in grayscale display mode; the controls for manipulating color values are unavailable.

When you add an alpha channel to a grayscale image, the image is automatically converted into a Multichannel image.

Indexed Color Modes

Indexed color modes are used when you want to limit the number of colors used to display an image: An indexed color image has a specific color lookup table, or fixed palette. A Macintosh II with a 4-bit video card can display up to 16 colors, while an 8-bit video card allows 256 colors: in both cases, there are two types of color palettes that can be used:

1. The standard system palette (8-bit) or uniform palette (4-bit) consists of a predetermined set of colors that are supposed to be supported by any application following the standard Apple programming guidelines. Object-oriented PostScript software such as Freehand and Adobe Illustrator use the standard System palette to display their entire color range on 8-bit displays. By dithering, or mixing, the colors in special patterns, it's possible to simulate intermediate shades of the colors found in the indexed palette, resulting in more colors than are actually in the palette.

2. Adaptive palettes are optimized to best represent the colors found in an image. When converting a 24-bit image to 8-bit indexed color, Photoshop analyzes the colors in the 24-bit image and creates a 256-color palette that best represents the colors found in the 24-bit file. An image with an 8-bit adaptive palette tends to look very much like the 24-bit image onscreen; we've fooled more than one person into believing that adaptive palette 256-color images created by Photoshop were actually 24-bit images.

Dithering is used in computer graphics to fool the human eye into thinking that there are more colors on a screen than the computer can actually produce. The technique involves mixing different colored pixels in close proximity to produce intermediate shades that aren't necessarily present in the currently available palette. Dithering is used primarily for two purposes: to create smooth color gradations using as few colors as possible, and to reap the maximum number of colors out of an 8-bit palette. Obviously, in a 24-bit environment there is no need for dithering, as the full possible color spectrum is available.

Dithering is applicable both to screen displays and printers; for example, the Tektronix 4693D color thermal printer uses a dithering scheme to more closely match the color range of the Macintosh II, and it's likely that future color printers will also utilize various forms of dot dithering to reproduce shading subtleties that cannot be handled by the limited number of colors of inks or wax transfer layers employed by current color printing technology.

For preparing images for screen presentations, it's preferable to use adaptive palettes. The problem is that some programs have problems dealing with custom palettes and expect images to be mapped to the Apple system palette. Programs such as MacroMind Director have the ability to import and work with different palettes. See "Animation," Chapter 9, for specific tips on moving adaptive palette images into MacroMind Director.

When you convert an RGB image into Indexed format, you can determine how the colors in the original image will be represented on the screen and the type of color palette that will be generated (Figure 3-32).

You can determine the number of bits dedicated to each pixel, which determines the number of colors in the color palette. Four-bit color can use up to 16 colors per pixel, while 5-bit color yields 32 colors (2 to the fifth power). The odd numbers, such as 3, 5, and 7

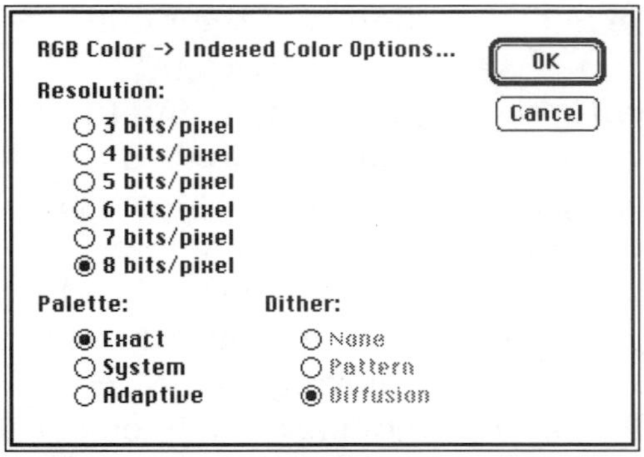

```
┌─────────────────────────────────────────────┐
│ RGB Color -> Indexed Color Options...  ┌────────┐ │
│                                        │   OK   │ │
│ Resolution:                            └────────┘ │
│     ○ 3 bits/pixel                     ┌────────┐ │
│     ○ 4 bits/pixel                     │ Cancel │ │
│     ○ 5 bits/pixel                     └────────┘ │
│     ○ 6 bits/pixel                              │
│     ○ 7 bits/pixel                              │
│     ● 8 bits/pixel                              │
│                                                 │
│ Palette:          Dither:                       │
│     ● Exact           ○ None                    │
│     ○ System          ○ Pattern                 │
│     ○ Adaptive        ● Diffusion               │
└─────────────────────────────────────────────┘
```

Figure 3–32   The RGB-Indexed color conversion dialog

are useful for saving images in some of the more esoteric modes, such as Amiga IFF and CompuServe GIF formats. The indexed color depths most used on the Macintosh are 2, 4, and 8 bits.

The palette and dithering options allow you to specify the type of palette that will result from the format conversion—either adaptive, system (8-bit) or uniform (4-bit) and the type of dither employed.

The "Exact" palette is useful only when there are less than 256 colors in the RGB image; in this case, no dithering is employed to create intermediate shades (in our experience with the program, we found that the "Exact" option is rarely available with detailed color images containing a variety of shades). System (256 colors), or Uniform (16 colors) palettes conform to the Apple standard color palettes for those respective color depths: Programs written to Apple's design specifications are supposed to utilize these fixed color palettes. Adaptive palettes are created when Photoshop analyzes the colors found in the 24-bit RGB file and creates an optimized set of colors that best represent the values found in the 24-bit file. Clearly, adaptive palettes yield the most true representations of the color range when RGB files are converted.

We find that regardless of the palette used, the diffusion dither tends to yield the smoothest image attainable. The pattern dither is useful for a certain effect, and the "none" option results in a heavily "quantized" appearance that is far from the original RGB image. (See

Figures 3-33 through 3-38 in this section, and their color versions in the color pages.)

You can view the currently active palette by going to the Color Table hierarchical menu in the Mode menu (Figure 3-39). Selecting the Edit Table... command opens a window that displays the currently used color palette (Figure 3-40).

You can save and load custom color tables using the Load and Save buttons in the right-hand side of this dialog; you can also change individual colors in the table by double-clicking on the desired color, which opens the standard Photoshop color picker. Option-clicking on the color brings up the standard Apple color wheel. If you change a color in the color table, all occurrences of that color in the image file will be updated to reflect the new color you chose.

You can also create gradients between two colors by selecting a range of colors in the Edit Table window; you'll be asked to specify beginning and ending shades, and Photoshop will automatically create the blend using the number of color cells selected. In practical use, we find this capability to be of limited usefulness.

The black body, grayscale, and spectrum color palettes are built into Photoshop. Selecting one of them replaces the current palette with the chosen palette.

Figure 3-33   Palette: System   Dither: None

Figure 3–34 Palette: System   Dither: Pattern

Figure 3–35 Palette: System   Dither: Diffusion

Figure 3–36 Palette: Adaptive   Dither: None

Figure 3–37 Palette: Adaptive   Dither: Pattern

Figure 3–38   Palette: Adaptive   Dither: Diffusion

In general, Indexed color mode is only used when exporting images from Photoshop to other 8-bit programs, or when creating images for use on other computers, such as the Amiga. Indexed mode does become important if you are using Photoshop as a processing tool for animation or presentation graphics. See Chapter 9, "Animation," for a full discussion of this application.

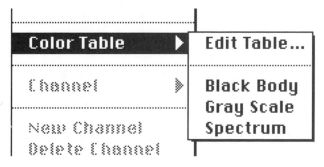

Figure 3–39   Color Table hierarchical menu

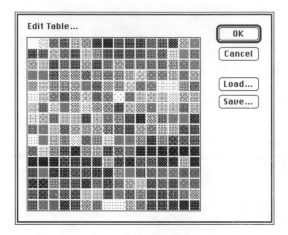

Figure 3–40   Edit Table window

The **Black Body** color palette has its origins in physics: This table displays a transition of colors based on the nature of how heat is radiated from a body (think of a star). As the body heats up, it goes from black to red to orange to yellow to white. If you were to heat a bar of iron over a hot fire, that would be the order of colors observed as the bar becomes increasingly hot. Desktop publishers probably won't get too much use from this color table, but scientists might find it useful for image analysis problems.

Grayscale replaces the color range with a smooth 256–shade transition of grays from black to white.

Spectrum is a color table based on the colors that make up white light: If you observe light passing through a prism, you'll observe a smooth transition between violet, blue, green, yellow, orange, and red.

RGB

RGB mode is the normal Photoshop working mode. When you open a 24-bit color scanned image (regardless of whether it's a 24-bit TIFF or PICT file) into Photoshop, you'll find yourself in the RGB display mode. RGB is also one of the default modes when new documents are being created. RGB mode gives you access to the full capabilities of all of Photoshop's tools and filters.

A 24–bit image can be described as three separate 8–bit images, one each of red, green, and blue, superimposed one on top of another to provide the full color spectrum. RGB display mode shows the three 8–bit channels superimposed, but you can also view the separate color components of an image by choosing them from the Channel hierarchical menu in the Mode menu. All of Photoshop's image processing commands and filters can be applied to any of the separate color component channels of an image.

When the monitor is running on a 24–bit video display card, RGB mode is displayed onscreen with the full 24–bit color range. On an 8–bit system, a pattern dithering scheme is used to display the image with the best possible 8–bit quality. All tools work at a full 24 bits, regardless of the pixel/bit depth of the video card driving the monitor.

CYMK

CMYK (Cyan-Magenta-Yellow-Black) mode is used for creating four-color process separations of a color image. Typically, you will be starting either from Indexed or RGB mode (most likely RGB) and converting to CMYK in order to output four separate layers, or plates, that are used to generate printing plates. When using CMYK mode, you can see the value of each of the layers as a black plate with the corresponding tonal densities, or represented by the actual colors of the layers. Use the Colored Separations control in the Preferences dialog to toggle this feature.

The process separation resulting from this conversion is also controlled by the parameters found in the Separations control in the Preferences dialog.

Printers use these four color inks to create the full range of printable colors; a full description of this technique can be found in Chapter 10, "Color Publishing and Retouching," dealing with four-color process printing.

▼ **Tip:** When you import images scanned on systems such as the Scitex, they are brought into Photoshop as CMYK separated elements; you may find that in such a situation, you'll want to convert the image to RGB mode for manipulation, and then convert back to CMYK display mode for output.

HSB and HSL (Hue, Saturation, Brightness —and Hue, Saturation, Luminance)

These display modes (HSB and HSL) break an image down into color, saturation, and brightness values. This is handy for adjusting the brightness of an image without affecting the actual color components of the image. After adjusting any of the channels, selecting the RGB display mode automatically converts the file back to the original RGB format.

Multichannel

The multichannel mode is probably the most "generic" display mode in Photoshop; a Photoshop document can consist of up to sixteen 8–bit channels, each essentially containing grayscale information. In an RGB document, three of the 16 channels are used for the three RGB layers, leaving 13 other 8–bit channels that can be used as alpha channels.

If you delete any of the component channels of an RGB image, or add alpha channels to an image in grayscale display mode, the image is automatically converted into multichannel display mode.

▼ **Tip:** If you are working with groups of grayscale images that are similar sizes, you might want to create a single multichannel Photoshop document with a different image in each of the channels. Using this technique, you can keep up to 16 related documents together in one file.

Creating New Documents

When choosing the New... command from the file menu, the dialog box shown in Figure 3–41 appears.

The default document size is 512 x 512 pixels. If there is an image on the clipboard, the default size of the new document will correspond to the size of the clipboard image. The clipboard image can then be pasted directly into the new document without the need to be cropped.

The image size is specified by separate height and width values. By clicking on the units field immediately to the right of the width value, you can specify the width in terms of pixels, inches, centimeters, points, picas, or columns. The height units can be specified in all these values, with the exception of columns.

The RGB radio button is selected as a default; any color image pasted into this document is automatically converted to a 24-bit RGB image, even indexed (256-color) images. If Grayscale mode is selected, any image pasted into this document will be stripped of color information while being pasted.

▼ **Tip:** If the image on the clipboard is a black-and-white or grayscale image, the grayscale radio button is automatically selected; if the image is a color image, then RGB mode is automatically selected.

The default image resolution is 72 DPI, which is the Macintosh screen resolution. You can specify a different default resolution if you know that you will want to work with images higher than 72 DPI. Resolution can be specified in terms of pixels/inch or pixels/centimeter. Set the units by clicking on the field to the immediate right of the resolution value.

▼ **Tip:** You can change the resolution of an image at any time by resampling the image. The resampling command is in the Image menu.

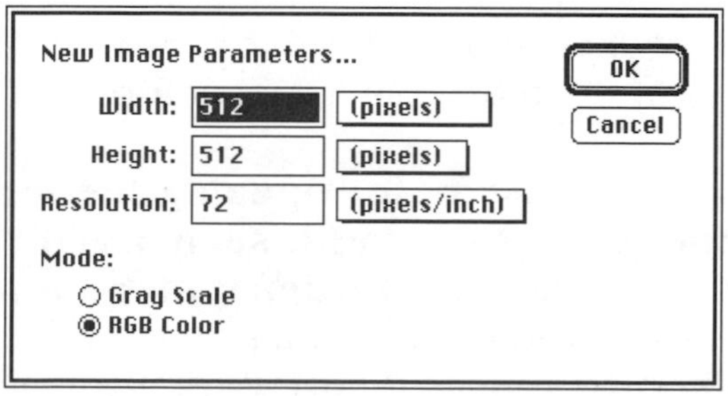

Figure 3–41   New Document dialog

Opening Existing Documents

Using the Open command in the File menu, Photoshop can directly open 14 different file formats. These include

- Photoshop

- RAW

- EPS (Encapsulated PostScript)

- TIFF

- PICT

- PICT Resources

- Amiga IFF/ILBM

- CompuServe GIF

- MacPaint

- Pixar

- PixelPaint (1.2, 2.0 and Professional)

- Scitex CT

- TGA/Targa

- Thunderscan

For a description of each of these, see Photoshop File Formats, page 77.

The Plug-in Acquire modules (which appear under the File menu) also open the door to allow Photoshop to be able to work with file formats that might appear in the future, such as compressed color formats.

The Open As... command is useful for opening file formats not normally used in the Macintosh world, such as TIFF files or Targa files created on the IBM PC. The default format in the Open As... command, Raw, is a generic format that can be used to open files that are likely to appear if you work with various types of computers. We have successfully used the Open As Raw command to open and view some great space shots that

When you select the Open command, Photoshop will display all documents in any of the above formats. As you click on the filenames, you can see the type and size of the selected file in the lower portion of the Open window, as shown in Figure 3–42.

we recently got from a CD-ROM disk of assorted image files from the Voyager missions.

Saving

Photoshop was originally conceived as a file format translation program, and as a result, it can save images in most of the formats

When opening an EPS file with a preview PICT (for example, an illustration created in Adobe Illustrator and saved with a Macintosh screen preview), Photoshop extracts the 72-DPI PICT screen preview information and imports it as a color bitmap. The resulting image looks exactly like Illustrator's own preview display mode.

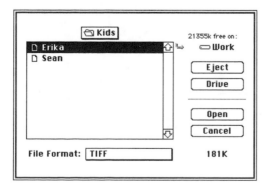

Figure 3–42 Open dialog with TIFF file selected

you're likely to ever want or need. The Save and Save as dialogs each contain a pop-up menu of the output file formats (Figure 3–43).

▼ **Tip:** Each of the different display modes presents you with different options when saving a file. You'll notice that some of the file formats in the Save dialog aren't available at times, depending on the display mode you're in when you select the Save command. Photoshop is smart in knowing what saving options will logically work based on the display mode—for example, to save a file in Scitex CT format, you need to be in CMYK display mode; if you're working on an image in Photoshop's normal RGB mode, you won't be able to save an image as a MacPaint file without first converting the display mode to grayscale and then to bitmap mode. See Appendix A for details on output file formats.

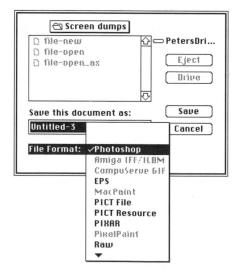

Figure 3–43 Save/Save as options pop-up menu

After you choose the file format you wish to output—and name the document—pressing the Save button will bring you to a dialog listing the options associated with the selected file format.

To get an idea of how large a disk file a saved image will create, look in the lower left-hand corner of the image window. The number there, which displays the amount of RAM an image occupies, typically indicates the amount of disk space the file will occupy when saved to disk.

▼ **Tip:** If an image doesn't fit on a floppy disk, Photoshop will automatically segment the file into multiple "chunks" and will prompt you to insert as many disks as needed to save the image. When opening an image saved in this fashion, Photoshop asks you to insert the disks with the segments, and rebuilds the single image file.

Photoshop File Formats

Photoshop

The native Photoshop format is preferable for saving either grayscale or color images that you don't plan to export to another application. When you are working in Photoshop, these files can be opened and saved much faster than any other file format. You can also save alpha or mask channels as separate layers together with the main image (see Chapter 5, "Image Selection and Masking," for more information on alpha channels).

Amiga IFF/ILBM

The Amiga Interchange File Format/Interlaced Bitmap format is a standard format for Amiga paint programs. The number of color bit

```
┌─────────────────────────────────────┐
│  Amiga IFF/ILBM Options...   ┌─────┐ │
│                              │ OK  │ │
│  Resolution:                 └─────┘ │
│                              ┌───────┐│
│    ○ 1 bit/pixel             │Cancel ││
│    ○ 2 bits/pixel            └───────┘│
│    ● 3 bits/pixel                     │
│    ○ 4 bits/pixel                     │
│    ○ 5 bits/pixel                     │
│    ○ 6 bits/pixel                     │
│    ○ 7 bits/pixel                     │
│    ○ 8 bits/pixel                     │
└─────────────────────────────────────┘
```

Figure 3-44   Amiga IFF/ILBM save dialog

planes can be from 1 (black-and-white) to 8 (256 colors), as shown on the dialog box in Figure 3-44.

CompuServe GIF

This format is useful for saving or opening files to or from the CompuServe Networks, a public telecommunications service. A number of microcomputers can read this file format. GIF files can contain from 1 to 8 bits of color information (Figure 3-45).

```
┌─────────────────────────────────────┐
│  CompuServe GIF Options...   ┌─────┐ │
│                              │ OK  │ │
│  Resolution:                 └─────┘ │
│                              ┌───────┐│
│    ○ 1 bit/pixel             │Cancel ││
│    ○ 2 bits/pixel            └───────┘│
│    ○ 3 bits/pixel                     │
│    ○ 4 bits/pixel                     │
│    ○ 5 bits/pixel                     │
│    ○ 6 bits/pixel                     │
│    ○ 7 bits/pixel                     │
│    ● 8 bits/pixel                     │
└─────────────────────────────────────┘
```

Figure 3-45   CompuServe GIF format dialog

EPS

EPS (Encapsulated PostScript) is one of the more useful formats for exporting color images to page layout programs. Using this format you can place color images into programs such as PageMaker and Quark Express for incorporation into full-page layouts.

▼ **Tip:** If you primarily use grayscale images in your layouts, then you should stick with using the TIFF format; a grayscale image saved in EPS format is appreciably larger than its TIFF counterpart.

An EPS file consists of a PostScript description and a PICT screen preview of the image. When saving an EPS file, you can choose to create either a 1-bit black-and-white or an 8-bit color screen preview of the image, or no preview at all (in which case, when imported into a page layout program, the image is represented by its bounding box). These options are shown in Figure 3-46.

The ASCII and Binary options are used depending on what program you plan on taking the EPS file into—PageMaker doesn't recognize binary EPS files, but Quark XPress can. An ASCII file is twice as large as an equivalent binary file, and therefore occupies more disk space and takes longer to save and print. The ASCII format is the default when saving a new EPS file.

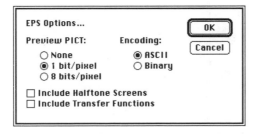

Figure 3-46 EPS Save options dialog

The halftone screen and transfer (dot gain compensation) values set in the Page Setup dialog can be saved with an EPS file; these values will override any screening or dot gain compensation utilized by the program importing the image. For example, if you move an EPS file saved with custom halftone information into Adobe Separator, the saved halftone information will override Separator's default halftoning values.

If you are in the bitmap display mode, and choose to save the image in EPS format, you also have the option to make the white areas of the black-and-white image transparent.

▼ **Tip:** If you decide to save a file in EPS format while in the CMYK display mode, a check box for the Desktop Color Separation option becomes visible in the EPS Save Options dialog (Figure 3–47). When this is chosen, the image is saved to disk as five separate files: four files representing the CMYK separations, and a plain EPS file that serves as a screen and low-resolution print preview. Used in conjunction with Adobe Illustrator/Adobe Separator and Quark XPress, you can place a full 24–bit color bitmap into those programs and separate it on a page with text and other art in place. Photoshop is one of the first graphics programs to support this powerful capability.

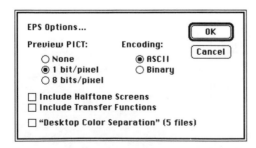

Figure 3–47   EPS Options in CMYK mode

PICT

The PICT file format is most useful for moving images into other Macintosh color painting programs, such as Studio/8, PixelPaint, Modern Artist, etc. Most Macintosh programs can import black-and-white and color PICT files.

You can save PICT images with various bit plane settings—anywhere from 1 bit/pixel (black-and-white) to 32 bits/pixel (full 24-bit color), as shown in Figure 3-48. Using the 8-bit system palette forces an image to conform with the standard Macintosh system palette; the image is dithered with a pattern dither.

▼ **Tip:** When you want to save a document as an indexed color file with a custom color palette, you need to convert the image to Adaptive indexed display mode before saving it—if you try to save an RGB image in 256-color indexed form, the file will be saved with the system palette. For the best results when saving an image with the system palette, use the diffusion dither option when converting the image from RGB to Indexed color, and then save the image with the system palette.

PICT File Options...   [OK]

Resolution: [Cancel]

- ○ 1 bit/pixel
- ○ 2 bits/pixel
- ○ 4 bits/pixel
- ○ 8 bits/pixel
- ○ 8 bits/pixel, System Palette
- ○ 16 bits/pixel
- ◉ 32 bits/pixel

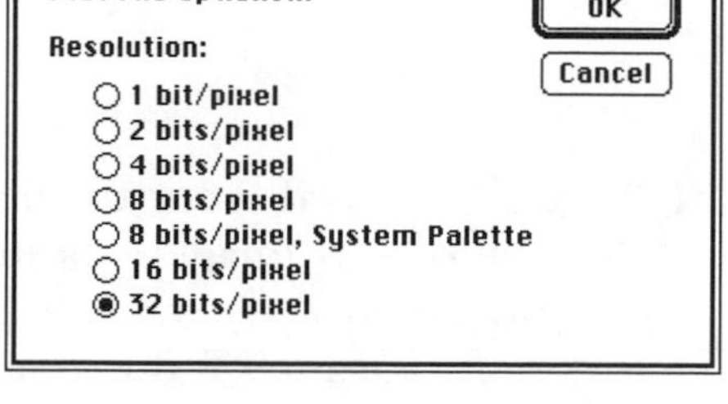

Figure 3-48   PICT save dialog

PICT Resource

This format is used to create custom startup screens and for creating PICT resources for inclusion in an application (programmers only need apply).

When you save a file as a PICT resource, you can specify the file type and creator, as well as the resource ID (0 for startup screens) and resource name (Figure 3-49).

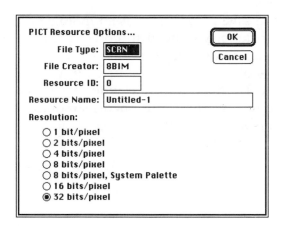

Figure 3-49   PICT resource save dialog

MacPaint

Black-and-white images in 72 DPI can be saved from the Bitmap display mode as MacPaint files. The size of this image is limited to an 8.5 x 11-inch letter-sized page. You can specify that the image appear either in the center or top left corner of the MacPaint document (Figure 3-50).

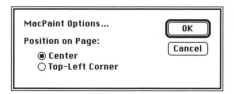

Figure 3–50   MacPaint save dialog

Scitex CT

Images can be saved in Scitex CT format from either the grayscale or the CMYK display modes; you can then transport an image to a Scitex workstation for high-end color separation and incorporation into page layouts. Currently, to use this option you will need to have access to the Quark XPress–Scitex communications system called Visionary. You might also be able to use in place of Visionary a communications program due to be released by Scitex in the near future.

TGA/Targa

In the IBM PC world, the Targa format is the standard for paintbox programs built to utilize the TrueVision Targa and Vista video boards. We were successful in opening compressed and uncompressed TGA files over a TOPS network, working on the file in Photoshop, and then saving the changes back to the PC-based file without ever having the Targa file reside locally on the Macintosh hard disk.

The maximum size of a TGA file is 512 x 482 pixels; files can be smaller but not larger than this size. TGA files can contain either 16, 24, or 32 bits of color information (in 32–bit files, the 8–bit alpha channel is in fact implemented for an overlay layer). Some programs expect the 24–bit RGB file to include an alpha channel, even though

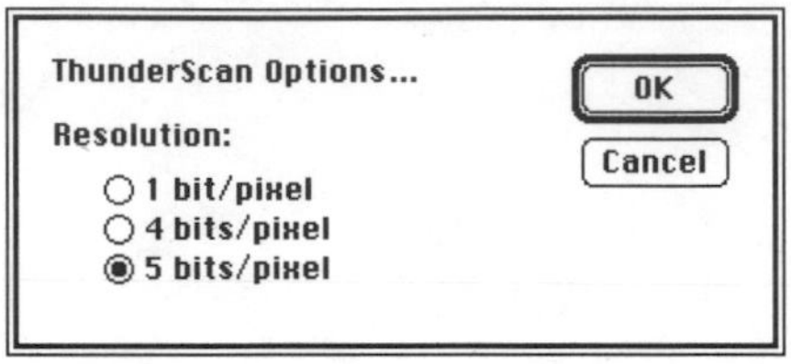

```
ThunderScan Options...        ( OK )
Resolution:                   [ Cancel ]
  ○ 1 bit/pixel
  ○ 4 bits/pixel
  ⦿ 5 bits/pixel
```

Figure 3–51   TGA save dialog

the alpha channel isn't recognized; hence the 32–bits/pixel option
(Figure 3–51).

ThunderScan

The ThunderScan was one of the first grayscale image digitizers to
appear for the Macintosh. You can save grayscale images with either
1, 4, or 5 bits of grayscale information, which can then be opened
in the ThunderScan software (Figure 3–52).

TIFF

TIFF (Tagged-Image File Format) is one of the more useful formats
for transporting color and grayscale images into page-layout
programs. TIFF is essentially a variable-resolution raster/bitmap file.

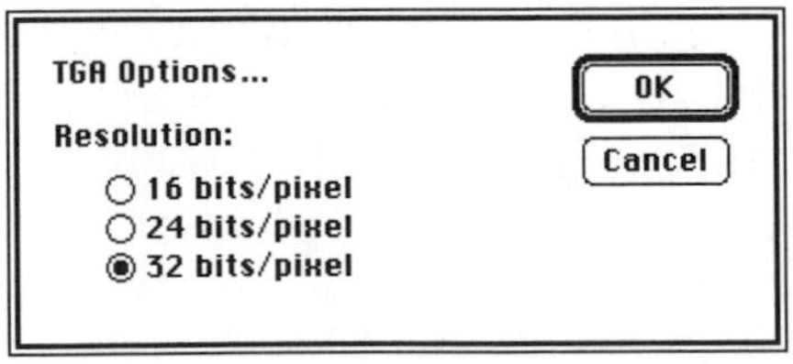

```
TGA Options...               ( OK )
Resolution:                  [ Cancel ]
  ○ 16 bits/pixel
  ○ 24 bits/pixel
  ⦿ 32 bits/pixel
```

Figure 3–52   ThunderScan save dialog

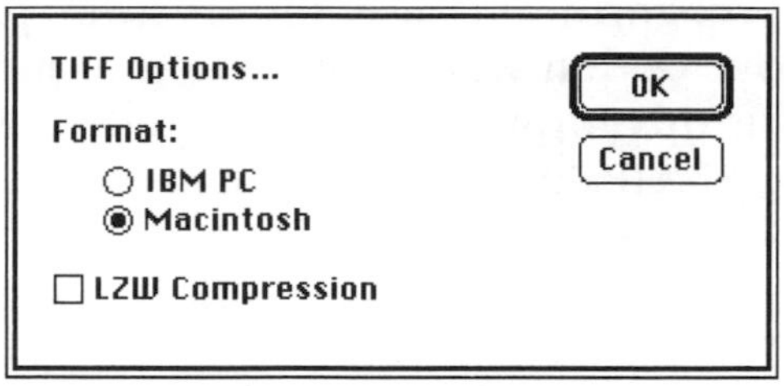

```
┌─────────────────────────────────────────┐
│  TIFF Options...            ┌─────────┐  │
│                             │   OK    │  │
│  Format:                    └─────────┘  │
│      ○ IBM PC               ┌─────────┐  │
│      ◉ Macintosh            │ Cancel  │  │
│                             └─────────┘  │
│   ☐ LZW Compression                      │
│                                          │
└─────────────────────────────────────────┘
```

Figure 3–53   TIFF save dialog

You can save TIFF files for use either on the Macintosh or on the IBM PC (Figure 3–53). We were successful in moving a PC-saved image over TOPS to PC PageMaker.

LZW compression yields smaller TIFF files. It's wise to be careful about using this feature, as many page-layout programs currently available can't read or generate LZW TIFF files.

PixelPaint

You can save images in PixelPaint 2.0 and PixelPaint Professional formats. You can choose the default document size (in pixels) and the position of the image in the document (Figure 3–54). Remember that PixelPaint 2.0 doesn't work in 24-bit color, so make sure to convert RGB images to indexed images before exporting to that

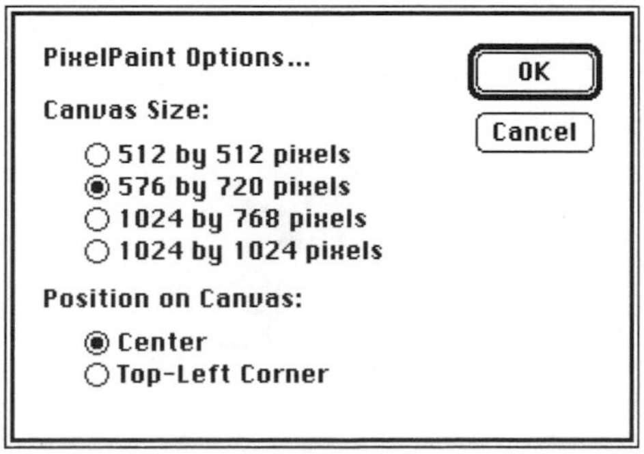

```
┌─────────────────────────────────────────┐
│  PixelPaint Options...       ┌────────┐  │
│                              │   OK   │  │
│  Canvas Size:                └────────┘  │
│      ○ 512 by 512 pixels     ┌────────┐  │
│      ◉ 576 by 720 pixels     │ Cancel │  │
│      ○ 1024 by 768 pixels    └────────┘  │
│      ○ 1024 by 1024 pixels               │
│                                          │
│  Position on Canvas:                     │
│      ◉ Center                            │
│      ○ Top-Left Corner                   │
│                                          │
└─────────────────────────────────────────┘
```

Figure 3–54   PixelPaint save dialog

program (PixelPaint will recognize and use the custom palette created by using the Adaptive option when converting to indexed color). RGB images saved in this format are recognized as 24-bit images when imported into PixelPaint Professional.

RAW

Raw format is a generic raster format, primarily for use in exporting images to other types of computers. We've been able to open raster files of satellite shots of the earth obtained from various sources.

4

Using the Tools

Some of the most obvious fixtures of Photoshop are the drawing and selection tools found in the main tool palette (on the left-hand side of the screen). In this chapter we'll concentrate on the painting and text tools and the various "floating palettes" (they can be moved to any position on the screen) that support the main tool palette (these floating palettes consist of the onscreen color picker and brush shape palettes), as well as the Fill command and the Paste Controls.

The selection tools (the circular and rectangular selection marquees, the lasso, and the magic wand) are covered in Chapter 5, "Image Selection and Masking."

When you first begin using Photoshop, you might want to try using the tools in their default state before changing some of the settings in their settings dialogs. Remember, each tool has myriad working modes, so proceed patiently.

Main Tool Palette

The main tool palette (Figure 4–1) contains icons for selection and drawing tools, as well as for the screen display modes (covered in Chapter 3).

Individual Tool Settings

Double-clicking or Option-clicking on any tool in the tool palette will open that tool's settings dialog (also refered to as the Options

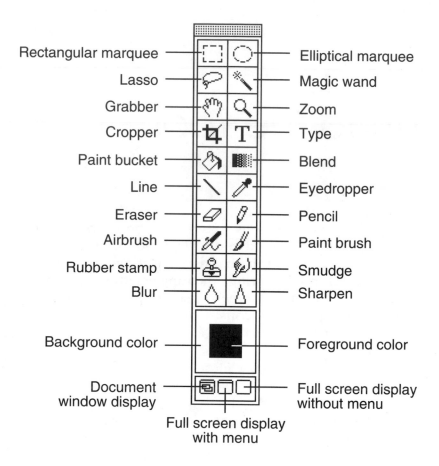

Figure 4-1 Main tool palette

window) allowing you to modify controllable parameters that affect the way the tool works. Although some of the settings in these dialogs are the same in all the tools, each tool has controls that are unique to it. For example, each tool has the same selectable brush shapes.

Factors That Apply to All Tools

Here are some factors that apply to the operation of all the tools in Photoshop.

- Each tool has a unique icon; normally, when you are using the tools on the screen, your cursor will be represented by the specific tool icon you're using. To provide maximum accuracy when using any of the tools, you can replace the tool icon with a precision crosshair. The center point of the crosshair is the "hot spot"; the effect of the tool will be centered on the crosshair's hot spot.

▼ **Tip:** To use a crosshair instead of the tool icon, press the Caps Lock key on your keyboard. While the Caps Lock key is activated, the crosshair indicator is active for all tools. If you decide that you like using the crosshair feature, just remember that if you save a file while the Caps Lock key is depressed, the letters will all be caps when you start typing the name of the file.

If you prefer to use the actual tool icons, Figure 4-2 shows the locations of the hot spots of each tool.

- If you want to use a tool to draw a straight line (or in the case of the softening or sharpening tools, to apply the effect in a straight line), you'll find that the Macintosh standard of using the Shift key while drawing to constrain

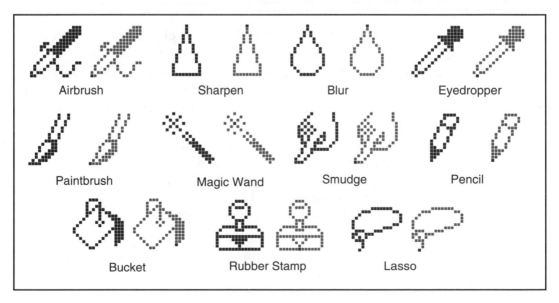

Airbrush	Sharpen	Blur	Eyedropper
Paintbrush	Magic Wand	Smudge	Pencil
Bucket	Rubber Stamp	Lasso

Figure 4-2 Tools and their hot spots

movement to 90-degree increments doesn't work as expected in Photoshop. Instead, you need to do the following:

1. Click the tool in the beginning position.
2. Release the mouse button.
3. Press the Shift key, and click the tool in the target location. The effect of the tool will be applied in a straight line between the first and second positions.

If the Shift key remains pressed, each successive click of the mouse will continue the effect or line from the last position. By releasing the Shift key, you can continue to use a tool in freehand mode, beginning from the last restrained position.

- While using the drawing tools, you can temporarily change the current tool into the dropper, in order to select a new foreground color from a color found in the image. Pressing the Option key turns the current tool icon or crosshair into the dropper tool or crosshair. Clicking on a color will make that color the active foreground color.

▼ Tip: While using the dropper tool, you can click on image windows other than the one you're currently working within in order to pick up colors not found in your working document; using this capability, you can make a document with your preferred/working color palette, and select colors from the document at any time. This technique overcomes the lack of a programmable palette window that is memorized by the program, a feature sorely missing from the current version of Photoshop.

Note that the crosshair for the dropper tool differs from the crosshair used by the rest of the tools (Figure 4-3).

- Each of the tools dialogs allows you to apply color in one of four techniques:

Normal   Color Only
Lighten   Darken

Figure 4–3   Dropper crosshair   Normal crosshair

The **Normal** mode is the default mode for all of the tools. When Normal mode is selected, the current foreground color is applied as a solid, opaque color fill using the current brush shape.

Color Only is extremely useful for tinting areas. In this mode, only the hue component (or actual "color") is applied to the image as the tool is passed over an area. When colorizing grayscale images, you would use Color Only to apply "transparent" tints of the current foreground color to grayscale areas. The brightness and saturation of the image remain intact, while the hue of the image changes.

The actual detail of an image is contained in its brightness and saturation values; these details are visible by their interplay with the light source directed at them, thus creating shadows. The shadows are simply different values of a particular color. When a tool in Color Only mode is passed over the shadows, those different values are tinted to a new color without losing their tonal differences.

Lighten Only applies a tool only to areas that are lighter than the current foreground color, with lightness measured as the luminosity value.

Darken Only applies a tool only to pixels darker than the current foreground color.

▼ **Tip:** The Lighten and Darken modes are found in other features of the program, such as the Paste Controls dialog and the Fill command. They work much the same way; the brightness of the foreground color sets the sensitivity, or threshold, of tinting and pasting a selected region or masked area. If you encounter a problem with tools that don't seem to be drawing on the screen when used, check your apply settings (darken, lighten, etc.) to make sure that you're not using a setting that prohibits the tool from applying paint as expected. Another important note: If an area of the image is selected with any of the selection tools, or through an alpha channel, tools will only work in the selected area. If for some reason you have a selected area with Hide Selection (Selection menu) turned on, tools may appear to not work properly. Remember that when an area is selected, the tools will only work within the selected area (this is one of the masking abilities of Photoshop).

Spacing controls the space between pixels being affected by the stroke of any particular tool. For example, if a spacing of 20 is set for the brush, then it will lay down color at every 20 pixels, leaving the pixels in-between untouched. This feature can be used to create dotted lines. If the spacing is set to 0, then the space between paint applications varies based on the speed of mouse movement: The faster you drag the mouse, the more space occurs between each paint application. Great for paint speckle and spatter effects. (See Figure 4–4.)

Fade-out is the factor that determines the distance the paintbrush or airbrush can go before the "ink" flow runs out. The overall effect is the ability to draw gradient strokes with the painting tools. In traditional methods, this is sometimes a handicap, or bug; in

Figure 4–4   Spacing set to 0   Spacing set to 25

Photoshop, it's a feature. It can be determined up to a pixel where the tool will start to fade out to nothing. The fade-out is gradual, as it would be with conventional tools.

▼ **Tip:** If the fade-out is set to a negative number, the paint stroke begins with the current foreground color and gradually blends to the current background color.

Paint Opacity is a control found in all of the paint tools with the exception of the airbrush. The percentage of opacity will determine the transparency of the color being laid down by a particular tool with respect to the underlying image. When a solid black is the Foreground color and the Opacity is set at 50%, the result will be a 50% gray with a blend of the image over which the tool is passed.

Pressure controls the "force" with which a tool is applied to the surface. For example, in the case of the smudge tool, a higher pressure setting will spread paint farther. With the painting tools, higher settings result in more paint applied to each stroke.

Repeat Rate can be found in all the tools except the pencil, line, eraser, and rubber stamp. This command controls how fast a tool will apply an effect or color while the mouse is motionless. If you set the paintbrush to a low opacity and a high repeat rate, the color is gradually built up as you hold the brush motionless over an area.

Brush Palette

The Brush palette is exactly like the brush shapes portion of each tool dialog, except that it's a floating window that can be left on the screen. When a tool is selected, the brush shape for that tool is reflected in the Brush window. If you've selected a brush shape from within the dialog of a specific tool, that brush is selected in the Brush window when the specific tool is selected. The Brush shape window overrides the settings in individual tool dialogs. You'll find that using the Brush window is the preferable way to select brush shapes during working sessions.

Custom Brush Shapes

Each tool has a variety of brush shapes and sizes. The different brushes are selected by simply clicking on them (Figure 4–5).

There is also a custom brush icon in the lower right-hand corner of the brush shapes display (which is empty if you've never defined

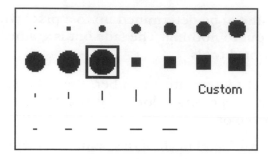

Figure 4-5   Generic brush shapes

a custom brush). Custom brushes can be created by any small (64 x 64 pixel) object on the screen:

- Make a small shape with any of the painting tools.
- Select the shape with the wand selection tool (you can use any of the selection tools to select the desired area).
- Choose the Make Custom Brush command from the Edit menu.
- Open any tool's control dialog.
- Look for the custom shape among the brush shapes.

If you try to create a brush larger than Photoshop can handle, you will see the message shown in Figure 4-6 immediately after you select the Make Custom Brush command.

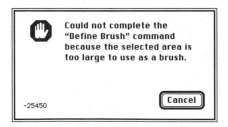

Figure 4-6   You'll see this warning if your selected shape is too large to become a brush.

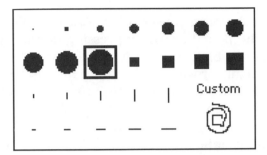

Figure 4-7 Brush Shapes window with new custom brush

Photoshop only allows you to use one custom brush at a time, and your custom brush appears in all dialogs that display brush shapes (Figure 4-7). There is no facility in the program to create libraries of custom brushes (you can cheat by creating a Photoshop document containing a number of custom brush shapes, and copying desired shapes from the document when necessary).

▼ **Tip:** Note that only the silhouette of the selected shape is used to create the actual brush; grayscale and color information is ignored in the process.

Individual Tool Overviews

Pencil

The Pencil tool works like the pencil found in almost every Macintosh graphics program: As you drag it across the screen, it paints. In Photoshop, the pencil is the only tool that isn't automatically anti-aliased; it's also the only drawing tool that works while you're in the Indexed display mode. You can set the pencil to automatically erase specific colored pixels to the background color by selecting the Auto Erase option. Make the starting point of the stroke the foreground color, and as you drag the pencil, all pixels of the foreground color are converted into the background color.

▼ **Tip:** When using the Wacom pressure-sensitive drawing tablet, you can vary the width of the pencil brush by pressing down on the stylus. If you use a Wacom tablet, you might wonder how it works with the pencil; the default brush size for the pencil is a single pixel, and while the pressure sensitivity is supposed to affect the pencil, when you first try it nothing will happen. You can make the size of the pencil tool change by choosing a large brush as the default brush. When this is done, the pencil will still draw a single pixel brush, but as you press down on the stylus, the brush size will increase up to the size of the larger default size you selected.

One of the main practical uses of the pencil that we've come across is for creating textures that begin with random pencil strokes and then are processed through some of Photoshop's special effects filters. Another essential use of the pencil is for pixel-by-pixel editing or retouching precise areas of an image.

The Line Tool

This tool's functionality dates back to the early MacPaint days. In Photoshop, it has undergone some evolutionary changes. The weight can be specified in pixels. The resulting line is anti-aliased. Arrowheads can be placed at the tips, either end or both. These arrow tips can be modified into various shapes and styles by adjusting their width, height and concavity (Figure 4–8).

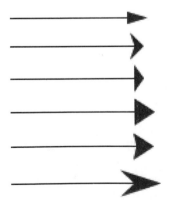

Figure 4–8   Examples of different arrowheads

The Bucket

This is another tool all Mac enthusiasts have grown to know. It uses the currently selected foreground color to fill the area over which it is applied. When you click over a particular color, it will fill the color area with a solid shade of color.

Unlike its predecessors in other paint packages, the bucket has Tolerance and Fuzziness settings. In most other paint programs, the bucket will fill only the color over which it is used. The Tolerance setting determines additional values that will be filled. The higher the tolerance setting, the farther a dropped paint bucket will spread. Let's say an image area is made up of three or four similar colors; if you've used the bucket in other programs in this situation you know the bucket will fill only tiny portions of the area, or only one of the three or four colors. With the Tolerance setting, the bucket can be set to fill the entire area.

The Fuzziness setting will make the outside edges of the fill anti-aliased: In general, the higher the setting, the smoother the edge.

Airbrush

The Airbrush is one of the more useful and seductive painting tools. Similar to the Paintbrush, this tool is for laying down gradual tones of color. The one main difference is how the stroke is laid down: The edges of the stroke are much softer than with the paintbrush. The result is a true simulation of the way a traditional airbrush works. Colors are applied as soft, subtle sprays, making it possible to add just a hint of color. Passing over a previous stroke gradually builds up the density of the paint.

One good application of this tool is adding make-up to skin tones. An example of this can be found in Chapter 10, "Color Publishing and Retouching," where a woman's face is retouched.

This tool can also be used to add highlights and shadows to an object. It can also simulate reflections on metal as in exercise 3 in Chapter 11, "Fine Art," where tones of varying grays are sprayed across the barrel of a traditional airbrush tool.

The Fade-out box in the Airbrush options window controls how far a stroke will go before it runs out of ink. Unlike its real-world counterpart, it can be controlled.

Airbrush Sparkle Recipe

The Airbrush tool is great for adding that little sparkle that your image might be missing—real sparkle, a little starburst shimmer that gives a polished surface that high-gloss look.

1. Start a new document and select Invert from the Map submenu of the Image menu. This turns the document into a black background.
2. Type a word in a large font size and bright red color.
3. Select a bright yellow color, which will now become the sparkle.
4. Double-click on the Airbrush tool to bring up the options window and select the third smallest brush size.
5. The setting for fade-out depends on the size of the area, but for this exercise, set the Fade-out to 80 pixels. Click OK.
6. Hold down the Shift key and click the tool at a tip of the last letter in your word.
7. Still holding the shift key, click about two inches away from the first click.
8. Release the Shift key and click once more on the original click point.
9. Hold down the Shift key and click two inches away but in the opposite direction.
10. Go back to the options window and reset the Fade-out to 40. Click OK.
11. Click again on the original point.
12. Hold down the Shift key and click one inch away at a right angle to the previous lines.
13. Release the Shift key and click once more on the original click point.
14. Hold down the Shift key and click one inch away but in the opposite direction.

The result should be sparkling!

▼ **Tip:** In traditional methods, an airbrush is used to achieve smooth gradients for large areas such as skies. In Photoshop, this is best achieved with the Blend tool. In Photoshop, the airbrush is for more detailed work.

Rubber Stamp

This is the most versatile tool in the tool palette. The options dialog, besides giving the size, opacity, spacing, and mode choices, offers a long list of additional options.

Clone

These options turn the Rubber Stamp into some extremely useful tools, the first of which is Clone (aligned and nonaligned). This effect is very useful when you are trying to retouch an area that has a texture.

Textures present a problem in retouching. Some of the more problematic textures are water, cloudy skies, skin, and any other texture made up of noncontinuous tones or shapes.

The best method for working with these textures is to use the textures themselves. A typical situation might be a boat in the water which has to be eliminated. Using the rubber stamp with the clone option does the trick.

1. With the option button depressed, click the cursor over an area showing the water texture.

> **NOTE:** This is the pick-up action telling the tool which area is to be cloned. Also notice that when the option button is depressed, the black triangular shape at the base of the rubber stamp tool becomes white.

2. Release the option button (the triangle at the tool's base goes back to black).
3. Move the cursor to the area to be covered—in this case over the boat.
4. Begin painting; the strokes will be made up of the water texture. Note the "ghost" cursor, which tracks the cloning.

Recently, we discovered a problem that was ideal for this technique. A sports figure was to be used for an ad, but the name of his team could not be used. The only photo available had the subject wearing his team's jersey. The jersey had a pattern of tiny vent holes with the team name across it. In traditional means the name would be painted out and then the pattern holes would be illustrated with painstaking attention to maintain the pattern. With Photoshop, the lower part of the jersey was simply cloned over the name. The overall color, hole pattern, and folds were all perfectly maintained.

When retouching skintones, it is important to note how sharp the image is. If the image is very sharp, then pores in the skin will be noticeable. If these pores are erased, the skin will take on a smeared look. To avoid this look in your retouching, you need to maintain as much of the original texture as possible. Again the clone rubber stamp comes into play. Here, however, it is necessary to clone areas very close to the area to be retouched. This is essential because the overall skin tone is not a flat color. Skin covers a curved area. Light hits it at different angles, thus producing a gradient effect. Many times when cloning an area, you will notice the change in color value. To avoid this, you must then choose an area adjacent to or at least as close in value as the area to be retouched.

There are two methods of cloning: *aligned* and *nonaligned.* In the aligned option, the distance and position between the sampled area and the tool remain constant. For example, you option-click in an area of an image to sample it and then start to clone it an inch up and to the right. If you now move your cursor somewhere else on the image, you will begin to clone the area an inch down and to the left of the new mouse position. The sampling cursor and painting cursor remain equidistant.

With the nonaligned option, no matter where you paint with the tool, it will always sample from the original point specified. This sampling occurs even if the sampling point is not visible within the working window.

A very important feature of the clone mode is that you can clone from another file. Even though the other file is not an active window, the rubber stamp can pick up information from any part of the file visible or not.

Revert

The next available option for the rubber stamp is Revert. This option allows you to revert areas to the last version saved on disk, complete with a soft edge on the brush strokes and control over transparency. This opens the door for some unusual effects. Recently an ad appeared showing a frosty bottle of beer. The moisture was wiped from the bottle across the center. Where the moisture was removed, a Blues band could be seen playing on a stage. This is a tough effect by conventional means. With Photoshop, it's a snap:

1. The image of the beer bottle is opened.
2. Select All is applied to the beer image.
3. The beer image is copied to the clipboard.
4. The Blues band is opened. It will serve as the base image.
5. The beer image is pasted on top of the blues band.
6. With the Rubber Stamp in Revert mode, strokes are applied over the image of the beer bottle. The result—the Blues band image will begin to show through the strokes.

▼ **Tip:** If the opacity of the tool is set at a low percentage, the image coming through will have a ghostly effect.

Texture

The texture option is great for painting with textures. Suppose you want to create a granite slab. Here's how to do it:

1. In Photoshop start a new file. Width 512, Height 512, DPI 72, and RGB.
2. With the Paintbrush, lay down a few strokes of different gray tones that overlap each other.
3. With the Rubber Stamp in the Texture option and the option button depressed on the keyboard, click in the area where the different grays overlap.
4. Release the option button and move the cursor over the area to be painted.
5. You can now paint with a stone-like texture.

Pattern

Pattern is the next option for the rubber stamp. Wallpaper designs, fabrics—the possibilities here are endless. Let's say the need comes up for a headline that has the word "WOOD" in it, which has to have a wood grain to it.

1. Scan in a wood texture.

▼ **Tip:** There are many sources for textures: Try scanning special papers, wood chip samples from furniture companies, wallpaper, textile swatches, slabs of marble, sweaters, and anything else you can get your hands on. We've had lots of success just laying cloth swatches and chunks of marble on a flatbed scanner. It's easy!

2. In Photoshop, open the scanned wood texture and choose Select All from the Select menu, or press Command-A on the keyboard.

3. Choose Define Pattern from the Edit menu.

The wood texture is now a pattern you can paint with.

4. Start a new file: Width 512, Height 200, DPI 72, and RGB.

5. With the text tool and a bold type font, type the word WOOD in 120 points. Make sure Anti-aliased is checked to assure a smooth edge to the type.

6. When the type appears in the window, it will come in selected, thus acting as a masked object.

7. With the Rubber Stamp and the Pattern option, paint over the word.

The result will be the word in a wood texture.

As with the Clone Options, the Pattern Option has an aligned and nonaligned choice. With aligned, when a pattern is created, the tool will lay it down as a tile in a fixed position. Painting over the same area will produce the same tile in the same position. The nonaligned option paints the pattern from the center out from where the tool's hot spot begins to paint.

Impressionist

The last of the options is the Impressionist. This option is great for creating organic-looking textures or patterns. It is also perfect for turning photographs into paintings.

To explain what is happening in this option, make believe an image is split into two layers. The first or base layer is the last version saved of the image. The second or paintable layer, which is on top, is the current image being worked on.

For this example, let's say we have a round brush shape five pixels in diameter. The brush has a one-pixel hot spot in the center. This hot spot looks at the color over which it passes on the base layer. It then spreads that color out to the edges of the five-pixel width of the brush over the paintable layer. The result is a smear of that color. Passage over multiple colors creates the effect of impressionistic brush strokes.

To get the painterly look to a photo, it is advisable to use a small brush size. The larger the size, the more chaotic the end result will be.

A very large brush will obliterate the image. This is, however, an excellent method for creating new patterns and textures.

- Over a very colorful image pass a large impressionist brush in short strokes.

This will result in a series of colorful swirls, which can be treated further through the use of filters to create some unusual backgrounds.

Blend

This is one of the most useful tools for creating realistic images. Unless an object is bathed on all sides with spotlights, no object in real life is a solid color to the viewer. If your surroundings are closely studied, you will notice that all objects in a room, including walls, are made up of gradients of color. The surface color of any object will diminish in intensity as it moves away from the light source. Even the subtlest of gradients will add dimensionality to an object.

Gradients are attained by selecting a starting and an ending color. The starting color is created in the Foreground color box. The ending color is in the Background color box. If a blue is selected as foreground and red as background, the result will be a range of purple shades blending from red into blue.

The Blend tool is also applied to create large gradient areas such as skies. This is an effect that by traditional means is achieved with an airbrush. When the tool is used, it is in a click-and-drag fashion. The first click lays down the foreground color. The drag of the mouse with the button depressed will produce a line that follows the movement of the mouse. The length of the line will determine the smoothness of the transition from one color to the next. The direction of the line will determine the direction of the fill. The position of the release of the mouse button will activate the fill, and at that point the background color will be used.

The way the Blend tool will apply a fill can be modified to create some unusual effects. There are two types of fills: linear and radial. The linear fill will create fills where the transition is in straight lines that follow the direction in which the fill was applied. The radial will make a fill of concentric tones, from the foreground color out, as in a sunburst effect.

In both types of fill, the Midpoint Skew can be defined. This sets up the point at which there is an even mix between the foreground and background colors—50% is the default. A lower percentage will set that midpoint closer to the starting point. For example, 25% will set the midpoint one-quarter of the way from the start to the end of the fill. A higher percentage sets it away from the start.

The Color Space can be determined. This specifies the way in which colors will be applied. There are three options: RGB, HSB CW, and HSB CCW. RGB will make the gradient between the foreground and background colors. The result in between is a direct mix of the two. For example, red to blue gives you a range of intermediate purple shades.

HSB will bring into the gradient any analogous colors appearing in the color wheel between the foreground and background colors. If you select red as a beginning color and magenta as the background or blend color, the blend will extend across a rainbow color spectrum. HSB has two possible directions, CW (clockwise) and CCW (counterclockwise).

To create a clear blue sky for instance, the Blend tool is used in this manner:

1. Select the starting color of a rich blue in the foreground color.
2. Select a lighter shade of blue in the background color box. This will serve as the color along the horizon, which usually appears to be lighter.
3. With the Blend tool, click and drag from the top down.
4. Release the mouse upon reaching the bottom of the sky area and the fill will be applied.

The first exercise in Chapter 11, "Fine Art," uses this technique to apply a background fall-off. Fall-off in a background is used often in product photography to add drama without distraction.

Paintbrush

Photoshop's paintbrush is smooth and anti-aliased. The brush edges are blended with the background as you paint.

Figure 4–9 Paint stroke with repeat rate set to 0 brush strokes

The repeat mode sets the space between strokes; when set to a high number, brush strokes appear as trails of soft, round dots. Set to low numbers, the stroke becomes more solid and line-like.

One useful application for a high setting is to create dotted lines. In retouching images, many times the need will come to rebuild some lost detail (such as a nose or part of a building). Tracing the area to be rebuilt with a light-colored dotted line will make it easier to apply the necessary strokes with whatever tool is then utilized.

▼ **Tip:** When the repeat rate is set to 0, the distance between the paint strokes becomes sensitive to the speed with which you move the mouse: the faster the mouse stroke, the larger the space. Using this setting, random spattered textures can easily be cooked up (Figure 4-9).

The paintbrush tool is "smart." If you paint while dragging the cursor very fast, Photoshop will force the paint stroke to follow the exact path of the brush, even though the drawing of the stroke lags behind your souped-up wrist action. This lag is very evident when painting on a Mac Plus or an SE, or when making broad, fast strokes on most Mac IIs. Photoshop is the only Mac color paint program we've seen with this capability.

The Cropping Tool

As the name implies, the purpose of this tool is to eliminate unwanted areas around the perimeter of an image.

The cropping tool is a more expanded version of the Crop command found in the Edit menu: You can determine the resolution of the final cropped image, and you can adjust the cropping area by the resizing handles before actually applying the command.

Drag the cropping tool over the area to be cropped; the very center of the tool is the "hot spot." Four handles appear at the

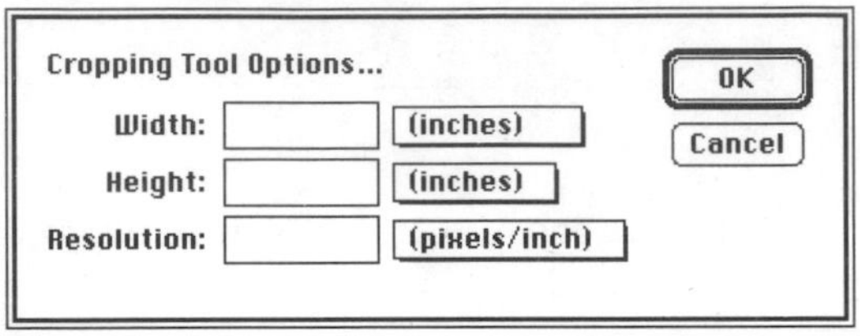

Figure 4–10   Cropping tool dialog

corners of the selection. You can click on and drag these handles, so that the selected area is redefined.

Once the area to be cropped is outlined, passing the cursor into the selected area will transform it into a little scissor. Click within the selection and the area outside of the selection will be eliminated.

▼ **Tip:** When an image is cropped, the crop will be the image size. If the desired effect is to have white space around an image, it is better to erase the unwanted perimeter.

If you double-click or Option-click on the Cropping tool, you are presented with the dialog shown in Figure 4–10.

By entering values into the width and height fields (which can be specified in a variety of units, selectable from the pop-up menus next to the fields), you can crop images to a predetermined size. The resolution field allows you to specify the final resolution of the cropped image. You can crop and resample the image in one step.

If you want to crop and rotate an area in one pass, press the Option key while clicking on a resizing handle: You can now rotate the cropping tool, using the selected handle as the central rotation axis. When you click inside the cropping area, the image is automatically rotated and cropped (Figure 4–11).

Eraser

The eraser will erase any portion of the image over which it is passed. If the Background color is other than white, the eraser will erase to that color.

Figure 4–11   Select area to crop, Option–click on handle, rotate, and crop.

▼ **Tip:** One of the fastest ways to change the background color, or canvas color, of an image is to set the background color to the desired shade and double-click the eraser tool. This is much faster than filling a background with a different foreground color using the Paint bucket tool or Fill command.

When the option key on the keyboard is depressed, the eraser becomes the Magic Eraser (Figure 4–12). This turns the normal eraser into a Revert tool: As you erase with the Magic Eraser, the image is reverted to its last saved version on disk, regardless of the changes made to the image since the last time it was saved.

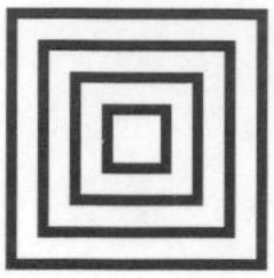

Figure 4–12   The Magic Eraser tool looks like this.
Press the Option key and eraser tool to activate it.

▼ **Tip:** The Rubber Stamp tool also has the ability to selectively revert areas of an image to the last saved version of a document. The difference is that the edges of the Magic Eraser tool are hard and jaggy, while the Rubber Stamp has anti-aliased edges.

Smudge Tool

This tool will bring you back to kindergarten days and the fine art of finger painting. The concept is the same as laying down a stroke in charcoal and using your finger to work it into shape.

The smudge tool picks up the color from where the stroke begins and pushes it in the direction that it's dragged. The pressure setting determines how far the color will be dragged: A low setting gives a slight push or blurring action, and a high setting can smear a color across an entire document.

▼ **Tip:** Although the smudge tool is perfect for small retouch areas, it is not advisable for retouching large areas of inconsistent shading.

Blur Tool

The Blur tool is useful for blurring harsh edges of an image, or areas containing undesirable detail. As you apply the Blur tool to an area, the contrast between the pixels in the area is decreased, resulting in an overall smoothing effect.

The Lighten Only and Darken Only settings for this tool can be very helpful. Use Lighten Only for smoothing out only dark shadow areas of an image, leaving brighter, more detailed areas sharp and defined. Or use the dropper tool to choose a color that represents the lightest portion of a shadowed area, and set the Blur tool to Darken Only. It will affect only the desired areas.

▼ **Tip:** When set at a small brush size, the Blur tool is good for softening the rough edge sometimes created when one image is placed on top of another.

Sharpening Tool

This tool is used to define soft edges in order to create the effect of enhanced focus, or clarity. As you apply the sharpening tool to an area, the contrast between the pixels in the area is increased, resulting in an overall sharpened effect.

If you continually drag the sharpening tool over a specific area, you'll probably end up stripping away all of the intermediate values in those pixels. While this might be used as an artistic effect, it is easily abused if all you meant to do was to reasonably sharpen a soft detail.

▼ **Tip:** The artistic effect part is fun: You can create smooth-edged, high-contrast portions of an otherwise detailed grayscale image. Similar effects can be obtained by applying the Threshold control over a paint stroke applied to an image through an alpha channel, but you will have less overall control.

Eye Dropper

The Eye Dropper is used to select the colors from open documents for the foreground and background values. As you press the mouse button and drag the color picker of an image, it picks up the colors. If passed over an inactive window, it will access any color within that document as well.

A color picked with the eyedropper will replace whatever color is in the Foreground color box. Press the option key and click on a color to set it to the Background color value.

The Color Picker

The standard method for choosing colors in Photoshop is through the Color Picker window (Figure 4–13). It replaces the standard Apple color wheel you've likely seen on a Macintosh II.

You can choose to use the Apple color picker by pressing the Option key while clicking on the foreground or background color swatches.

The first time you'll encounter the color picker is when you click on either the foreground or background color swatches in the lower portion of the main tool palette. If the foreground color is black and you click on it, you'll be brought into a color picker window with a large square area of red hues in the left-hand side of the Color Picker window. This is called the Color Field. Click in the upper right-hand corner of the Color Field, and the color spectrum will appear in the vertical strip immediately to the right of the color field. This strip is the Color Slider.

The default mode of the Color Picker is Hue; in this mode, the current color is displayed in the Color Field in all of its various brightness and saturation combinations. You can click anywhere in the Color Field to change the currently selected color, which is discernible in the Field by a little hollow circle indicator. By clicking on the various radio buttons in the Color Picker, you can change color display modes. The most useful are the first three—Hue, Saturation, and Brightness (H, S, and B). You also have RGB color spaces; but for most practical purposes, you'll find that the RGB modes are less useful than the default Hue mode and the Saturation and Brightness modes.

When in the Hue display mode, the Color Slider displays a full color spectrum of hues. By dragging the indicator arrows on either side of the Color Slider, you can change the current hue. When this is done, the colors in the Color Field are updated to show the saturation and brightness values of the newly selected hue. If you use the Saturation model (by clicking on the "S" radio button), the

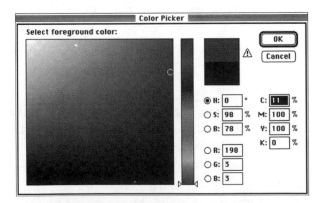

Figure 4–13   The Color Picker window

Sometimes a small warning/alert icon will appear immediately to the right of the small current color swatch (Figure 4-14). Photoshop knows that certain bright and saturated colors can't be properly reproduced with a four-color process separation. When you choose such a color, the warning icon appears. If you click directly on this icon, Photoshop replaces the selected color with the closest matching color that can be reproduced in a color separation. You'll almost always see this warning icon when the current color is a hot red or intense blue.

Figure 4-14   The Alert indicator

Color Field displays a color spectrum starting at full brightness at the top and gradually blending into black at the bottom of the field. The Color Strip displays the current hue blending to white. When Brightness is toggled on (the "B" radio button is selected), the display switches to show the blend of the spectrum for full saturation blending—to white in the Color Field—and the hue blending—to black in the Color Strip. We've found that these three models are the most useful for creating any variation on a specific hue, though we usually end up using the color Palette window (you'll find out more about this window in the next page or so).

Note that at any time you have the option to change the current color in many ways: You can change the CMYK and RGB values by simply typing percentages directly into the appropriate value field. As you type in new numbers, Photoshop automatically recalculates the new color and updates the entire window with the new values for all of the various component indicators. You can learn a lot about color theory from plugging different numbers into the fields and studying the results and the interactions between the numbers.

There are two small color swatches in the upper central part of the Color Picker window. These display the original starting color (the lower swatch) and the current selected color (the upper swatch).

The Color Palette

Photoshop's onscreen color palette is a quick way to choose from a default set of colors, as well as to use the full range of Photoshop tools to create new colors. You can reach it by choosing the Show Palette command in the Windows menu (Figure 4–15). It definitely doesn't give you the full power found in the more complete Color Picker, but the tradeoff is immediacy and the ability to mix custom colors by hand.

In the color palette there are three rows of colors; the top row has the main colors of the spectrum (red, yellow, green, magenta, blue, and purple) and some spots for custom colors, and the remaining two rows contain a grayshade blend between black-and-white. These are the default colors for the palette window. This selection is meant to give you a place to start making your own colors, as well as a grayscale range (necessary for mixing darker and lighter shades of a color).

As you pass the cursor over these color boxes, it turns into the dropper tool, allowing you to click on a color cell and make it the current color (which is indicated by the color swatch located below the RGB and Fore/Back buttons). You can also drop the current color (the larger color swatch in the lower box) into a color cell in the palette by pressing the Option key, which turns the dropper into a paint bucket.

There are also two pop-up menus and a set of slider controls in the palette. If you're working on a standard color Photoshop document,

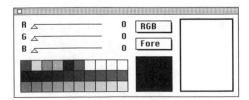

Figure 4–15   The Color palette

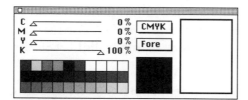

Figure 4-16   CMYK palette display

the sliders will probably be labeled RGB; by using the mouse to move these slider controls, you can vary the amount of each component in the current color (the values, displayed to the right of the sliders, range from 0 to 255—no saturation to full value). The pop-up control (labeled RGB in Figure 4-15) allows you to vary the color model used by the sliders. You have

- RGB (as shown in Figure 4-15).

- CMYK (cyan, magenta, yellow, and black); (Figure 4-16).

- HSB (hue, saturation, and brightness); (Figure 4-17).

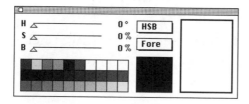

Figure 4-17   HSB palette display

It's quite nice to be able to switch between color models at the click of a button. For example, you can find out the CMYK values of a color selected in the RGB mode.

▼ **Tip:** HSB mode is quite useful in everyday work; for example, by setting the saturation and brightness to fixed values and moving around the Hue slider, you can create a set of consistent pastel colors, or use the Brightness sliders to make lighter and darker shades of a fixed color.

The other pop-up control determines whether you are editing the foreground (FORE) or background (BACK) colors. As you create new colors, note that the current color appears in the foreground/background color swatches in the main tool palette.

The large scratch area in the right-hand side of the palette window is the custom color mixing well. In this area, you can use any of the painting tools to mix colors the way you might using a real-world (wood) artist's palette. The magnifier works in this scratch area, so that you can zoom in or out for precise color selections.

Using the Brush tool, you can apply two different colors to the mixing area; with the Smudge tool, these two colors can be mixed together to create new colors. For example, mixing a red and a blue will result in a spectrum of purple tones.

The Blend tool also works in this scratch area. By setting the color space in the Blend tool dialog to either HSB-CW (clockwise) or HSB-CCW (counterclockwise), you can create a hue rainbow in the mixing area. This gives you access to the full spectrum without having to use the Color Picker window.

To apply a blend:

1. With FORE appearing in the pop-up menu box, click on the red square, which is the first of the colors in the three rows.
2. Change the pop-up menu to read BACK.
3. Choose the yellow, which is next to the red.
4. Double-click on the Blend tool.
5. In its options box, select HSB either CW or CCW. Click OK.
6. Back in the Palette window, apply a fill from one corner of the scratch box to the opposite corner.

The rainbow will appear within the box. The eyedropper will then select any of the colors within it and place them in either the FORE or BACK position any time you wish.

You can also use the clone tool to copy a portion of an active document into the scratch area.

▼ **Tip:** The tool, mixer, and brushes palettes can be moved around the screen; and on a multiple screen system you can place the palettes on one screen while working on another.

Text in Photoshop

Like most other bitmapped graphics programs, Photoshop allows you to create bitmapped type for use in your illustrations. Unlike those other programs, you can create type in a variety of resolutions and onscreen type that is anti-aliased, or smoothed against the background (more on this in a moment). Also, using the special-effects filters, you can create simply outrageous display faces in myriad colors and flavors.

When you select the type tool and click anywhere in the active document window, the dialog appears as in Figure 4–18.

The controls are fairly obvious: You can specify the font and size, leading (line spacing), letter spacing, alignment (justification), and

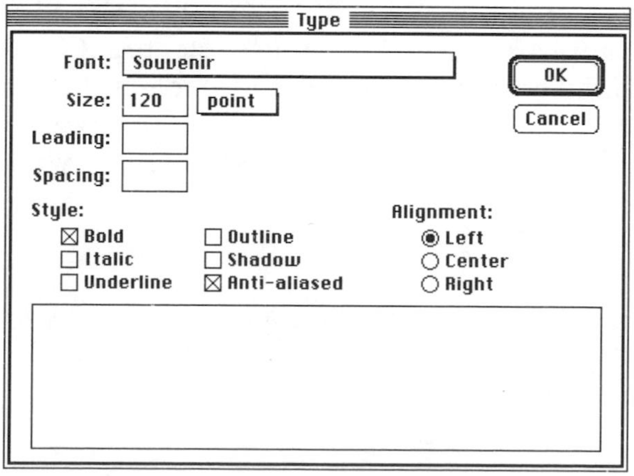

Figure 4–18 Text tool dialog

style. Type size is specified in either pixels or points (you choose which by clicking on the pop-up menu next to the size number field and selecting the desired unit). You can create type in sizes between 4 and 1000 points or pixels (Figure 4–19).

Text is entered by clicking in the text field in the lower portion of the text dialog and typing with the keyboard. Standard Macintosh editing techniques apply here, and although the Edit menu isn't available while you're in the text dialog, you can use the keyboard equivalents for Cut, Copy, and Paste (Command X, C, and V, respectively) on text that you've highlighted.

The text field will hold up to 255 characters; all style specifications apply to all of the text in that text field. To create blocks of type with different styling, you'll have to make multiple blocks of type and combine them manually (after all, no one ever claimed that Photoshop is a page-layout or typographical-effects program!).

When you're finished, pressing the OK button returns you to the main image screen, and the text appears. What really happens is that the text is pasted into the active image in the position where you originally clicked the text tool; the text is selected, so that you can move it around the screen, delete it by pressing the Backspace or Delete key on your keyboard (which won't disturb the image behind it), or use any of Photoshop's tools or controls to change or modify it.

To create and manipulate some text:

1. Select the desired color for your text (the current foreground color), and click the Text tool on an image.

2. Type in some text, choose your font—size and style. Click OK.

3. When the type appears on the image, it's selected. Change the current foreground color to another shade, select the Fill command from the Edit menu, and press OK. You can also press the Command and Backspace/delete keys on your keyboard for

Figure 4–19   Font size units pop–up menu

a quick fill using the current foreground color. You can continually change the color of the type as long as you don't deselect it (if you click anywhere on the background image outside of the text, the text will be deselected).

4. Choose the Stretch command from the Effects command in the Image menu. Handles appear on the four edges of the type. Click on a handle and stretch the text to a new size.

Any Photoshop command or filter can be applied to selected text for endless visual experimentation and fun. You can change the color of text by using the hue/saturation controls in the Image menu, apply strange filters, paste bizarre textures into or behind type, or discover a new kind of elemental particle. Just about any known visual phenomenon can happen in this program.

▼ **Tip:** While the text is still selected immediately after creation, you can open the Paste Controls dialog (Edit menu) and change the way that the text interacts with the underlying image. For example, using Paste Controls, you can vary the transparency of the text, allowing the background to show through; or by using Color Only/Lighten/Darken, you can apply the type as a tint or drop it out of the background.

Adobe Type Manager and Photoshop Text

Adobe Type Manager (ATM) is software that enhances scaled sizes of all Type 1 fonts for maximum onscreen quality. It does this by using the printer description files in the System folder as a foundation to calculate and draw screen fonts (Figure 4-20). When used

Figure 4-20 Close-up of normal scaled text, scaled/ATM, anti-aliased scaled

in conjunction with Photoshop, ATM opens the doors to a wide world of smooth, high-quality, bitmapped type.

▼ **Tip:** Remember, Photoshop text is not normal outline PostScript text when you save and print it. Don't expect to achieve the quality of normal object-oriented text typically produced by illustration programs such as Illustrator and FreeHand.

If you are running ATM normally with the rest of your system, it will automatically be used by Photoshop. To get the highest quality type, though, make sure to activate the anti-aliased checkbox in the text creation dialog.

When you create anti-aliased text directly on a detailed background, the nonsolid anti-aliased edges of type are automatically averaged with the background to achieve the maximum smoothness on the edges of the type. While the type is still selected, you can move the text around the screen, and the averaging will remain active until you deselect the type. Remember, once you deselect the text and start using another tool, you cannot edit or change the text—it becomes part of the image.

▼ **Tip:** If you want to see the way type will look on a background without deselecting it, use the Hide Edges command in the Select menu; even though the "marching ants" selection effect is hidden, the type remains selected and can be moved into a new position.

When creating large-sized type, it's preferable to specify the size in the text creation dialog versus stretching the type with the dynamic stretching command; stretched type is much coarser than large sizes that are specified in the text creation dialog.

Fill

The Fill command is located in the Edit menu. This feature allows you to fill a selection or border around a selected area with either the foreground color or any specified pattern.

The selected area is determined by the use of any of the selection tools. A feather can be applied to the selection to give the fill a soft outer edge (see "Feather" in Chapter 5).

▼ **Tip:** You can quickly fill any selected area with the current foreground color at 100% opacity by pressing the option and backspace/delete keys. This shortcut doesn't use any of the settings in the Fill dialog.

Selecting the Fill option from the menu brings up its dialog box (Figure 4–21).

Three options are available for the Fill: Normal, Pattern, and Mode.

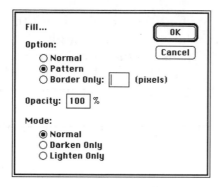

Figure 4–21   The Fill dialog

Normal

The Normal option will take whatever foreground color is currently being used and fill the selected area with that color.

Pattern

With the second option, Pattern, the fill will use the currently defined pattern to fill the selection. To create a pattern you follow these steps:

1. With the Marquee selection tool, select an area to be a pattern.
2. Choose Define Pattern from the Edit menu.

▼ **Tip:** Each time you create a new pattern, it replaces the previous pattern. You can only have one pattern at a time, and patterns can't be saved; so you might want to create a document consisting of pattern swatches for subsequent pattern creation.

If the pattern is smaller than the selected area to be filled, the pattern will be tiled to form a mosaic of the pattern swatch.

When Border Only is selected, only the border of the selected area is filled. This is a great way to make frames around selections. When using Border Only, you're asked to specify the width of the border in pixels: The acceptable value range is from 1 to 10 pixels.

▼ **Tip:** If you want to make wider borders around selections, you'll need to use the Fringe command in the Selection menu. Refer to Chapter 5, "Image Selection and Masking," for this procedure.

The Opacity of a fill can be specified. This enables you to set a transparency to the fill effect; the fill can become a ghost or tint over the selection. Whether the fill is a color or a pattern, the underlying image will show through. The visible amount of the underlying image is determined by the amount of opacity. At 100%, the fill is opaque, and the background is invisible. At 50%, the fill is a perfect blend between the color or pattern and the background image.

Mode

The third and final entry in the dialog box is the Mode for the fill. The main modes found in the tools dialog boxes are described here.

The **Normal** mode is the default mode; when selected, the current foreground color is applied as a solid, opaque color fill, or transparent if the opacity is set at a low percentage.

Color Only applies only the hue, or color portion of the fill, leaving the brightness and saturation values of the underlying image unmodified. Think of this mode as a tinting fill, which can be controlled using the Opacity setting—the higher the opacity, the higher the saturation of the fill color.

Lighten Only applies the pixels of the fill color or pattern only where they are lighter than the underlying image. For example, if you had some black text on a white background, and you wanted to fill the text with a pattern but leave the white background undisturbed, you would use Lighten Only.

Darken Only applies the pixels of the fill color or pattern only where they are darker than the underlying image. For example, if you had some white or light text on a black or dark background, and you wanted to fill the text with a pattern but leave the background undisturbed, you would use Darken Only.

Paste Controls

Any object being pasted in from the clipboard comes in on a plane that floats over the underlying image. It can be moved around and modified until it is deselected. Once deselected, it obliterates any portion of the original image that lies underneath it. The same thing applies to any floating selection that is dropped into place. The Paste controls in the Edit menu allow you to control the interaction between a floating selection and the background behind it until the floating selection is deselected. (Figure 4–22)

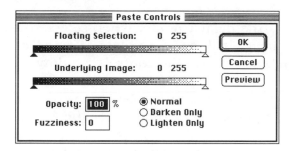

Figure 4–22   The Paste Controls

The Paste Controls in the Edit menu become active

—the moment an image is pasted into a document.

—immediately after you move any selected area.

—when text created with the text tool appears on the screen.

Anything you specify in the Paste Controls can be previewed before committing the change to the image by using the Preview button.

The first controls available employ sliders to determine which pixels in the floating selection replace those in the underlying image. These sliders, Floating Selection and Underlying Image, correlate to the mode selected at the bottom of the window. The modes are

- Normal

- Color Only

> The full range of the Paste Controls is available in RGB mode only. Certain features are not available in other modes: For example, the red, green, and blue radio buttons aren't present when Paste Controls are used on grayscale images.

- Darken Only
- Lighten Only

The **Normal** mode is the default mode; when selected, all the pixels in the floating image will appear unless affected only by whatever other option is selected in the controls window.

Color Only will affect only the hue value of the floating selection; only the color of the floating selection is applied to the background, without affecting the brightness or saturation of the background pixels.

Darken Only and **Lighten Only** let you compare the brightness values of the pixels in the floating selection and the underlying image to determine which pixels in the floating selection will appear.

The sliders will also let you further determine which pixels will appear by specifying a brightness range for the pixels.

The values in the sliders range from 0 (black) to 255 (white). If a value is specified and the values of the floating selection fall within the specified values, they will be pasted in. Values not falling within the range are eliminated.

A great use of this feature is when pasting an object that has been anti-aliased against a white background. White and light shades of gray many times will appear on the outer edges of the floating selection. By bringing the white triangle at the right end of the Floating Selection slider inward to about 250, the whites and grays will disappear.

You can also choose to have certain brightness ranges of the underlying image cover the pixels of the floating image. The Underlying image control varies the visible range of the underlying image.

The floating selection's Opacity can be controlled. By lowering the percentage in the Opacity setting, the floating selection can be turned into a ghost over the underlying image. The lower the percentage, the less the floating selection will be seen.

The Fuzziness setting in Paste Controls works differently from the way it does in the paint tools. In this case it controls how sharp the transition between colored pixels will be. This parameter is only applied in conjunction with the Floating Selection and/or Underlying Image sliders. When a color range is specified with the sliders, pixels that do not fall into the range do not appear. If the fuzziness is set at higher values, the eliminated pixels will appear but with only a part of their original color (though the optimum fuzziness setting depends on the brightness difference between the floating selection edger and the background brightness). It sets a transparency for those pixels so that they blend in with the new pixels, making the transition smoother.

▼ **Tip:** One practical way to use the Paste Controls is to apply a gradient tint to a grayscale image with a color gradient.

1. Start with a grayscale image. Convert to RGB display mode.
2. Select the entire image and Copy.
3. Create a new document, and create a color gradient covering the area of the new document. Select All and Copy.
4. Make the RGB converted grayscale image active, and paste the color gradient into the document.
5. Without deselecting the pasted-in gradient, open the Paste Controls. Select Color Only and click OK. See Figure 4–23 in the color pages for the results of this exercise.

5

Image Selection and Masking

One of the most basic functions found in any graphics program (and especially paint programs) is that of selecting portions of an image to be manipulated. If you've used other Macintosh painting programs, you have probably grown used to using the standard Macintosh Marquee and Lasso tools for selecting portions of an image. In Photoshop, the selection tools are more powerful and complex than what you're probably accustomed to—they can do things you've never been able to do easily (or at all!). In this chapter, we'll explore their full power.

The Selection Tools

Photoshop has four basic palette tools to select portions of images:

- The Lasso
- The Rectangle Marquee
- The Circular Marquee
- The Magic Wand

These tools work in conjunction with the commands found in the Select menu. Double-clicking or Option-clicking on any of their icons in the tool palette brings up a settings dialog. You can change the way each selection tool works by changing the values of the controls found in these dialogs.

Using the selection tools in Photoshop, you can quickly:

- Create complex photomontages with elements from different sources.

- Place objects against any background and create seamless smooth edges between foreground and background objects.

- Construct on-the-fly masks for applying tint and color correction changes to specific portions of an image.

- Create vignettes—like soft borders around selected areas or objects.

Macintosh users who have followed the progress of graphics software since MacPaint can tell you that things haven't changed much in all these years—the Lasso and Marquee are still the standards for selecting images on the screen. In the world of MacPaint and other black-and-white paint programs, screen pixels can be one of either two colors: black or white. Selecting a black-and-white image with a Lasso is a straightforward affair; the Lasso zooms in on the black pixels, slipping over the surrounding white pixels in the process. In some of the more sophisticated implementations of this capability, the Lasso knows that white pixels inside the solid black-pixel boundaries are supposed to be transparent. For example, in Studio/8, when selecting onscreen bitmapped text, you can specify that the Lasso (or Marquee) consider all white pixels to be transparent. With this feature, you can select text with the Lasso, move the text over a textured background, and the background will show through the white portions of the type (such as the inside of an "O").

When color painting programs began appearing, the standard Lasso and Marquee went through an evolutionary stage— color on the screen made things a bit more ambiguous. Programs such as Pixelpaint and Studio/8 dealt with more than just black-and-white values for pixels; hence, the concept of choosing a portion of an image became more complex. In Studio/8, for example, you can select a range of colors that are ignored when the Lasso or Marquee tools are used, making it possible to automatically lasso an area or object located on a complex background (where the background is made up of either a single color or multiple colors).

Photoshop takes the entire concept of selecting images to the next level of capability/functionality (and consequently, complexity). To understand how to properly use the selection tools in Photoshop, you'll need to temporarily forget how other Macintosh paint programs work in this regard. The familiar Lasso and Marquee tools found in Photoshop are far more intelligent and powerful than their counterparts in other Mac graphics programs.

Here are some basic points to remember.

- For selecting a specific isolated image against a solid colored background, you'll probably use the Wand tool. It effectively takes the place of the functionality of the Lasso tool normally found in bitmapped paint programs.

- If you are in a magnified view and your current drawing tool doesn't seem to be working, make sure that you don't have an area selected that is outside of your view. Remember, this is forcing the tool to draw only within the selected area. If that selected area is outside of the magnified view, then the current drawing tool will work only within that selected area.

- While any area is selected, it is automatically masked; whatever you do will only work within the selected area. Paint tools, filters, and color correction controls only work within a selection, unless nothing is selected, in which case the entire document is affected. This is the golden rule of Photoshop masks. Learn it well—even the mighty alpha channels spring from this simple notion.

- While using any of the selection tools, you can actually adjust or move the active selection "shape" by pressing the Command and option keys while dragging from the inside of the selected area. This moves the selection area without moving the *contents* of the selection. With this technique, you can "nudge" a selection Marquee if it's slightly off when you make the actual selection.

▼ **Tip:** With this technique, you can create "cookie-cutter" masks consisting of the shape of a selected area. By moving the custom selection area onto another part of the image and using color correction controls or filters, it's easy to generate special ghosting and shadow effects.

- When using any of the selection tools, you can add and subtract from the current selection range by using key commands in conjunction with the tools on the screen.

  —By pressing the Shift key, you can add to a current selection range. For example, if you started to make a selection with the Marquee tool, you could add to the selection area by using the Shift key and choosing more of the image on the screen with any of the other selection tools. This also allows you to select discontinuous portions of a document for any image processing or filtering enhancement.

  —The Command key is used to subtract from the current selection range.

  —The combination of the command and shift keys is used to calculate the intersection of two overlapping selection ranges.

▼ **Tip:** The selection modifier keys work with all of the selection tools all of the time; you can begin selecting with one tool, and add or subtract to that selection area with any other selection tool.

- When moving a selected image into place, deselecting it will place it over the background and make it part of the background image. If you undo the Deselect, you can delete the floating image by pressing the Backspace or Delete key on your keyboard, or selecting Clear from the Edit menu. This will delete the floating selection and return the background to it's original state. In many other Macintosh graphics programs, this same action will remove the floating image while erasing the background behind it.

- Any selected area can be "nudged" in any direction, one pixel at a time using the keyboard's cursor keys. This can also be used in conjunction with the Command and Option keys in order to nudge selection areas without moving the contents of the selection.

- Like most other Mac graphics programs, pressing Option while dragging a selection moves a duplicate of the selection, leaving the original intact.

The Lasso

The Lasso tool works differently from what you might expect: It doesn't automatically close in on an object against a solid background (the old MacPaint way). Only the Wand tool is capable of "autoselecting" the continuous color area it's clicked in (see the discussion of the Wand tool for more details). Instead, everything inside of the area created by your dragging the Lasso is included as part of the active selection.

Photoshop's Lasso also has an additional mode, which allows you to toggle between the normal freehand mode and a rubber-band straight-line mode.

▼ **Tip:** Hold down the Option key while using the Lasso, and you will be able to draw straight rubber-band lines; releasing the Option key closes the current selection with a straight line in between the first and last click. You can continue adding to the selection by using the Lasso and Shift keys. It's easy to isolate and select odd-shaped objects closely surrounded by other objects.

Double-clicking or Option-clicking the Lasso tool icon in the tool palette opens the feathering control (Figure 5–1).

You can specify a default feather amount for the Lasso. We suggest that you set this value to 1 for most basic selection tasks. This allows you to automatically avoid having a harsh edge around the border of the selected image or area.

▼ **Tip:** A feather value of 1 is quite good for most default selection operations; this will assure that the edges between two composited objects are always smooth, without the full possible effect of higher feather values.

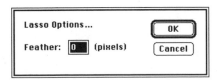

Figure 5–1 Lasso dialog

Figure 5-2 Rectangular
Marquee icon

Figure 5-3 Elliptical Marquee
icon

The Rectangular and Elliptical Marquees

There are two Marquee tools in Photoshop: the rectangular and the
elliptical Marquees (Figures 5-2 and 5-3). These tools allow you to
select portions of an image for manipulation. The rectangular Marquee works much like you would expect it to, with some added
capabilities. Those of you who have used Digital Darkroom will
most likely have used that program's circular/elliptical selection
tool.

The options available for these two selection tools are very
similar. Double-click or Option-click on the icons in the tool palette
for the controls dialogs (Figures 5-4 and 5-5). Both tools have
constraint parameters that allow you to select portions of an image
with a predetermined selection size, as well as a fixed height-to-
width ratio.

The fixed-size button forces the selection to be the specified size:
When you click the selection tool in the image, the predetermined

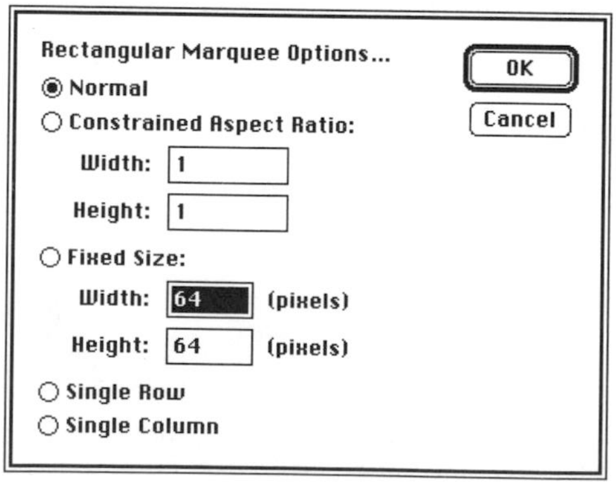

```
Rectangular Marquee Options...          [ OK ]
⦿ Normal
◯ Constrained Aspect Ratio:             [ Cancel ]
    Width:  [ 1      ]
    Height: [ 1      ]
◯ Fixed Size:
    Width:  [ 64     ] (pixels)
    Height: [ 64     ] (pixels)
◯ Single Row
◯ Single Column
```

Figure 5-4 Rectangular Marquee dialog

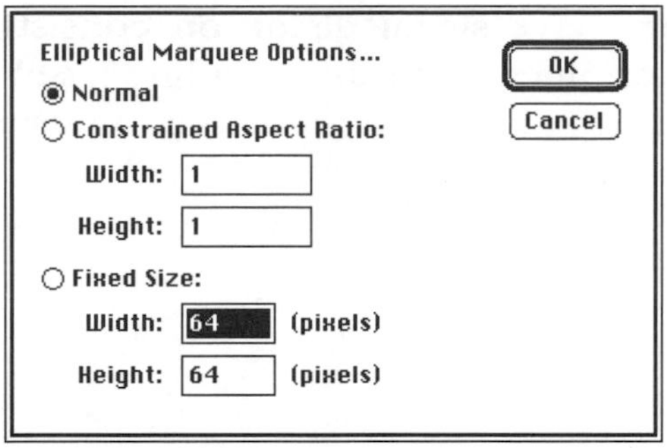

Figure 5-5   Elliptical Marquee dialog

Marquee appears onscreen, and can be moved to the desired location on the screen. Clicking the mouse button applies the selection.

▼ **Tip:** If you are preparing images for boilerplate layouts, chances are that you have already created sized placeholders for graphic images that are optimized for the layout; by predetermining the size and aspect ratio of these two selection tools, you can save time moving the image back and forth between the Photoshop and whatever page-layout software you're using.

The fixed ratio is invoked when the Shift key is used with the Marquee for selecting. A standard in the Macintosh graphics world, the Shift key usually constrains drawing tools to drawing perfectly symmetrical squares and circles. When you use a Shift ratio of 1:1, the selection tool will always be constrained to perfect squares and circles. The variable ratio allows you to expand this capability by determining separate width/height (horizontal/vertical) values.

You can choose to draw a selection area :

—diagonally, from corner to corner, as you drag the mouse.

—from the center of the selection out. Click and drag while holding the Option key; the beginning click determines the central axis of the selection.

The rectangular Marquee can be used to select individual one-pixel-wide vertical and horizontal bands of an image. This is useful for retouching images captured with video digitizers and frame grabbers, which sometimes have signal distortion consisting of slightly shifted or offset scan lines.Once the scan line is selected, you can "nudge" it a pixel at a time in any direction by using the cursor keys on your keyboard.

The Magic Wand

The Magic Wand is one of Photoshop's more impressive tools. The Wand is used to select contiguous areas of similar colors. Clicking on a color will automatically extend the selection to the borders of the color; the sensitivity of spread factor is adjustable.

Double-clicking or Option-clicking on the Wand tool icon in the tool palette brings up the Wand dialog (Figure 5–6).

The Tolerance control determines how far the selection area will spread. The values range between 0 and 255; the lower the value, the smaller the area the Wand will search—the higher the value, the farther out the Wand will search (Figures 5–7 and 5–8).

The Fuzziness parameter controls the smoothness, or anti-aliasing, of the edges of the selected area. Generally, lower numbers in the Fuzziness parameter result in harsher, more abrupt edges of a Wand-selected area. Higher numbers generally yield smoother edges. If you plan on copying a Wand-selected area and pasting it into a complex background, stick with the default Fuzziness value or try using higher numbers to achieve smoother blends between the pasted object and the background.

By using the Wand and the Marquee tools, you can easily isolate distinct elements against a background by using a variation of the intersection command. Here's how:

Figure 5–6   Magic Wand dialog

Figure 5–7 Low tolerance

Figure 5–8 High tolerance

1. Select the area surrounding an object with the rectangular Marquee tool (Figure 5–9).
2. Click the Wand tool anywhere in the background area enclosed in the rectangular selection while pressing the Command key (Figure 5–10).
3. Note that the object is selected on its outside border. Try using higher values for the Fuzziness setting in the Wand tool to increase the anti-aliasing of the selected border (Figure 5–11).

Figure 5–9 Area selected with Marquee

Figure 5–10 Magic Wand tool clicks on area to be deselected

Figure 5–11 Final selection

You can now easily copy and paste the object into a different background or another image and retain a soft edge on the object.

The Select Menu

The Select menu (Figure 5-12) works in conjunction with the selection tools in the tool palette; using the commands in the selection menu, you can

Select	
All	⌘A
None	⌘D
Inverse	
Grow	⌘G
Similar	
Fringe...	
Feather...	
Defringe...	
Hide Edges	⌘H
Selection->Alpha	
Alpha->Selection	

Figure 5–12 The Select menu

All of the commands in the Select menu work only when an image or area is selected on the screen except for the Alpha → Selection Command.

- Extend the selection area.

- Create "vignetting" effects with the feather command.

- Copy a selected image into an alpha channel.

- Hide the "marching ants" of a selected area while maintaining the selection.

Select All

This command selects the entire currently active document, regardless of the current magnification. If the entire document isn't visible, the Selection Marquee will extend beyond the visible boundaries of the window.

▼ **Tip:** It's mentioned elsewhere in this book, but we'll tell you here: If you want to rotate or flip an entire document, *don't* use the Select All command to select the whole document for rotation; this will result in a cropped image.

None

This command deselects any selected area. Once applied, you can be sure that nothing is selected in the current document. Command-D is the keyboard equivalent for this command.

▼ **Tip:** You can also deselect a selection by clicking anywhere outside of the selection area (inside of the actual document) with the mouse.

Inverse

Inverse selects the exact opposite of the current selection; if you are working on a selected portion of an image and decide that you want to leave the image alone and change the coloring of the rest of the picture, you would use the Select Inverse command. You can switch back to the exact original selection by choosing Inverse again.

Hide Edges

When you select this command, the "marching ants" animation of the selection border is hidden, even though the selection remains. This command is useful for applying masked painting tools to a selection without seeing the selection edges, for seeing how text looks immediately after creating it without deselecting the text, or for previewing an area processed with any of Photoshop's commands without the distraction of the animated selection effect. If you use a painting tool in a selection while the Hide Edges command is active, the selection animation will return when you release the mouse button.

The Hide Edges command is a toggle: when you turn it on, the menu command turns into "Show Edges," implying that the next selection will turn it off. Command-H is the keyboard equivalent for this command.

Feather

Feathering is one of the more useful selection modifiers—it allows you to precisely determine how an object's edges blend together with the background. Using the Feather command, you can create variable soft edges for a selected area, resulting in stunning "vignette" effects.

When you choose Feather from the Select menu, a dialog appears in which you can specify the degree of feathering (Figure 5-13). Accepted values are 1 to 64. Higher numbers yield softer edges (Figures 5-14 and 5-15).

▼ **Tip:** Feathering applies when duplicating an object with the option key, moving an object, or copying an object to the clipboard.

Figure 5-13   Feather dialog

Figure 5-14   Soft feathered image against white background. Feather radius is set to 3.

Figure 5-15   Heavily feathered image. Feather radius is set to 15.

Everything from a smooth border to a glowing halo effect can be achieved by using the Feather command alone or in conjunction with other selection commands (see the technique for creating glows around objects by combining the Feather and Fringe commands in Chapter 7, "Advanced Photoshop Techniques"). Examples are shown in Figures 5-16 through 5-20.

▼ **Tip:** Using a small Feather value (0.1-1.0) when isolating an object can be done all the time for smooth edges. Double-clicking on the Lasso tool opens the feathering factor dialog to be used as a default with the Lasso tool: you might want to set it to 0.5 or 1 at the beginning of work sessions.

Figure 5–16   Feather set at 0

Figure 5–17   Feather set at 1

Figure 5–18   Feather set at 3

Figure 5–19   Feather set at 15

Figure 5-20   Feather set at 30

You can feather selections and use them as masks for any of Photoshop's painting tools. See Chapter 7, "Advanced Photoshop techniques," for examples.

Fringe

Fringe Select is used to isolate and select the border of a selected area. The Fringe command can be used to select the edges of a floating selected object and apply a blur filter to enhance and blend the edges of the object with the background. With a fringe selected, a color can be filled to give an object an outline.

When you select the Fringe command, you're presented with a dialog that allows you to specify the thickness, in pixels, of the fringe (Figure 5-21). Photoshop will let you know when an entered value is too large (which occurs if the border is larger than the image, or when there are no pixels in the resultant selection area).

▼ **Tip:** By using Fringe and Feather together, you can create smooth glows around the edges of objects. See Chapter 7, "Advanced Photoshop Techniques," for details.

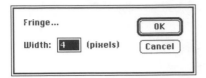

Figure 5–21   Fringe dialog

Grow

When an area is selected, choosing the Grow command causes the selection to expand outward into neighboring pixels. The Grow command is very useful when you've selected an area with the Magic Wand tool and discover that the Wand didn't select as much area as you want. By choosing Grow, the selection area will be expanded to adjacent pixels. The amount of the additional expansion as well as the degree of anti-aliasing on the edge of the selection area is based on the tolerance setting in the Magic Wand dialog.

Similar

When an area is selected, choosing the Similar command causes Photoshop to search thoughout the document and select all colors that are similar to the originally selected colors. As in the Grow command, the sensitivity of the Similar command is set in the Magic Wand dialog.

Defringe

When the Wand tool is used to select an object and copy it into another document or to place it on a different background, a common problem is that the outer borders of the selected object tend to display leftover traces of colors from the original background. By using the Defringe command, you can have Photoshop analyze the inner adjoining areas of a selection edge and extend those areas to the edge, covering the offending pixels (Figure 5–22).

▼ **Tip:** After using the Defringe command, you might want to use the Fringe command in conjunction with the Blur filter to anti-alias the sharp defringed edge with the background.

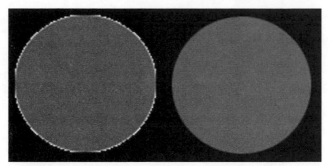

Figure 5-22 The Defringe command extends the inside pixels of a selection to the edges.

Paste Commands and Masking

The Paste Into and Paste Behind commands in the Edit menu are directly tied into Photoshop's masking capabilities. These commands are used when an object or area is selected.

Paste Into

The Paste Into command is used when an area is selected and an image exists on the clipboard; instead of the normal Paste command, the Paste Into command pastes the clipboard inside of the current selection area. In effect, the pasted image is masked by the boundaries of the selected area.

To use the Paste Into command:

1. Copy a texture or image into the clipboard.
2. Select an area of a blank document with the rectangular Marquee selection tool.
3. Choose the Paste Into command; if the clipboard image doesn't appear within the selected area, you'll see its bounding box in the center of the document.
4. Move the pointer within bounding box of the pasted image, and move the image into the area of the original selection area. You'll see the image within the selection area as you drag it around. Once you're satisfied with the position of the pasted image, release the mouse button.

Paste Behind

Paste Behind pastes an image behind the current selection area (Figure 5-23). This allows you to place new backgrounds against a set of selected foreground images.

▼ **Tip:** Immediately after you've used the Paste Into and Paste Behind commands, you can

- Move the pasted selection to precisely position it.
- Use the dynamic controls to stretch/distort, rotate, show perspective, and skew to modify the pasted image.
- Apply any filter or color control to the pasted image. Any modification will affect only the pasted selection and not the surrounding area.

When you modify the pasted image, you can undo the effect without undoing the actual Paste Into or Paste Behind. Once you deselect the pasted image, it becomes part of the bitmap and cannot be manipulated.

Figure 5-23   Selected objects with a background pasted behind the selection

Alpha Channels

One of the most powerful capabilities of Photoshop is also one of the most misunderstood: Alpha Channels. Most Macintosh users think of the alpha channel as the unused portion of 32-bit Quick-Draw; in Photoshop, the alpha channel is the gateway to a myriad of special effects.

In general terms, the alpha channel is a mask. Masks are useful for isolating certain portions of an image and applying color changes, filters, or any other image manipulation command to just those parts of the image. While you can use any of Photoshop's selection tools to temporarily mask portions of an image, alpha channels are masks that can be saved independently with an image file for later use.

▼ **Tip:** Alpha channels are essentially selection areas that can be saved with an image for use at any time.

One of the major differences between "object-oriented" programs (MacDraw II, FreeHand, and Illustrator) and bitmapped programs (MacPaint, PixelPaint, Studio/8) is that the object programs allow you to maintain a complex image as individual components, where the components can be modified at any time without disturbing surrounding elements. With bitmapped software, changing your mind about the shape or color of an element usually means that you have to redraw the element from scratch over and over until you're satisfied. The alpha channels allow you to designate certain portions of an image as separate entities, which in essence emulates this advantage of the object-oriented world. Alpha channels can also be used to "superimpose" images onto a background in a highly controlled fashion.

To fully understand the functionality of an alpha channel, it's important to understand the basic structure of a Photoshop document. In general terms, Photoshop works with multiple layers, each with 8 bits of information, or 8-bit images. Programs such as PixelPaint and Studio/8 can use up to 256 colors at a time—these programs are "8-bit" paint programs. In Photoshop, which allows you to create and edit full 24-bit color pictures, the image is actually made up of three 8-bit channels, or layers—one each for red, green, and blue. When viewed as a composite image, these RGB layers display the full spectrum of viewable colors. Your television set works in much the same way. This method is known as "additive" color, because the system works from the the lack of saturation of the red, green, and blue signals (which create a pure black) and adds value to each component in order to reproduce a range of colors. In the world of color printing, exactly the opposite is true—the CMYK printing model is "subtractive," because you achieve color by mixing diluted combinations of the four process colors.

Photoshop has the ability to work with documents containing up to 16 channels of 8-bit data: With a 24-bit image, three channels are occupied (for the RGB layers), leaving 13 channels unused. These unused channels are all alpha channels; they can all be saved with the 24-bit color image in a single Photoshop document. Whenever you open the document that was saved with alpha channels, the alpha channels are always available for use.

So what's the catch? As expected, disk space. Each alpha channel of an image is

- 1/2 the size of a main grayscale document.

- 1/3 the size of a color document.

That can add up to a large amount of disk space for images saved with all 13 alpha channels. Also consider that alpha channels are the full resolution of the main image—large, high-resolution images have large, hi-res alpha channels.

Alpha channels can be used for

- Isolating individual elements of an image.

- Overlapping image compositing effects.

- Selective image control and image processing, based on selected regions or color values.

The basic concept of the alpha channel is this: Each alpha channel contains 8 bits of grayscale information. The white areas of the alpha channel are transparent, the black areas are opaque, and grayshades are varying degrees of opacity. When an alpha channel is overlayed on another image (either another grayscale channel or a color RGB image), all of Photoshop's tools and commands work only on the transparent parts of the alpha channel. Any paint tool and filter can be used in an alpha channel, and any image can be imported or pasted in. By selecting and creating alpha channels for a number of individual elements making up a single image, you can change any aspect of each element at any time, without disturbing the surrounding image.

Creating and Deleting Alpha Channels

You can create new blank alpha channels by selecting New Channel from the Mode menu. You can put a seleceted area into an alpha channel by selecting it and then choosing Selection→Alpha from the Select menu.

Once you have completely finished compositing and manipulating an image, you can delete the alpha channel(s) to reduce the size of the final document by using the Delete Channel command in the Mode menu.

You can select which alpha channel to overlay onto an image by using the Channel hierarchical submenu in the Mode menu. In a color image, the RGB composite channel can be accessed by pressing Command-0; the red, green, and blue channels are accessed by Command-1, 2, and 3, respectively; and the first alpha channel is channel 4, which can be accessed by pressing Command-4. A second alpha channel would become channel 5, accessible through Command-5. You can also choose the various channels by selecting them from the Channels hierarchical menu. When an alpha channel is visible onscreen, you use the Alpha → Selection command in the Select menu to overlay it onto the main color image.

▼ **Tip:** In the case of grayscale documents, making an alpha channel converts the grayscale image mode to multichannel mode. Multichannel images consist of multiple 8–bit grayscale images. You can use the Split Channels command to make separate documents from a multichannel grayscale document.

▼ **Tip:** You can use any tool, filter, or control that normally works in grayscale mode in an alpha channel.

Most people will use the alpha channels to create custom masks for specific areas of a color or grayscale image. While this is great, be aware that there is much more that you can do with the power of alpha channels. The multitude of applications would fill many pages, so let's look at some specific examples that translate well to the black-and-white printed pages of this book.

Note: These examples assume that you have had some working experience with the program.

1. Open the Flowers demo file, and choose a flower by using the Magic Wand tool.

2. Once the flower is selected, make an alpha channel by choosing the Selection→Alpha command from the Select menu.

3. You now see a black screen with a white silhouette of the selected flower. You're now looking at a grayscale document and screen; remember, alpha channels are 8-bit grayscale documents. Note that the edges of the flower mask can be made soft if you've feathered the selected flower before copying it into the alpha channel.

4. You can now overlay this mask back onto the image with the Alpha→Selection command in the Selection menu.

5. Once back in the main menu, you'll notice that the flower is selected. Actually, the mask of the flower is selected. Any command or painting tool will only be applied to the inside of the selection. Try using the Sharpen, Blur More filter, or Invert command on the selection.

▼ **Tip:** Only the luminosity and saturation values are useful for the alpha channel; if you paste a color image into an alpha channel, it's automatically converted into a grayscale image.

By pasting scanned paper textures or specialty papers, you can make grayscale textures become a foundation for Photoshop painting tools.

1. Create a new blank RGB document.

2. Choose Select All and Selection→Alpha from the Select menu.

3. Paste a scan of wrinkled paper into the alpha channel (Figure 5-24).

4. Select Alpha→Select from the Select menu.

5. Return to RGB mode and select Hide Selection (Select menu). Click on the Paintbrush. Choose the desired foreground color and paint away—you'll notice that the texture of the paper (the white areas in the alpha channel) is gradually revealed by the paint brush (Figure 5-25).

Figure 5–24   Scanned paper pasted into alpha channel

Here's another alpha channel exercise for creating composite type effects:

1. Make a new grayscale image, and fill it with a texture created with Photoshop's noise and blur filters. This gives us a nice, complex background to work with (Figure 5-26).

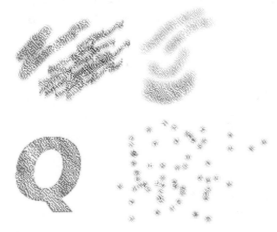

Figure 5–25   Paint tools applied through wrinkled–paper alpha

Figure 5–26   Noisy texture

2. Next, select the entire image with the Select All command and choose the Selection→Alpha command, both located in the Select menu. This will make an alpha channel of the same size as the image window.

3. You're now looking at an alpha channel. It's empty, so we'll create some type with the text tool and place it in the channel. Make sure that you have ATM (Adobe Type Manager) installed in your system, and that you use an installed PostScript typeface (with both the screen and printer versions of the face in the proper places). Click the text tool on the screen. Select the "anti-aliased" option in the type dialog. Make a word in a larger size (Figure 5-27).

4. In the alpha channel, white is transparent and black is opaque (more on this in a moment); so we'll invert the entire image, resulting in a black background and white text, as in Figure 5-28.

5. Choose the Alpha→Selection command from the Select menu. This will bring us back to the background pattern, with the white portions of the alpha channel (in this case, the text) appearing as an actively selected outline (Figure 5-29).

Figure 5–27   Text in alpha channel

Figure 5–28 Inverted text in alpha channel

6. By filling the alpha channel with different shades of gray (using the Fill command in the Edit menu), we can experiment with different type shades without recreating the type from scratch. You can also paste images from the clipboard into the alpha type, creating textured type, or use the Fill command to create pattern-filled text. Remember, this stuff works with *anything* overlayed through the alpha channel (Figure 5–30).

Once you overlay an alpha channel onto an image, you can add to or subtract away from its selection area by using any of Photoshop's selection tools.

1. Create a word with a large letter "O" in it, as in Figure 5–31.
2. Deselect the text, and click the Wand in the center hole of the "O" (Figure 5–32).
3. Select the Grow command a couple of times, to expand the selection of the "O" hole.
4. Choose the Alpha → Selection command from the Select menu. You now have an alpha channel for the hole (Figure 5–33).

Figure 5–29 Main texture image with text alpha superimposed

Figure 5–30   Examples of filled alpha text

BOAT

Figure 5–31   RGB image with letter "O"

Figure 5–32   Select the center of the letter "O" with the Wand tool.

Figure 5–33   Alpha channel with the center letter "O"

Figure 5–34   Selected "O" hole in main image

5. Apply the alpha back onto the main image with the Alpha→Selection command. The "O" hole is now selected (Figure 5–34).

6. Use the rectangular Marquee while pressing the Shift key to add a large vertical selection to the right half of the "O" hole (Figure 5–35).

Figure 5–35   Add to the alpha selection with the rectangular Marquee tool.

Figure 5-36   "O" with image Pasted Into the selection area

7. Open and copy a portion of an image to the clipboard, which we'll paste into the "O" hole.

8. Make the "O" document active again, and select the Paste Into command from the Edit menu. Position the pasted image so that it appears to be coming out of the "O" hole. Note that the left side of the image is masked by the alpha channel, while the right side of the image appears in front of the right side of the "O" character (Figure 5-36).

One fun way to use the alpha channel is to create a black-and-white checkerboard in an empty alpha channel of an image, and use it to composite two versions of the same main image together. For example, if you have two copies of an image (one normal and one that has been mutilated with a few filters), apply the checkerboard

Figure 5-37   Checkerboard composite image. Too much fun!

alpha channel onto the normal image, and use the Paste Into command to place the strange version of the image into every other cell of the checkerboard. As long as the images are exactly the same size, you'll end up with a great composite (Figure 5-37).

These are basic examples of creative uses of Photoshop's alpha channels. Look at Chapter 7, "Advanced Photoshop Techniques," for more Alpha channel tricks. The galaxy of potential effects is limited only by your imagination and the amount of free disk space on your system.

Case Study 1, Chapter 10.

The image on the left, is the original unretouched photo. Right, is the final retouched image of the record album cover.

Case Study 2, Chapter 10.

Lower left, the original unretouched photo. Right, is the final comp for a liquor ad.

Case Study 3 & 5, Chapter 10.

The image of the woman's face on the upper right of the page, is the original unretouched photo.

Upper left, is the final retouched image.

Lower left, the same image altered as described in Case Study 5 in the same chapter.

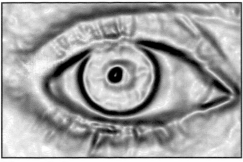

Figure 7-8
Color image pasted over metal image

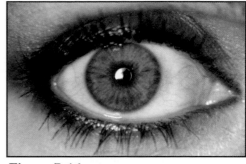

Figure 7-16
vertical crossfade from color to grayscale

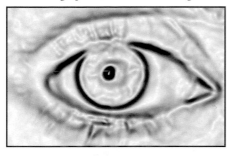

Figure 7-9
Gold metal
(left) and
Copper metal
(right)

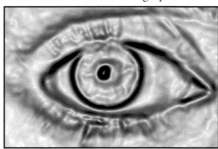

Photo: FAITH ECHTERMEYER

Figure 7-10
The image below was created by inverting
the Huechannel of the image above

Image: BERT MONROY

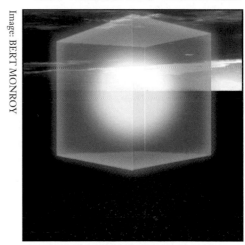

The image of this light filled cube was
created entirely with levels control of
selected areas. The background consists of
manipulated scans. The cube was created
by selecting the shapes that make up the
cube and lightening them with the Levels
control. A slight blue tint was applied with
the Hue/Saturation control. The light
source in the middle was an elliptical
selection with a heavy Feather that was
then lightened to the point of being pure
white. The haze of light on the ground is
also a lightened feathered selection.

Figure 3-33
Indexed color,
System Palette,
Dither-None

Figure 3-34
Indexed color, System
Palette, Dither-
Pattern

Figure 3-35
Indexed color, System
Palette, Dither-
Diffusion

Figure 3-36
Indexed color,
Addaptive Palette,
Dither-None

Figure 3-37
Indexed color,
Addaptive Palette,
Dither-Pattern

Figure 3-38
Indexed color,
Addaptive Palette,
Dither-Diffusion

Case Study 4, Chapter 11. Completed image.

Tutorial 2, Chapter 2.
Completed image.

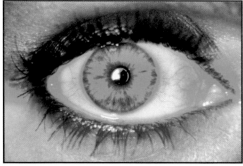

Figure 4-23
A blend done between red and
magenta using the CCW option in
the Blend tool is pasted onto a
grayscale eye using the Color
Only option in the Paste Controls
dialog. The result is a rainbow -
tinted eye.

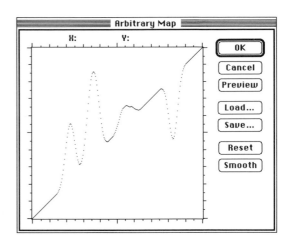

Color solarized image. Opposite: smoothed arbitrary map for the same image.

Figure 8-13
Illustrator 3.0 file with EPS separation from Photoshop trapped within circular mask.

Jo.before and **Jo.after**
A restoration by John Knoll. This is an excellent example of the retouching capabilities of Photoshop.

6

Image Processing

Image processing, a term loosely thrown around the computer graphics world, can mean many things. In scientific circles, image processing is used to analyze images in order to "see" things that aren't immediately apparent; and the prepress world's "color correcting" techniques are actually image processing in disguise. In this chapter, we will discuss the tools and commands for changing an image. These controls consist of

- Posterization effects: the Map commands

- Color correction controls: Levels, Brightness/Contrast, Color Balance and Hue/Saturation

- Filters

- Resizing and Resampling: image resizing, document resampling, dynamic effects (Flip, Rotate, Distortion, etc.)

The Image menu is the place to find commands for all of the above effects. Also found in the Image menu is the Calculate command, which is used to manipulate various channels of an image. You can find information regarding the practical uses of the Calculate commands in Chapter 7, "Advanced Photoshop Techniques."

Image processing is important to many Photoshop users. For desktop publishers, it's the ability to have fine-tuned control over every aspect of the image. For scientists, image processing reveals things about an image that might otherwise elude detection.

A few basic points regarding the image-processing capabilities of Photoshop:

- All of the image-processing controls, with the exception of the Resizing and Resampling commands, are only applied to the selected portion of an image. If you have selected an area by using an alpha channel or any of the other selection tools, any filter or color correction control will be applied to only that selected area.

- When working on an 8-bit video display, all of the image-processing slide controls work in real time; for example, as you drag a slider control of the Levels command, the image on the screen dynamically brightens and darkens. On 24-bit displays, some of the image-processing controls work in real time, while others don't. Make sure that the "VideoLUT animation" command is set to "On" in the main Photoshop Preferences dialog—this will assure that all real-time controls that can work will work on a 24-bit display.

- Many of the image-processing control dialogs (such as the Hue/Saturation, Levels, and Brightness/Contrast dialogs, among others) have a Preview button (Figure 6-1). When you use any image-processing control dialog, you'll notice that the change or effect of a command is applied to the entire screen. The Preview button is used to apply the changes exclusively to the currently active document or selection area. If you are applying a command specifically to a selected area, the Preview button is useful for trying out different values in dialogs and seeing the results in the selected area of the active document without leaving the current image-processing dialog. All of the image-processing controls in

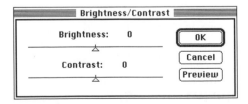

Figure 6-1   Brightness/Contrast dialog, Preview button

the Map and Adjust submenus (with the exception of the Invert command) have Preview buttons.

▼ **Tip:** Before you press the Preview button after changing a slider or other control, you can do quick before-after comparisons of the change over the entire screen by clicking on the title bar of the control dialog that you're using. The screen will temporarily revert to the normal, unaffected display mode. When using a 24–bit video display, you'll notice that after the Preview button is pressed for the first time to see a change on a selected area, it seems to go dead. Subsequent changes you make to the controls seem to have "lost" the real-time preview capability. You can reset the Preview button to work again by holding down the Option key on the keyboard while clicking on the Preview button.

• While you are in an image-processing dialog, the current document's scroll bars, as well as the Grabber and Zoom tools, are active and can be accessed. You can scroll around a document and zoom into an area to see the effects of an image-processing change without closing the dialog.

• If you're running Photoshop on a black-and-white machine (Macintosh SE or Plus), most of the interactive map and adjust controls aren't interactive: You have to use the Preview command to see the changes made. Not that we expect you to be doing color correction work on a black-and-white machine, mind you!

• If you are processing a number of images through the same type of color and brightness correction settings, you can create custom global maps of the settings in the Levels, Color Balance, Invert, Threshold, Arbitrary, Hue/Saturation,and Posterize windows. Here's how:

1. Make copies of the "Custom Map/B&W" and "Custom map/RGB" files that came with the original Photoshop disks. You'll modify these files to create the custom correction templates.

2. Select an image that will be the calibration "control" image. You'll be saving the changes you make to this image into a Custom Map file.

3. Make the desired changes to the calibration image, making note of the order and values of the applied controls.

4. Open the Custom Map file (you'll use either the black-and-white or RGB template to create separate maps for the two types of images), and apply the same changes to the controls using the Cutom map as the active document.

5. Using the Save As command, save the Custom map in the RAW file format, specifying "8BLT" as the File Type, and "8BIM as the File Creator. If this is an RGB map, make sure that the non-Interleaved button is turned on. Save the file.

6. You can now apply this custom map to any other image by opening the desired target image and choosing the Arbitrary Map command from Map submenu in the Image menu. Click Load and load the desired Custom map. Click the OK button, and the map will be applied to the image.

Posterization Effects: The Map Commands

The commands found in the Map submenu in the Image menu allow you to modify the number of colors or brightness levels in an image, as well as create custom maps of the input/output relationships of brightness values. In this Map menu you'll find

- Invert
- Equalize
- Threshold
- Posterize
- Arbitrary

Invert

This command inverts the values of the pixels in an image or selection area. You can make a positive image into a negative, or take a scanned negative and create a positive image. This command works in both black-and-white and color.

Equalize

One of the more useful commands, Equalize essentially balances the brightness and contrast values of an image to optimum settings. For example, if a scanned image appears darker than the original, you might want to use the Equalize command to automatically redistribute the balance of brightness and contrast values, resulting in a lighter, more balanced image. When applied, Equalize finds the brightest and darkest values in the image, and averages the entire spectrum of brightness values so that the darkest value actually represents full black (or the closest equivalent), and the brightness value represents full white. All other values in between are redistributed respectively.

The Equalize command is typically used in conjunction with the Histogram in order to observe "before-and-after" brightness values in an image (see the discussion of the Histogram farther ahead in this chapter).

In this example, the original scanned image was a bit dark, but with the Equalize command, we were able to automatically compensate and lighten the image accordingly (Figures 6-2, 6-3).

Normally, the Equalize command is applied to the entire image. If there is a selection area of any type when the Equalize command is chosen, you'll see a dialog as in Figure 6-4.

You have the option of either equalizing the selection without affecting the rest of the document (the default selection), or equalizing the entire image based on the range of values found in the selection area. When using this latter option, be aware that if a

Figure 6-2, 6-3   Image before and after Equalization

Figure 6–4   The Equalize selection dialog

selection area contains predominantly brighter values, the entire image will be equalized to a brighter weight; if the selection area contains darker values, the entire image will generally be darkened.

▼ **Tip:** Although Equalize is a great way to begin correcting a scanned image, you might find that the results are often much brighter or darker than you expect. Remember, the Equalize command is a starting point, and depending on the brightness range of the scanned image, Equalize might yield unusable results. If this is the case, try using the Brightness/Contrast or Levels controls as a starting point. For examples of the Equalize command and its relation to the Histogram window, see the discussion of the Histogram farther ahead in this chapter.

Threshold

Threshold allows you to create high-contrast black-and-white versions of a grayscale or color image. When this command is selected, the screen goes into a 2–bit black-and-white display mode, and the Threshold dialog appears, as in Figure 6–5.

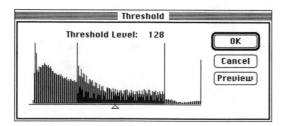

Figure 6–5   The Threshold dialog

This dialog displays a histogram of the brightness values in the current document or selection area, and by manipulating the slider control, you can determine the level of detail in the high-contrast image. The position of the slider determines the brightness level that Photoshop uses to determine whether a pixel should be converted to black or white when Threshold is applied (the numerical brightness value is displayed at the top of the Threshold dialog, and changes—updates—as you drag the slider). Try dragging the slider back and forth—the functionality will become obvious (Figures 6–6, 6–7, 6–8).

 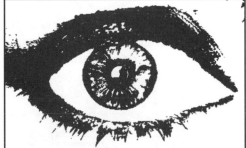

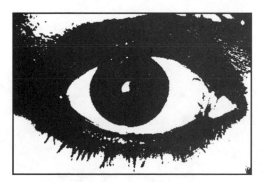

Figure 6–6, 6–7, 6–8 Three different Threshold settings with the resulting images

▼ **Tip:** If you are using this command on a 24–bit display, you'll find that when you use the Threshold control, the screen might not convert to black-and-white display mode. On most of the 24–bit video cards we've used with Photoshop, the screen goes into a pseudo-posterized mode, using chunks of solid colors instead of just black-and-white. In this situation, you'll have to use the Preview button to see the effects of the desired Threshold setting before clicking on the OK button.

Posterize

The Posterize command allows you to reduce the number of colors or grayshades to represent an image or selection area. While typically used to reduce the number of grayshades in a grayscale image, the Posterize command is quite useful for special color effects. When selected, a dialog appears as in Figure 6-9.

As you type numbers into the dialog, Photoshop automatically changes the number of shades or colors used in the image (Figure 6-10) to the number of specified shades. We've found that this

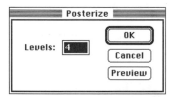

Figure 6-9   The Posterize dialog

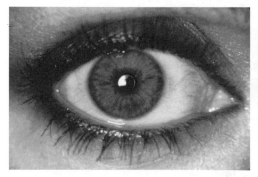

Figure 6-10   Grayscale image with 256 shades and posterized to 3 gray levels

"type-ahead" preview isn't quite as accurate as the image when previewed by clicking on the Preview button.

Arbitrary

The Arbitrary Map control allows you to precisely control the input/ouput relationship of the color and brightness values of an image. When opened, dialog appears as in Figure 6–11.

If the current image is a color RGB document, the Arbitrary dialog will display radio buttons for the separate channels. You can adjust the map for the overall image (brightness or grays) or for each individual color channel.

When you first open the Arbitrary Map dialog with an active image, you'll notice a line in the mapping area is a straight diagonal vector, going from the lower left to the upper right. This represents a normal distribution of brightness values (Figure 6–12).

NOTE: Please refer to the discussion of the Arbtitrary command in the Photoshop user manual for a detailed explanation of the intricacies and technical mechanics of this command.

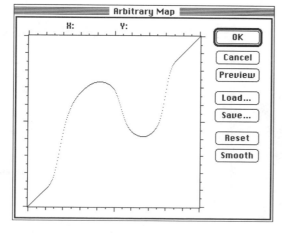

Figure 6–11   The Arbitrary Map dialog

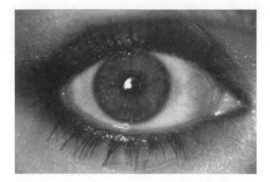

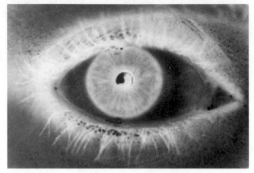

Figure 6–12 Image with normal map

Figure 6–13 Image with inverted map

When you move the cursor into the map area, it turns into a pencil tool. You can draw a new curve with this pencil, which will change the way brightness values are represented in the image. Using the Shift key, you can draw straight lines with the pencil. Click the pencil in the upper left corner of the map area, hold down the Shift key, and click the pencil in the lower right-hand corner of the map area. This will draw a straight line that is exactly the inverse of the normal map, resulting in an inverted, or negative image (Figure 6–13).

By using the pencil to draw irregular maps, you can achieve a wide variety of solarization effects (Figure 6–14a/b).

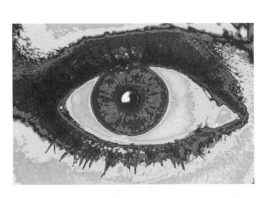

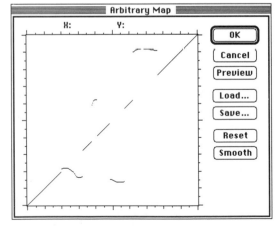

Figure 6–14 Image with solarization effect map

The Smooth button smooths out the abrupt transitions between map level changes. This is most useful for smoothing out the color transitions of solarized and other irregular maps (Figure 6-15a/b).

▼ **Tip:** The Arbitrary command attempts to display the new mapping effects as you drag the pencil tool in the map area; but you'll want to use the Preview button to see the true changes of the new maps you create. This is especially true when the Smooth control is used.

Color Correction Controls: The Adjust Commands

The commands found in the Adjust submenu include

- Levels
- Brightness/Contrast
- Color balance
- Hue/Saturation

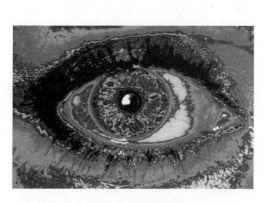

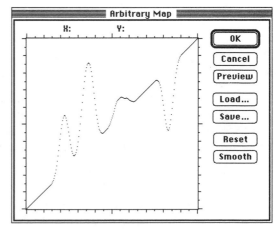

Figure 6–15   Image with smoothed solarization map

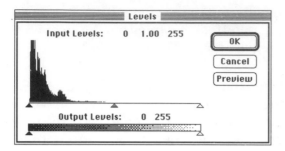

Figure 6–16   The Levels dialog

Levels

The Levels control is the most accurate tool for precisely adjusting the brightess and contrast levels in an image. When it is opened, the dialog in Figure 6–16 appears.

This control displays a histogram for the current document or selection area, and if the image is a color RGB document, there are radio buttons for the overall values "Master" as well as separate controls for each of the RGB channels. The left side of the histogram represents the darker areas of the image, and the right side represents the lighter areas. Remember, a value of 0 is black, 255 is white, and numbers in between correspond to varying degrees of brightness.

Immediately below the histogram are three triangular sliders. The black slider represents the darkest value, the gray triangle the midtones, and the white triangle is for the brightest value. At the top of the Levels dialog, you'll find three numbers, which correspond to the actual values of the three triangular slider controls. The positions of the sliders with respect to the histogram represent the Input Levels: the relationship of the darkest and brightest possible shades with respect to the actual values in the image. In an optimum situation, the darkest actual value in the image (pure black) would be right over the black triangle, and the lightest value in the image (pure white) would correspond to the position of the white triangle.

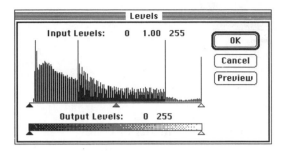

Figure 6-17 The Levels control with a dark image

Let's say we have a scanned image that we know is darker than the original artwork. When opening the Levels control, we find that the brightest mapped value in the image is located to the left of the white triangular indicator (Figure 6-17).

By dragging the white triangle slider to the left, the image is gradually lightened. Once the white triangle is directly underneath the right edge of the visible histogram, we'll have a much more balanced brightness component. You may find that it becomes necessary to slide the gray midtone triangle to the right to compensate for the newly brightened image.

At the bottom of the Levels dialog is the Output Levels indicator with a black slider and a white slider on a gradient bar; using this control, you can adjust the overall output contrast of the image. The two sliders determine the lowest and highest overall output brightnesses. As you drag the black slider to the right, you are effectively decreasing the contrast of the image, although in reality this is affected by the values set in the Input Levels sliders. If the white and the black triangular sliders are both set to the same value (note that the values of each of the sliders are displayed immediately above the gradient bar), then only that value will be output, resulting in a solid shade of gray.

Brightness/Contrast

The Brightness/Contrast controls work exactly as you might expect: You can control the overall brightness and contrast values of either an entire image or of a selected area. The current values are displayed numerically above the respective controls (Figure 6-18). While these controls are straightforward, you'll find that you'll want

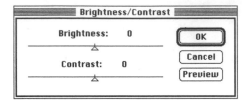

Figure 6–18   The Brightness/Contrast controls

to experiment with the Levels control, which offers much more control over the process. Use Brightness/Contrast for simple adjustments and move up to Levels. Once you become accustomed to the Levels control, you'll probably never use the Brightness/Contrast controls again.

Color Balance

Each pixel in an image is a color made up of a mixture of the three primary colors: red, green, and blue. The Color Balance feature allows you to adjust the balance of these colors.

The Color Balance is found under the Adjust submenu of the Image menu and works with both RGB and Indexed images. It will affect an entire image or any selected portion. Using the Color Balance control, you can adjust the relationship of RGB and CMY for three brightness ranges: shadows, midtones, and highlights. These components represent the three brightness ranges.

Many times in photography, certain colors will be contaminated by other colors in the image. An example might be a woman wearing a yellow coat standing next to a bright red curtain. Light bouncing off the red curtain will change the yellow of the coat. With Color Balance, these areas of contamination can be corrected by pulling out the unwanted colors.

There are times when a particular color appears dull or muted. Color Balance will allow you to enhance that color (the first exercise in Chapter 10 uses this feature to enhance the color of trees in the image).

Hue/Saturation

The Hue/Saturation control is found under the Adjust submenu of the Image menu. With it, you can change the hue (color) or the saturation (purity of color) of an image or selection area. You can also tint an image or selection area with a solid shade by using the Colorize command (found in the lower right side of the dialog). This is very similar to filling an area with the Color Only option (except that you can dynamically change the color by using a slider control—much more convenient than filling with different colors).

Essentially, using the Hue command is equivalent to sliding all of the values in an image or selected area along a color wheel. As you drag the Hue slider, all of the colors change with respect to one another. By using this technique, you can easily create multiple complex color variations of a specific image without much effort. It gets better. Let's say that you have a grayscale image with some color text overlapping the image. More specifically, let's say that the text consists of three copies of a word in semi-opaque red, white, and blue (created by using the Paste controls when creating the text). By using the Hue command to change the overall colors in the image, we are able to get variations on the red, white, and blue text that are perfectly harmonious. By adjusting the Saturation control, you can create pastel tones from brightly saturated colors.

The photographic process depends on many factors to achieve an accurate color representation. Lighting is not the only consideration: There are times when two objects of the same color but different materials will photograph totally differently.

Recently we had the need to photograph a shoe care kit. The shoebags were made of a lime-green nylon. The polishing cloth was the exact same lime-green but made of felt. In the shot, the shoebags came out the right shade of lime-green but the cloth came out a brownish green. By selecting the cloth and working the hue control, the proper green tones were regained.

The need might arise to totally change the color of an object. We recently had to photograph a sweater for inclusion in a mail-order catalog. The manufacturer, meanwhile, discontinued the particular color used in the shot. Because of this, the sweater required a total change in color. The Hue/Saturation window has a Colorize option available. This option allows you to remap the hue levels of all of the pixels in an image to a specific color. With the Colorize option

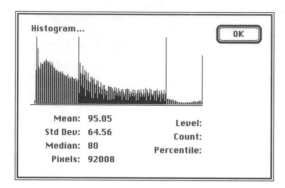

Figure 6–19   Histogram window

chosen, the sweater was selected, and the color was completely changed.

The Histogram Window

The histogram window (Figure 6-19) displays a visual analysis of the brightness component of the current selection (if an area is selected with any of the selection tools) or of the currently active document (if nothing is selected).

Te be exact, the histogram shows the relative amplitudes of brightness and saturation values for the overall image, or specific amplitudes for the red, green, and blue values of an image. Ouch! In other words, this window shows you the balance of distribution of brightness and darkness levels in an image. The histogram is a gauge by which you can adjust the picture for optimum brightness and contrast settings.

A Dark image typically has a histogram with a heavy emphasis on the left side of the spectrum (Figure 6-20). Lighter images display uneven balances toward the right side of the spectrum (Figure 6-21).

> If an area is selected when the histogram dialog opens, the histogram will display the information pertaining only to the selected region

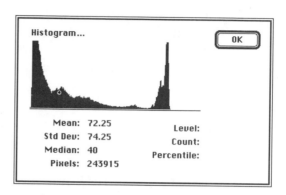

Figure 6–20 Dark image   Histogram

As you move the mouse over the graphic portion of the histogram window, the numerical readout below informs you of the brightness value and amplitude of the current pointer location. Clicking on the red, green, blue, and gray channel buttons changes the display to show the luminosity values of the separate respective channels. Other information in the dialog includes the average brightness value of the selection or document, the amount of differentiation of brightness (Std. Dev.), the number of pixels in the whole selection/document, the number of pixels at the currently selected brightness level, and more.

To fully appreciate the importance of knowing how to "read" histogram feaures, let's try a simple exercise.

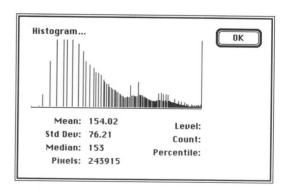

Figure 6–21 Light image   Histogram

1. Start with a deliberately dark scanned image. You can darken the Flowers demo file and start with that. Open the Histogram dialog and observe the graphic-heavy dominance in the darker (left-hand) region of the luminosity spectrum (Figure 6-22).

2. Choose the Equalize command from the Image menu (Figure 6-23).

3. Open the Histogram window. Notice that the graphic distribution is much more balanced/symmetrical. The top of the curve should optimally resemble an arch, or bell, curve (Figure 6-24).

Filters

The large variety of filters found in Photoshop is virtually unequalled by any other Macintosh graphics program on the market; it's easy to get lost in the Filters menu for hours at a time. Sometimes the effect of a particular filter is very subtle—sometimes it's overwhelming. Many of the filters are highly useful for everyday production tasks, others yield unexpected and visually arresting artistic results, and some are downright strange. The only way to truly appreciate the power of the filters is by using them individually or in combinations on many types of images.

The filters found in Photoshop can be one of two types: built-in or modules. The built-in filters are the standard filters that are programmed directly into Photoshop; they cannot be removed from the program. By contrast, modular filters are separate little programs that can be added to the Photoshop filter menu at any time: Simply place a filter module in the same folder as Photoshop's Prefs file, and it will appear in the Filter menu in the program. No special installation procedure is required. We have already seen that Adobe and third parties sell separate add-on filter module sets as accessories to the main program.

If a filter module doesn't appear in the Filter menu, make sure that the filter file is in the same folder as the active Photoshop Preferences file; if it still doesn't appear, chances are that the filter file has been corrupted—unlikely but possible. Try installing a fresh copy of the filter file.

The Photoshop package includes some fantastic modular filters—Ripple, Twirl, Spherize, ZigZag, Pinch, and Wave—which you should make sure to put in the main Photoshop folder of your hard

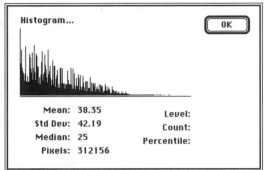

Figure 6–22   Histogram window with dark image

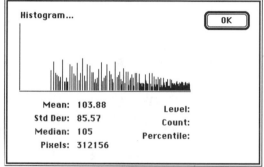

Figure 6–23   Equalized image

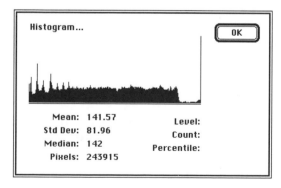

Figure 6–24   Histogram with perfect EQ curve

disk. You can verify which plug-in effects modules are currently loaded by opening the About Photoshop menu command under the Apple menu and clicking on the Plug-In button. Credits for each plug-in will appear on your screen.

Another differentiating characteristic of Photoshop's filters is that some are immediate and others have user-specified parameters. For example, while Blur and Blur More are immediate and begin processing right after you select them from the menu, Gaussian Blur has a control dialog that asks you to specify the degree of blurring (a first in a Macintosh graphics program—more on it later).

When you select a filter that has a control dialog, you can choose to cancel the action before the filter begins processing by clicking on the Cancel button in the control dialog. Hitting the return key on the keyboard will choose the OK button, and processing will begin. If a filter is going to take more than a few moments to process, you'll be presented with a graphic progress meter as the filter chugs away. The meter displays the relative percentage of completion of the filtering process.

Some of the filters in Photoshop are fairly straightforward, while others are somewhat esoteric and unusual. Don't be discouraged if you don't immediately pick up on the relevance or usefulness of the Convolve or Offset filters, for example—they are quite useful for things that aren't immediately obvious. Sometimes the scientific background of Photoshop's authors shows in the program—High Pass filtering is common in the worlds of image processing and audio engineering, but you won't run into it too often in the desktop publishing world (or traditional publishing, for that matter). Still, used properly, some of these effects can be employed in practical, creative ways. The Convolve filter, for example, can be configured to create effects as diverse as blurring, relief/emboss effects, and sharpening. All from the same Convolve command.

There are some things to keep in mind when working with Photoshop filters:

- Filters don't work in two graphics modes: Bitmap and Indexed color. To apply a filter to a black-and-white bitmapped image, you must first convert it to a grayscale image. To apply filters to an imported PICT file (which is brought into Photoshop as an indexed color image), you must first convert the indexed color file to RGB display format, apply the desired filters, and then convert the file back into indexed color format. There is no loss of data of the original image in this process.

- Filters can be applied to any selected portion of an image; as you have learned, there are many ways to select areas in Photoshop. As a result, filters can be applied to masked areas and through the alpha channel. This allows you to specifically determine what parts of an image will be affected by the filter—and when using the alpha channel, you can save sets of filter masks that can be used at any time.

Unlike the color correction and brightness controls, there is no preview mode for effects. Unlike these controls, filters aren't interactive (filters don't work in real time, unlike many of the color correction controls). Since you can undo a filter immediately after applying it to an image, this is a minor inconvenience.

- After the Mac starts processing an image through a filter, the process can be instantly halted by pressing the Command-Period keys. When this is done, the image reverts to its prefiltered state.

- Sometimes it's helpful to zoom into an area of the affected image and use the Undo command to get a quick before-after appraisal of an applied effect.

Filter Menu Structure

The Photoshop filters are found in a hierarchical pop-up Filter menu selection in the Image menu (Figure 6–25). The last filter that you apply to an image is remembered, and it appears immediately underneath Filter in the Image menu. By pressing Command-F on the keyboard, you can reapply the last filter used.

▼ **Tip:** Some of the filters have control dialogs that appear when selected; others are "immediate" and are applied to the image without an intermediate control dialog. In the case of those filters with control dialogs, pressing Command-Option-F will reopen the last filter's control dialog and allow you to change the parameters before reapplying the filter.

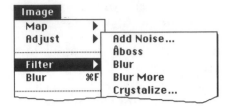

Figure 6–25 Filters menu command in Image menu

If you abort a filter while it's processing (by pressing Command-Period), it will still be remembered as the last filter selected and will appear in the menu.

If there are more filters in the pop-up menu than can be displayed onscreen at once, the list will scroll up as you move the mouse down.

Add Noise

The Noise filter adds "random" pixels to an image. While this doesn't obviously seem like a good thing, noise can be used for creative effects that would otherwise require tedious work to produce. Television static, or "snow," or unusual textures can be created instantly. When processed through some of the other filters, such as Blur, Gaussian Blur, and Find Edges, noise can become a useful source for organic patterns otherwise difficult to create from scratch.

You can specify the amount of noise applied to the image by typing in numbers ranging from 1 to 999. The differences between the "Uniform" and "Gaussian" settings are subtle: Uniform noise tends to be less chaotic, or more ordered, than noise created by the "Gaussian" method. Gaussian noise also applies a slight lightening effect to the image, resulting in a brighter noise effect than the Uniform setting.

Results of some noise applied to a 50% gray fill and magnified by 200% are shown in Figures 6–26 through 6–29.

Applying small amounts of noise (amount set between 10 and 40) to grayscale images enhances the overall texture, resulting in a stippled effect.

Figure 6–26 Normal noise with amount at 5

Figure 6–27 Normal noise with amount at 200

Figure 6–28 Gaussian noise with amount at 5

Figure 6–29 Gaussian noise with amount at 200

Noisy backgrounds are useful when placed behind headlines of bold, sans serif type. Images processed with the noise filter are also good as background for title effects.

Applying noise to single RGB channels of an image results in controlled color noise.

Blur

The Blur filter is the most basic smoothing filter found in Photoshop. Blur works by lightening the pixels found next to the hard edges of well-defined lines and shaded regions. The Blur filter effect is subtle, when compared to Blur More and Gaussian Blur.

The Blur filter can smooth out large regions of noise from a less-than-optimum scan; the blur tool is more useful for touching up small regions of noise in scans.

Perhaps the most useful application of Blur is called into play when pasting an individual image or object onto a complex background. Normally, the edges of the pasted image stand out in harsh contrast to the receiving background. By using the Blur filter in conjunction with the Fringe command in the Select menu, you can effectively blend the edges of the pasted object with the background.

Blur More

Blur More is essentially equivalent to multiple passes of the normal Blur command. The difference is that it's slightly faster than applying the Blur command multiple times (Figures 6–30, 6–31).

Much of the time, we'll automatically use Blur More instead of the normal Blur when compositing an object against a background with the Fringe feature. The edges of objects that have been manually separated from a background are usually quite rough, and for smoothing those edges into a new background, the Blur More command will typically yield better results.

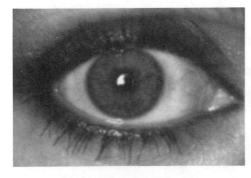

Figure 6–30   Normal Blur

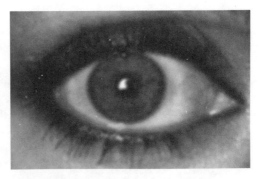

Figure 6–31   Blur More

Figure 6-32 The Custom filter dialog

Custom

The Custom filter is a programmable convolution matrix. With the Custom filter you can create various special effects, as well as custom blurring and sharpening filters (in fact, many of the blurring and sharpening filters in Photoshop are essentially hardwired convolution matrixes). You can save and load custom filters using the corresponding buttons in the Custom filter dialog (Figure 6-32).

The mathematical aspects of the Custom filter are explained in the Photoshop user manual, so we won't get into them in this book. Instead, we'd like to share the following neat Custom filters with you (See figures 6-33 through 6-40). Thanks, John Knoll!

Emboss

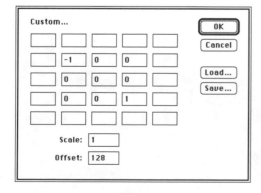

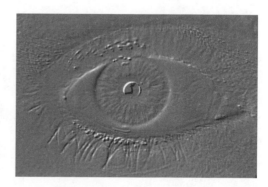

Figure 6-33 Filter matrix   Image sample

Blur

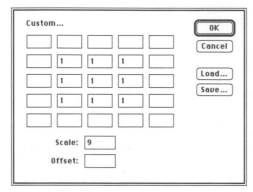

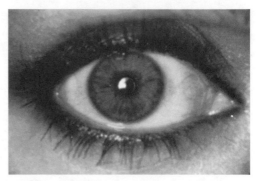

Figure 6–34   Filter matrix   Image sample

Slight Blur

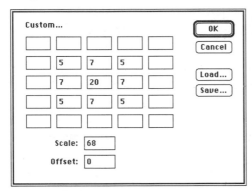

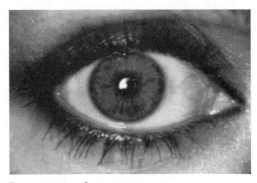

Figure 6–35   Filter matrix   Image sample

Sharpen

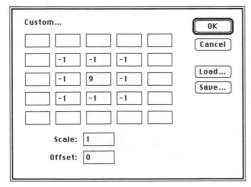

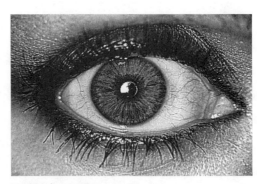

Figure 6–36   Filter matrix   Image sample

Laplacian Edge Detector

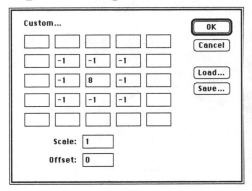

Figure 6–37   Filter matrix   Image sample

East Directional Gradient

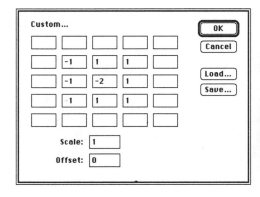

Figure 6–38   Filter matrix   Image sample

Horizontal Line Segment Dectector

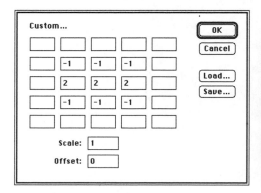

Figure 6–39   Filter matrix   Image sample

Horizontal Line Segment Enhancement

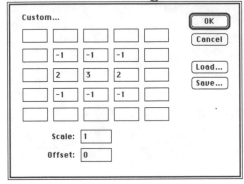

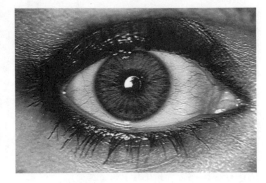

Figure 6–40   Filter matrix   Image sample

Despeckle

The Despeckle command is a type of blurring command that doesn't affect distinct areas of contrast. Specifically, Despeckle finds the distinct edges in an image and slightly blurs everything except the edges (Figure 6–41). This filter is great for removing unwanted noise from an image without affecting major areas of detail—old photographs are prime candidates for the Despeckle filter as a first step in restorative retouching. Try it on satellite or space shots. It's

Figure 6–41   Noisy image, despeckled

also good for beginning to stabilize images captured from video sources with a frame grabber.

Diffuse

The Diffuse filter randomly "jitters" the pixels in a selected area. Diffuse shifts the pixels in a selection in various directions. As you repeatedly apply this filter, the image gradually breaks up and starts to look as if it were drawn with a crayon or charcoal. The effect of the normal Diffuse command is shown in Figures 6-42 through 6-45.

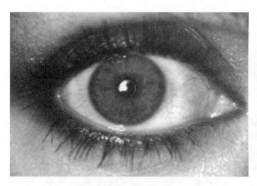

Figure 6-42   Normal image

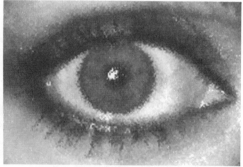

Figure 6-43   Diffuse applied once

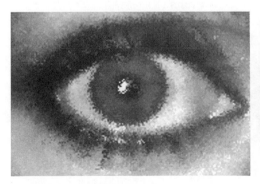

Figure 6-44   Diffuse applied twice

Figure 6-45   Diffuse applied 8 times

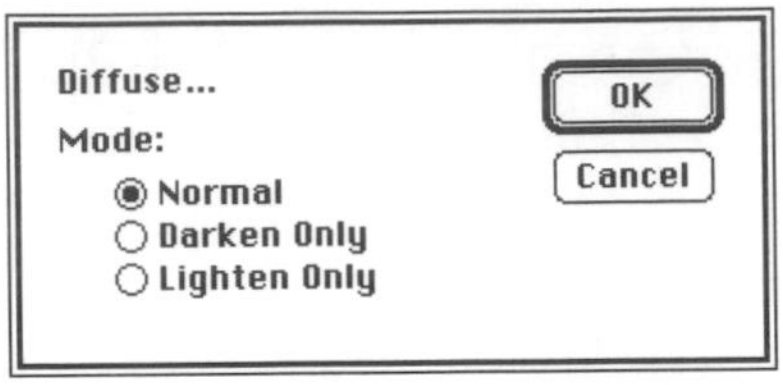

```
Diffuse...
                          ┌─────────┐
Mode:                     │   OK    │
  ◉ Normal                └─────────┘
  ○ Darken Only           ┌─────────┐
  ○ Lighten Only          │ Cancel  │
                          └─────────┘
```

Figure 6–46   Diffuse dialog

There are three options in the Diffuse dialog (Figure 6–46): **Normal** breaks up all of the pixels in the image.

Darken Only replaces light pixels with darker pixels; darker parts of the image break up more than the light parts (Figures 6-47, 6-48).

Lighten Only replaces dark pixels with lighter ones; lighter parts of the image break up more than darker parts (Figures 6-49, 6-50).

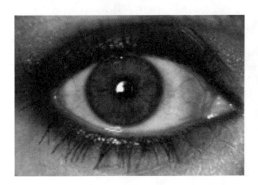

Figure 6–47   Normal Image

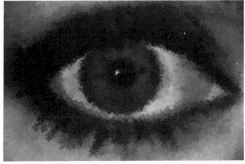

Figure 6–48   Darken Only applied 4 times

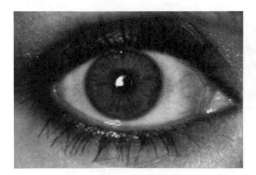

Figure 6–49   Normal Image

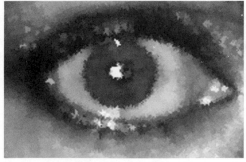

Figure 6–50   Lighten Only applied 4 times

Try using Diffuse in conjunction with the blurring filters to get soft chalky variations of a filtered image. If you use the Diffuse filter on high-resolution images (200 DPI and up), notice that the effect is subtle if the output is on a high-res imagesetter.

Facet

The Facet filter is unique: It can make a scanned image look "painted." This filter analyzes a picture, determines major areas of solid or similar colors, and emphasizes them. The result is that any scanned image can be turned into what appears to be a hand-painted rendering (Figure 6–51).

By applying this filter multiple times to an image, you can convert a photo-realistic image into an abstract painting with minimum effort (Figures 6–52, 6–53, 6–54).

Another useful way to use the Facet filter is to select only a portion of an image with any of the selection tools, and process only the selected area with Facet. If you have a full-page image and want to put type into a column that will cover half the page, try applying multiple passes of the Facet filter on the area where the type is to be located.

For filter fun, try processing a Faceted image through the Trace Contours, Find Edges, and Diffuse filters. Also, Faceted images are good candidates for color substitution through the Hue/Saturation controls.

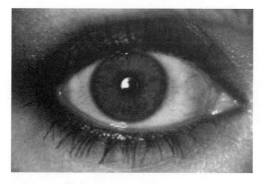 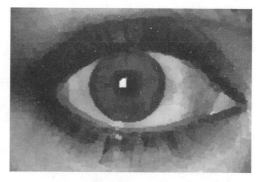

Figure 6–51 Facet–Before   Facet–After

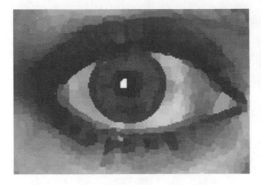

Figure 6–52   Facet – 1 Pass

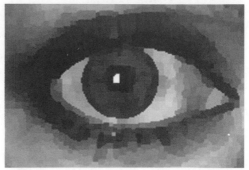

Figure 6–53   Facet – 10 passes

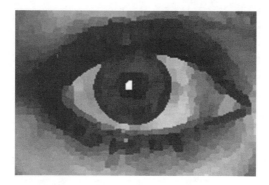

Figure 6–54   Facet – 3 passes

Find Edges

Find Edges is used to find the areas of significant brightness transitions in an image and emphasize them. The result of using the Find Edges filter is that an image turns into a series of light strokes against a dark background.

Find Edges is a fun, creative filter. For example, you can instantly turn a human eye into a scary monstrosity by applying Find Edges (Figure 6-55).

Find Edges is also great when you paste the results of the filter back onto the original image and use the Paste Controls command

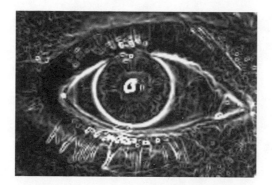

Figure 6-55 Eye after the Find Edges filter

to make the black portions of the floating filtered image transparent (Figure 6-56). Instant weirdness!

Try applying the Find Edges filter to a single channel of an RGB image. Strange stuff. Look at Chapter 7, "Advanced Photoshop Techniques," to learn how to use the Find Edges filter in conjunction with the Gaussian Blur and Invert commands to convert any image to molten metal.

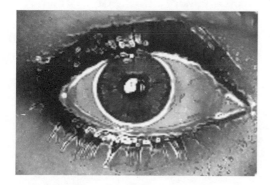

Figure 6-56 Eye with Find Edges of itself pasted back on top, transparent black

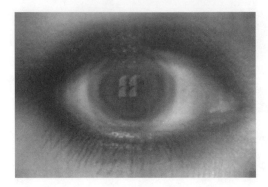

Figure 6–57 Samples of Fragment filter

Fragment

Fragment takes an image, makes four copies of it, and lays them back down, slightly offset from each other—very similar to a photographic "star" filter. Use it for weird effects. Apply it to a single pixel or paintbrush dab for a glimmer effect (Figure 6-57).

Gaussian Blur

The Gaussian Blur is a variable smoothing filter (Figure 6-58). Unlike the other blurring filters, you can specify the degree of blurriness. Accepted radius values range between 0.1 to 100 (yes, you can type in fractional values—3.4, for example).

Using this filter, you can create very subtle or overwhelmingly blurred variations of an image (Figures 6-59 through 6-62).

Using Gaussian Blur on an individual RGB component channel of an RGB image can result in eery glowing effects (try the Guassian

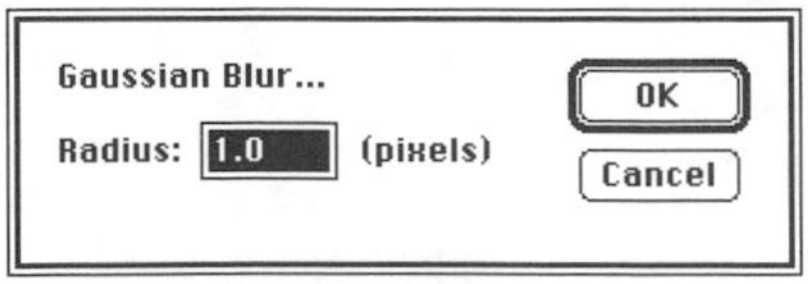

```
Gaussian Blur...
Radius: 1.0  (pixels)      OK
                           Cancel
```

Figure 6–58 The Gaussian Blur dialog

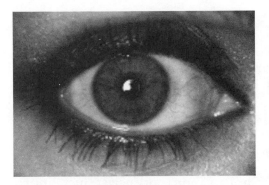

Figure 6–59 Normal Image

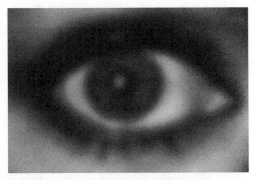

Figure 6–60 Gaussian Blur = 3

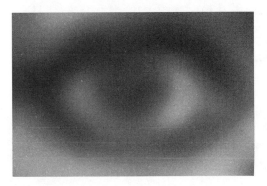

Figure 6–61 Gaussian Blur = 8

Figure 6–62 Gaussian Blur = 20

Blur on the red channel of a scanned human face—radiant radioactive rash, as we so fondly call it). Gaussian Blur is also a natural for animation (see Chapter 9) and soft dropshadow effects (Chapter 7). And it's great for creating soft areas on a detailed image for text overlays.

High Pass

High Pass is a filter with origins in engineering. It allows the high-frequency portion of a signal to get through, blocking out lower frequencies. (See the dialog in Figure 6–63.) If you have an audio equalizer (or a graphic equalizer on your home or car stereo),

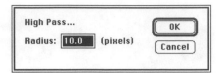

Figure 6–63   The High Pass filter dialog

this filter is like lowering all of the bass attenuation sliders while pumping up the treble. (If you're not an audio enthusiast, just ignore that.)

The High Pass filter finds areas of major brightness and highlights them, while it increases the apparent contrast of areas with less contrast differentiation. The accepted range of values is 0.1 to 100: generally, the lower the number, the more apparent the effect of the filter (Figures 6–64 through 6–67).

High Pass is useful for creating filtered images for use as alpha channels: When you overlay a High Pass alpha image back onto the source image, you can apply effects (such as tinting and filtering) that accentuate the lighter portion of an image (Figure 6–68). When doing this, you'll want to try to bring the darkest value in the alpha channel down to black using the Levels Control, so that only the lighter areas of the High Pass alpha are the masks.

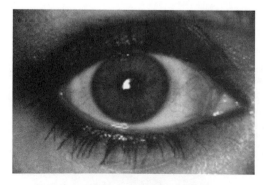

Figure 6–64   Normal image

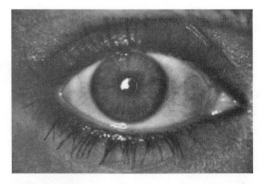

Figure 6–65   High Pass = 10

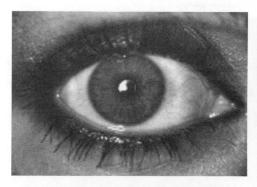

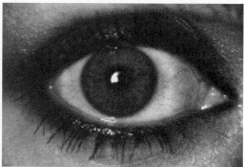

Figure 6–66　High Pass = 25　　　**Figure 6–67**　High Pass = 60

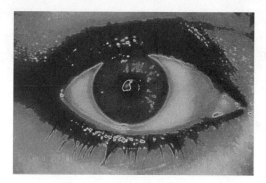

Figure 6–68　Example of High Pass
alpha mutilated images

Maximum

Maximum blows out the lighter portions of an image and makes dark shadows murkier—instant wild, jittery images. You can specify the thickness of the effect in pixels (acceptable range: 1 to 10). The dialog box is shown in Figure 6–69.

Maximum amplifies and exaggerates the bright areas of an image (Figures 6–70, 6–71).

Try creating a Maximum-filtered version of an image, paste the results into an alpha channel, apply the alpha channel onto the normal source image, and try the Gaussian Blur filter, Hue shifts with the Hue/Saturation control, and Find Edges filters. Sample results are shown in Figure 6–72.

Another great use of the Maximum filter is to thicken the thin lines resulting from the Trace Contours filter (Figure 6–73).

Figure 6-69   Maximum dialog

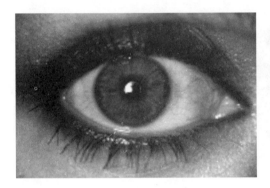

Figure 6-70   Normal image

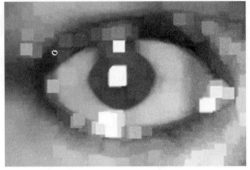

Figure 6-71   Maximum = 4

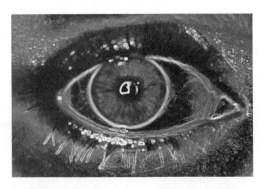

Figure 6-72   Sample of Maximum alpha filter effect

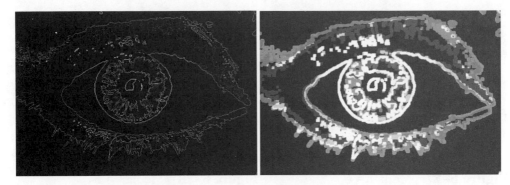

Figure 6-73 Trace Contour   Trace Contour with Maximum = 2

Median

The Median filter averages the brightness values of adjacent pixels (Figure 6-74). It's a good starting point in getting rid of digital "noise" in an image, especially video frame grabs.

The accepted value range is 1 to 16 pixels. The higher the value, the more averaging you get, which makes the image look more blurred (even though the effect is distinctly different from the Blur filters). Examples are shown in Figures 6-75, 6-76, 6-77, 6-78.

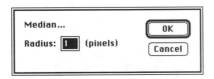

Figure 6-74 The Median dialog

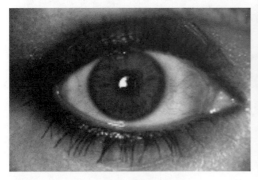

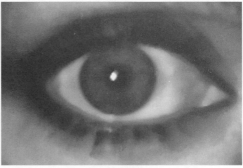

Figure 6-75 Normal Image   **Figure 6-76** Median = 2

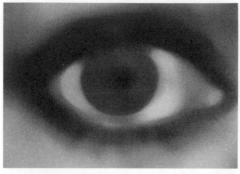

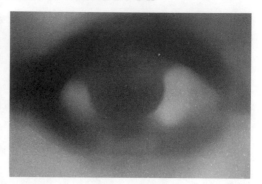

Figure 6–77   Median = 6   **Figure 6–78**   Median = 14

Minimum

Minimum blows out the darker portions of an image, and deemphasizes light areas (Figure 6–79). Instant dark, jittery images appear. You can specify the thickness of the effect, in pixels (acceptable range: 1 to 10).

Minimum amplifies and exaggerates the dark areas of an image (Figures 6–80, 6–81).

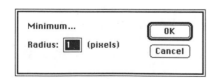

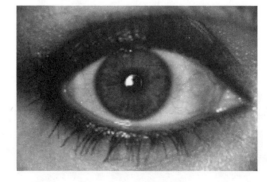

Figure 6–79   Minimum dialog   **Figure 6–80**   Normal Image

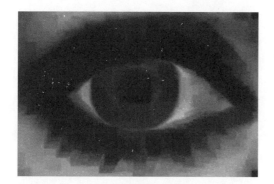

Figure 6–81   Minimum = 4

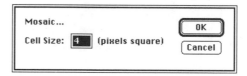

Figure 6–82   Mosaic dialog

Mosaic

The Mosaic filter turns an image into pixelated squares (Figure 6–82). You can choose the size of the square "cell"; values range from 2 to 64 (Figures 6–83 to 6–86).

You can create variations on the square cell by

—resizing the image by 50% horizontally or vertically, applying the Mosaic filter, and then resizing the image back to the original size. This creates rectangular cells (Figures 6–87, 6–88).

—rotating the image by an arbitrary number of degrees, applying the Mosaic filter, and then rotating the image back to the original orientation (by applying the same rotation in the opposite direction) (Figure 6–89).

Try using the Trace Contours filter after applying Mosaic to an image. Also, Mosaic is fun for animation—see Chapter 9 for more details.

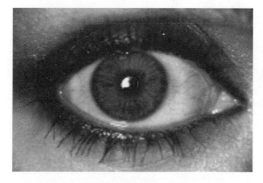

Figure 6–83   Normal image

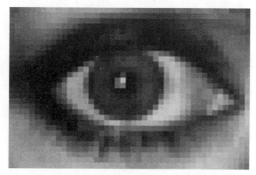

Figure 6–84   Mosaic = 4

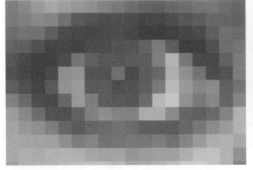

Figure 6–85 Mosaic = 10

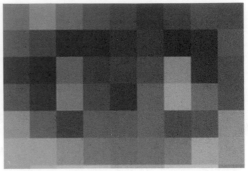

Figure 6–86 Mosaic = 20

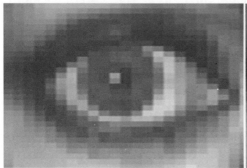

Figure 6–87 Horizontal cells

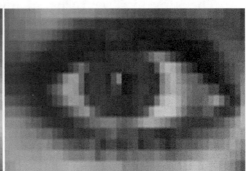

Figure 6–88 Vertical cells

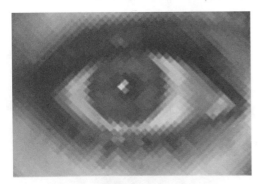

Figure 6–89 Rotated image by 45 degrees CW, applied Mosaic filter with value of 5, rotated image 45 degrees CCW

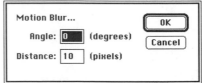

Figure 6–90 The Motion Blur dialog

Motion Blur

Motion Blur creates the illusion of movement. As perceived by the human eye, moving objects are never exactly in focus—they are somewhat distorted. Objects move at a certain speed, in a specific direction. Motion Blur allows you to simulate this effect (Figure 6-90).

There are two variables—angle (degrees: acceptable value between -90 and 90) and distance (pixels: acceptable values between 1 and 32). These control the direction and amount of blurring (Figures 6-91, 6-92, 6-93, 6-94).

A scene of race cars thundering down the track can easily be captured on video. The sense of speed in a still image is a bit trickier

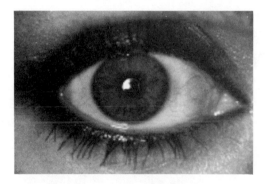

Figure 6-91   Normal image

Figure 6-92   Motion Blur
45 degrees, 10 pixels

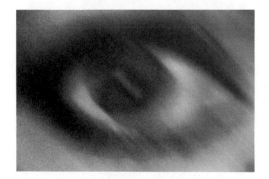

Figure 6-93   Motion Blur
45 degrees, 25 pixels

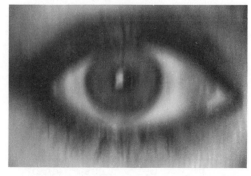

Figure 6-94   Motion Blur
90 degrees, 10 pixels

to achieve. The Motion Blur filter is designed to give a still image the feeling that it is racing through space.

The example described here is an illustration of a bullet flying through space. We took artistic license and sent the bullet's casing flying as well.

- The bullet is illustrated using Photoshop's painting capabilities (Figure 6-95).

- The bullet is then selected with the Marquee selection tool, making sure to select portions of the surrounding background. With the Option button depressed, a copy is made. The copy remains selected (Figure 6-96).

- The Motion Blur filter is called up from the Filters submenu in the Image menu (Figure 6-97).

- Since the movement will be a lateral one, it is not necessary to enter an angle. The distance required to create a sense of high velocity is great. The filter has a distance limit of 32 pixels—which is not enough, so a distance of 25 is applied twice.

- The new blurred image is pasted over the original bullet and left selected.

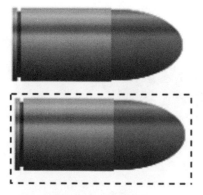

Figure 6-95 Illustration of bullet

Figure 6-96 Copy of bullet is created.

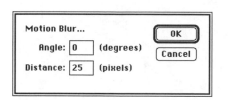

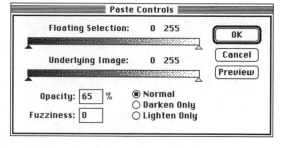

Figure 6–97 Motion Blur dialog   **Figure 6–98** Paste Controls dialog

- Paste Controls are called up from under the Edit menu (Figure 6-98).
- The Opacity is brought down to 65%.

The result is a speeding bullet (Figure 6-99).
Another great use of the Motion Blur is a technique we've discovered for creating a useful streaking pattern.

1. Create a New document; fill background with 50% Gray (Figure 6-100).
2. Apply Noise filter with 150 value, either Uniform or Gaussian (Figure 6-101).
3. Apply Motion Blur with 45-degree angle, 25 pixel distance (Figure 6-102).
4. Use the Equalize command (Image menu, Map submenu) (Figure 6-103).

Figure 6–99 Speeding bullet

Figure 6–100   New document
with 50% grayfill

Figure 6–101   Gray with noise value
of 150 applied

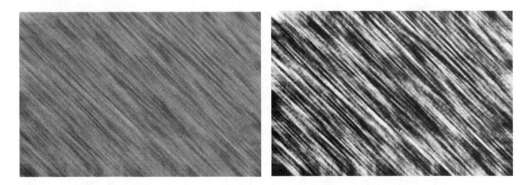

Figure 6–102   Motion Blur applied

Figure 6–103   Equalized image

This texture is useful on its own, or even more fun if you throw it into the alpha channel of an image and use it as a mask. Try applying an appropriately sized version of the texture as an alpha channel applied onto a color image, and

—Fill with a solid color (Figure 6-104).

—Use the Paste Into command to place a mutilated version of an image back on top of the main image (Figure 6-105).

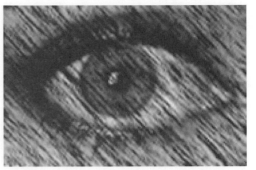

Figure 6–104 Streak pattern applied to image through alpha channel, filled with solid color

Figure 6–105 Normal image composited onto effect image through alpha streak (image on cover, second eye down on left)

Sharpen

The Sharpen filter is used to sharpen blurry images. It does this by increasing the contrast of adjacent pixels (Figures 6–106, 6–107).

Try sharpening an image once too many times (Figure 6–108). Neat Neuromancer effect (seminal William Gibson cyberpunk book).

Sharpen Edges

Sharpen Edges applies a sharpening filter only to the areas of major brightness change—the same edges that the Find Edges filter picks up (Figures 6–109, 6–110). It's quite useful for sharpening an image without affecting smooth areas of minimal differentiation.

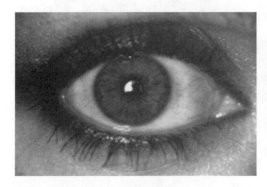

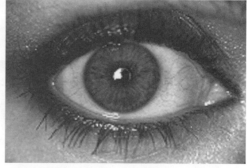

Figure 6–106 Normal image

Figure 6–107 Sharpened image

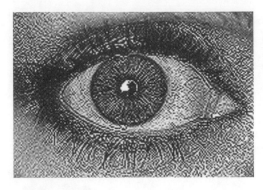

Figure 6–108 Image with too much sharpening. Brash and technofunkadelic.

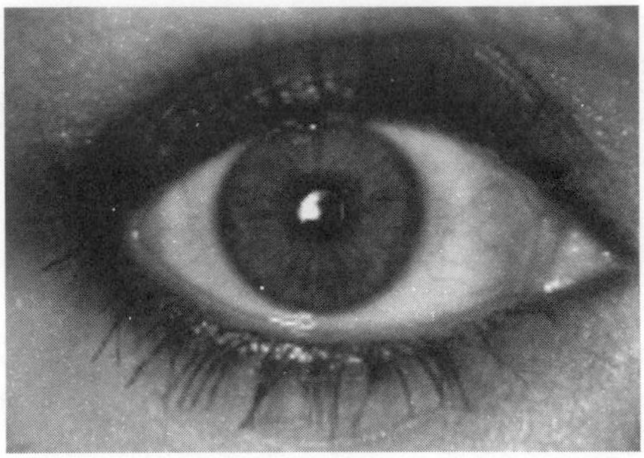

Figure 6–109 Normal image

Sharpen More

Sharpen More is simply equivalent to applying the normal Sharpen filter a couple of times—more contrast differentiation for the same money (Figures 6–111, 6–112).

Trace Contour

Trace Contour finds the areas of major brightness changes and draws thin lines around them, while making the remainder of the image black. You specify the threshold level and which side of the edge it highlights (Figure 6–113).

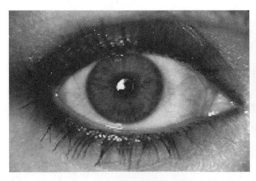

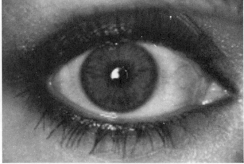

Figure 6–110 Sharpen Edges image

Figure 6–111 Normal image

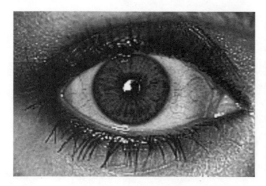

Figure 6–112 Sharpened More image **Figure 6–113** Trace Contour dialog

How do you use this command? Well first of all, the difference in the Upper and Lower results is really quite minimal, so don't fret over it. Use either one. The real key is to know how to find the best Level value to use in order to bring out the desired details of an image. Here's how (see Figures 6–114 to 6–118):

1. With the desired document open, select the Threshold command from the Image menu, Map submenu.

2. Using the slider in the Threshold dialog, find a level that reveals the detail that you wish to highlight. Take note of the numerical value displayed in the readout at the top of the Threshold dialog. Click on the Cancel button.

3. Open the Trace Contour filter, and type the threshold value into the Levels field. Click OK.

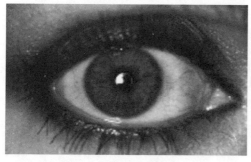

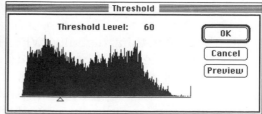

Figure 6–114 Normal image **Figure 6–115** Threshold dialog #1

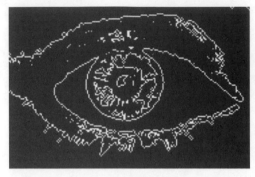

Figure 6–116   Trace Contour
results #1

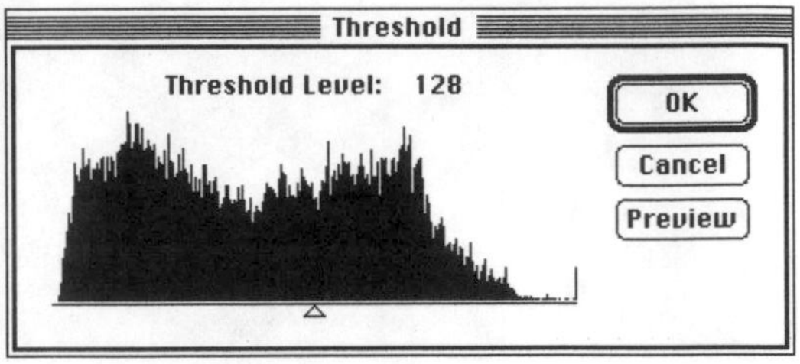

Figure 6–117   Threshold dialog #2

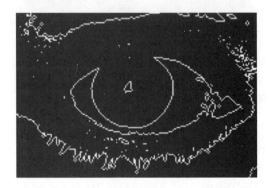

Figure 6–118   Trace Contour
results #2

Unsharp Mask

Unsharp Mask is the most accurate way of creating a controlled sharpening effect. It has its origins in the traditional noncomputer techniques developed to sharpen images on film. The process essentially consisted of taking a film negative, creating a blurred positive version of the image, sandwiching the two together, and shooting the results onto a higher-contrast photographic paper.

Photoshop's Unsharp mask filter Figure 6–119) essentially does the same thing digitally. When the filter is used, the image is copied, made negative, blurred, and averaged with the original image. The results are then brightness balanced, and the image comes out sharpened only in the areas where there is substantial brightness differentiation (you control the threshold value). Think of it as a very smart Sharpen Edges filter.

Unsharp Mask...

Amount: [50] %

Radius: [1.0] (pixels)

Threshold: [0] (levels)

OK

Cancel

Figure 6-119   The Unsharp Mask dialog

You can specify the radius of the blur (acceptable values: 0.1 to 99.9) — the higher the radius, the stronger the sharpening effect that is applied to the areas of brightness differentiation. Lower radius numbers produce less noticeable sharpening.

The Amount of the blur controls the weight of the blend between the blurred and normal images. This means that higher percentages result in more pronounced sharpening (within the areas affected based on the radius setting). The acceptable range of values for Amount is 1 to 500 (see Figures 6-120 through 6-126).

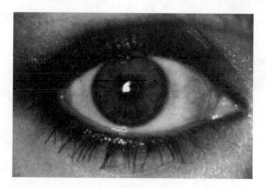

Figure 6-120   Normal image

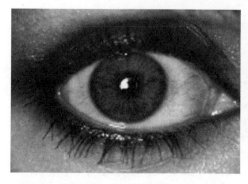

Figure 6-121   Amount = 20%, radius = 2

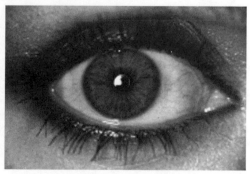

Figure 6-122   Amount = 20%, radius = 4

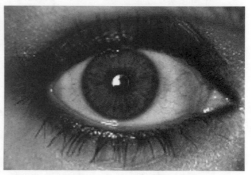

Figure 6–123   Amount = 50%, radius = 2

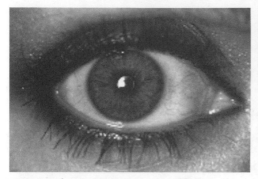

Figure 6–124   Amount = 100%, radius = 2

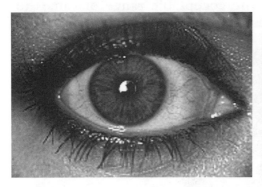

Figure 6–125   Amount = 250%, radius = 2

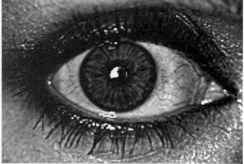

Figure 6–126   Amount = 250%, radius = 5

Knoll Software Filters

In your Photoshop package you'll find an envelope marked "Third Party Software." This envelope contains some very special filters that were created by John Knoll and are included free with Photoshop, along with documentation on how to use the filters. *Make sure that you find this stuff—we know many Photoshop owners who don't even realize that this envelope is in the box.* These filters are just wild—you'll have hours of fun with them. We

All of these filters work on either the entire image (if nothing is selected) or the image in the selection area. Try selecting different areas of an image—the effect of the filters may vary dramatically, based on the position selection area. The filters also work well with feathered edges—the amount of the effect of the filter decreases as the feathered edge blends with the background. If for any reason you are informed by Photoshop that you don't have enough memory to run the filter on an RGB image, try applying the filter to the RGB channels of an image individually, and then view the results in the RGB display mode.

suggest that—to have a full understanding of how each filter works—you review John's documentation before reading our descriptions of the filters. Make sure that you install the filters in the same folder as the Photoshop Preferences file. You should note that technical questions regarding these filters need to be directed to Knoll Software; their phone number is listed in the documentation included with the package. Try not to call too late at night, though—you might wake up little Sarah (John's daughter!).

Spherize

Spherize maps a selected area onto an imaginary spherical surface. Instant fisheye effects are achieved (Figures 6–127, 6–128).

Twirl

Twirl spins your image down toward the center of the selection area (Figure 6–129). Down the digital drain!

You can specify values between -999 and 999. Positive values yield a "right-hand" twist, while negative numbers result in a "left-hand" twist (Figures 6–130 to 6–134).

Try applying the Twirl filter to a single RGB channel of a color image. This effect works especially well if the main color image is composed in such a manner that the center of the image is a natural aesthetic focal point (such as our eye image—the pupil and iris are

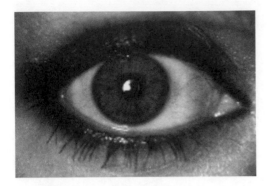

Figure 6–127 Normal image

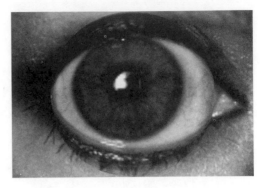

Figure 6–128 Spherized

Figure 6–129 Twirl dialog

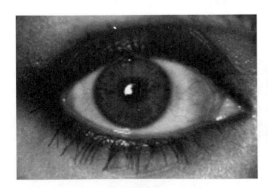

Figure 6–130 (a) Normal image

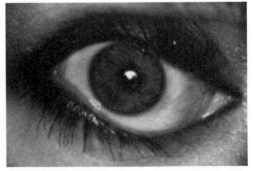

Figure 6–131 (b) Image twirled to +75

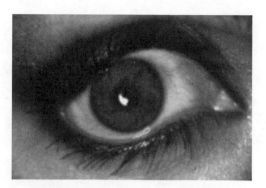

Figure 6–132 (c) Image twirled to -75

Figure 6–133 (d) Image twirled to +350

Figure 6–134 (e) Image twirled to -350

centrally located. When using the Twirl command on the Red channel of this image, we can make make it look like a red glow is twirling away from the center of the pupil).

Ripple

Ripple breaks up an image with a very fluid, liquid effect (Figure 6–135).

The accepted values range between 1 and 999. You can also choose the size of the ripple effect—small, medium, or large (Figures 6–136 to 6–142).

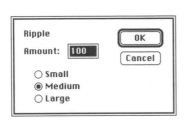

Figure 6–135 Ripple dialog

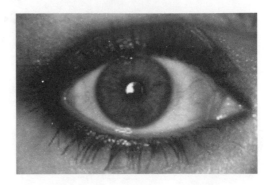

Figure 6–136 Normal image

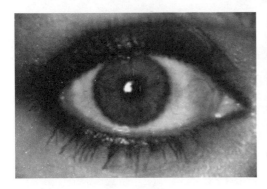

Figure 6–137 Ripple —
Small/50

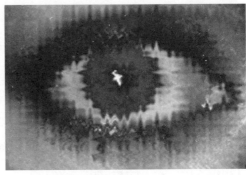

Figure 6–138 Ripple —
Small/350

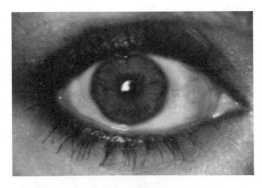

Figure 6–139 Ripple —
Medium/50

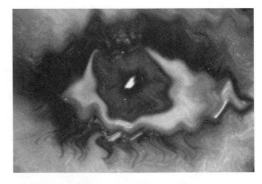

Figure 6–140 Ripple —
Medium/350

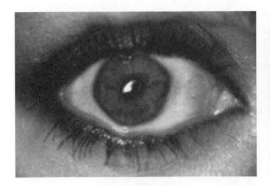

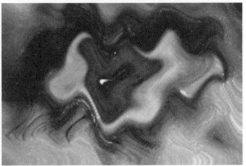

Figure 6–141 Ripple —
Large/50

Figure 6–142 Ripple —
Large/350

Figure 6–143 Rippled noise pattern. Weird wool!

This filter is great for creating textures. For example, a noise pattern rippled with Small/50–150 begins to look like digital wool (Figure 6–143).

ZigZag

ZigZag is like dropping a rock into the center of a glass disk filled with water which is sitting on top of an image—the waves ripple away from the point where the rock hits the water (Figure 6–144).

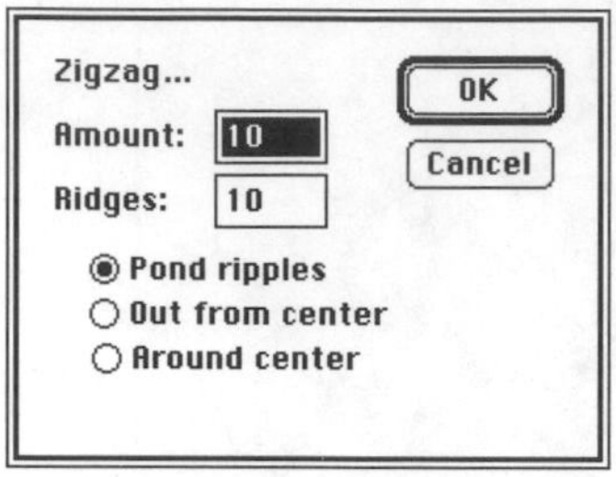

Figure 6-144   ZigZag dialog

You can specify the amount of the effect (1-999) and the "ridge" of the waves (1-999). The larger the amount, the more evident the waves; the larger the ridge, the more wavy the edges of the waves.

You also have three different types of ZigZag: pond ripples, out from center, and around center. Each changes the orientation of movement of the affected pixels (Figures 6-145 to 6-156).

Pinch

Pinch distorts an image toward or away from the center of a selection area (Figure 6-157).

Accepted values range from -100% to +100% (Figures 6-158 to 6-160).

Pinch is great on human faces and text characters.

Wave (1.1)

Wave is a unique filter that can automatically create dense, rich textures unlike anything you've ever seen on a Macintosh. It works like a highly programmable Ripples filter. The textures created by Wave are very organic. The effect is called "turbulence," a mathematical concept based on chaos theory.

Turbulence abounds in the natural world:

- The wisps of smoke dissipating from the end of a lit cigarette.

- The patterns formed by pressurized water coming out of a small opening, such as the end of a pipe.

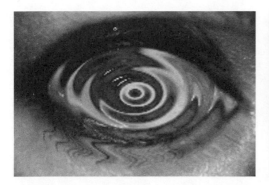

Figure 6–145 Pond ripples – direction

Figure 6–146 Amount = 20, Ridge = 10

Figure 6–147 Amount = 150, Ridge = 10

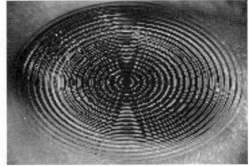

Figure 6–148 Amount = 150, Ridge = 40

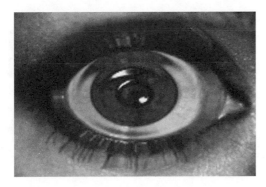

Figure 6–149 Out from center – direction

Figure 6–150 Amount = 20, Ridge = 10

Figure 6–151   Amount = 150, Ridge = 10

Figure 6–152   Amount = 150, Ridge = 40

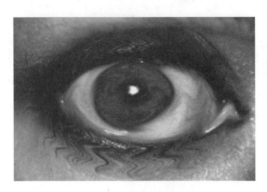

Figure 6–153   Around center – direction

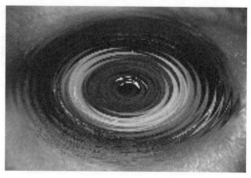

Figure 6–154   Amount = 20, Ridge = 10

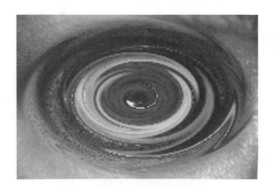

Figure 6–155   Amount = 150, Ridge = 10

Figure 6–156   Amount = 150, Ridge = 40

Figure 6-157 Pinch dialog

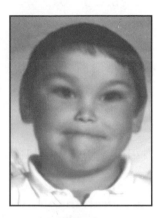

Figure 6-158 Normal image

Figure 6-159 Pinch = 75%

Figure 6-160 Pinch = -75%

- The mixture of fluids of different densities, such as oil and water.

The Wave dialog has a number of controls (Figure 6-161).

The Number of Generators specifies how many "strange attractors" will be used for a wave pass. You can specify up to 100 generators. Higher numbers of generators produce more complex patterns (Figures 6-162 and 6-163).

▼ **Tip:** You'll find that the Wave filter is like a Ripple filter when applied once; however, multiple passes begin to yield smooth, liquid effects. As you apply the filter more than once, each pass modulates the previous pass. Think of a pond of water, where you can drop many pebbles into the water at once. Even though each splashing pebble produces a simple radial wave pattern, the com-

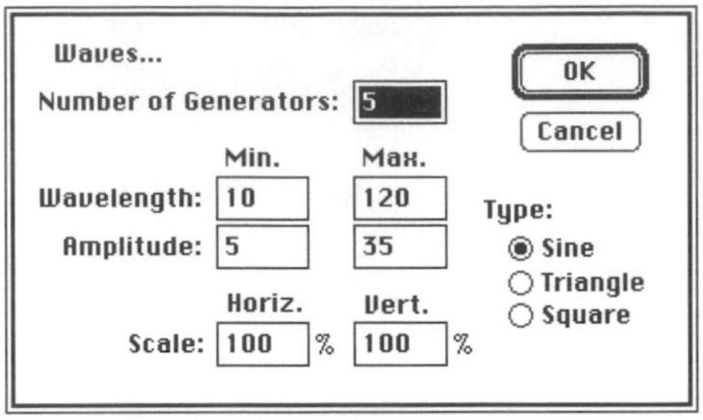

Figure 6–161 Wave dialog

bined effect of many radial waves crashing into each other produces more complex patterns. Each generator is a virtual pebble!

The Wavelength and Amplitude fields allow you to enter minimum and maximum values: Photoshop randomly uses the values within the specified range on each of the generators. Each generator is applied with a different value, adding to the chaotic effect. In general, the more of a range between the Min and Max values, the more random and chaotic the resulting effect.

The Random Start Phase checkbox determines the type of "seed" used by Photoshop. When this box is checked, each pass of the filter is based on a different set of locations for the generators. While this is OK for print design, if you're creating animation with the Wave

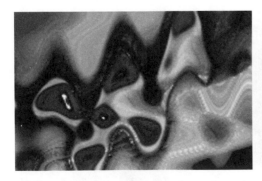

Figure 6–162 4 Generators

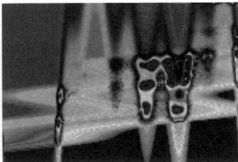

Figure 6–163 40 Generators

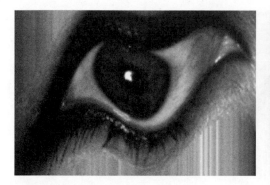

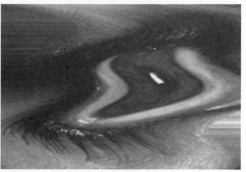

Figure 6–164 100% vertical, 0% horizontal

Figure 6–165 0% vertical, 100% horizontal

filter, you'll want to make sure that this option isn't selected, so that each incrementing pass of the filter will be based on the same kernel.

The Scale values allow you to determine the separate horizontal and vertical emphasis of the filter effect. You can clearly see the separate effects of the horizontal and vertical values by trying each with 100% while the other is set to 0% (Figures 6–164, 6–165).

You can specify the type of waveform used by by the effect: Sine, Triangle, or Square. Each yields an entirely different effect (Figures 6–166, 6–167, 6–168).

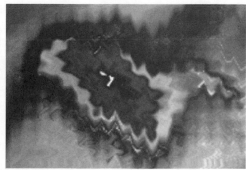

Figure 6–166 Sine

Figure 6–167 Triangle

Figure 6–168　Square

You can also choose to Wrap Around the pixels in a selected area or Repeat Edge Pixels. This determines what happens on the edges of the selected areas as the filter is applied. Most of the time you'll probably want to use Wrap Around, as this preserves the visual continuity of the effect. Repeat Edge Pixels creates a distinctive border on the edges of the filtered selection (Figures 6-169, 6-170).

Figure 6–169　Wave with Wrap Around

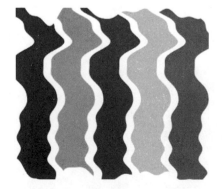

Figure 6–170　Wave with Repeat Edge Pixels

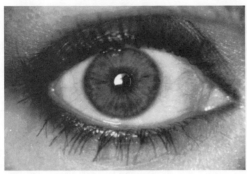 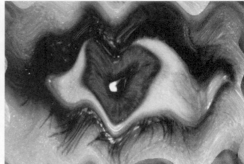

Figure 6–171   Normal image   **Figure 6–172**   Waved

Figure 6–173   Heavily waved

One of the main uses of the Wave filter is to create what we call "Alien Metallic Liquid." We've found that this tends to work best on images with large amounts of detail. The trick is to apply the Wave filter multiple times, changing some of the values slightly on each pass. After two or three passes, the alien liquid begins to pour (Figures 6-171, 6-172, 6-173).

Dynamic Effects

In the Image menu you'll find the commands that allow you to flip, rotate, stretch, skew, and distort portions of images. While the functionality of these commands is fairly self-evident (and because of this, we won't discuss each command individually), there are some basic rules to remember:

- The Interpolation method specified in the Preferences dialog affects the rendering quality of all of the dynamic effects. Nearest Neighbor is the fastest method with the poorest results, Bilinear is a reasonably fast method with reasonable quality, and Bicubic is the slowest method with the best quality. The difference between the interpolation methods is highly visible (Figure 6–174).

Figure 6–174 Image distorted with Nearest Neighbor, Bilinear, and Bicubic interpolation

- In any of the dynamic commands, CW stands for "clockwise" and CCW means "counterclockwise." This simply refers to the direction of the effect; for example, you'll find these in the Arbitrary Rotate command.

- The acceptable value range for the Arbitrary Rotate command is -359.9 to 359.9 degrees. Note that you can specify fractions of a degree.

- When you use the Free Rotate command, the axis of rotation is determined by the handle you click on when beginning to apply the effect. You can select any of the four handles to change the rotation axis.

- The Flip, Rotate, and Effects (otherwise referred to in this section as the "dynamic" effects) commands can be applied to any kind of a selected area. You can make selections with any of Photoshop's selection tools (Circular and Rectangular Marquees, the Magic Wand, the Lasso, and alpha channel selections) and use these effects.

- The Flip and Rotate commands are usually applied to a selected area, but there are times when you might want to rotate an entire image. If the document size is the size of the actual image, then you should get into the habit of *not* selecting any of the image when applying any of the rotate commands: If you select the entire image (with the Select All command), and apply an arbitrary or a 90–degree rotation, the resulting image will be cropped. The same effect applied to an image with no selection range will rotate both the image and the document, with no cropping (the dynamic effects aren't available unless an area or image is selected). If necessary, Photoshop will automatically make the document area larger to accommodate the rotated image. This is one of the more common problems encountered by Photoshop users, so take note.

- When using the Stretch, Distort, Perspective, and Skew commands, you can continually change an image with a specific command (release the mouse button, wait for the effect to be applied, study the result, click on a handle, and continue dragging the handle into a new position). If you Undo the effect, all of the consecutive changes of the specific command will be undone, bringing the image back to its initial state. The same will happen if you abort any part of this process by pressing the Command-Period key (you might think that this would just abort the most recent change of the effect, but in fact it works exactly like the Undo command).

- When any of the manual dynamic effects are used (free rotate, stretch/shrink, distort, perpective and skew), handles appear on four corners of a selection's bounding box. As you drag the corner handles into the desired position, the image redraws itself when you release the mouse button. If you hold down the Option key while selecting and dragging handles, the image will not redraw itself until you have placed all of the handles where you want them and released the Option key. This is very handy when you want to distort a high-resolution image into a predetermined shape.

- When using the Skew command (skew allows you to slant an image in a vertical or horizontal direction), you'll find that the first time you use the command, the horizontal and vertical pairs of handles are "coupled," so that moving one handle moves the coupled handle also. After the command has been applied for the first time, the handles become "decoupled": You can choose an individual handle and drag it into place (which causes the Skew command to behave like a constrained Distort). You can "recouple" the handle pairs by pressing the Shift key while clicking on and dragging a handle.

Resizing and Resampling

The relationship between the size and resolution of an image isn't immediately obvious to the casual user; but in Photoshop, this relationship is essential.

The size of an image is measured by the number of pixels or inches or centimeters that make up the dimensions of an image. An image that is 3 inches by 4 inches takes up that much physical space when printed.

The resolution of an image deals with the pixel density of that image: For example, our 3 x 4–inch image might vary in terms of the number of pixels in that area, even though the size is fixed. An image with a resolution of 72 DPI takes up much less disk space, and contains far less detail, than the same size image with 300 DPI. The resolution is usually determined by two factors:

1. The resolution at which the image is scanned.

2. The reslution of the output device.

For printing purposes, the output resolution of an image should be twice the desired linescreen value. For example, if you're going to print an image with a linescreen of 133, you should be working with a 266-DPI image. Using the Size/Rulers command in the Page Setup menu, you can have the image resampled at output time, leaving the original image at a lower resolution.

▼ **Tip:** If you are scanning images for 300-DPI laser output, note that you don't necessarily have to have all of the information in the 300-DPI scan for the best output quality; you might want to scan at 300 DPI and then resample the image down in Photoshop.

Resizing

You'll use the Resize command when you want to rescale an entire image and the working document canvas, or make your workspace canvas larger without affecting the size of the image (Figure 6-175).

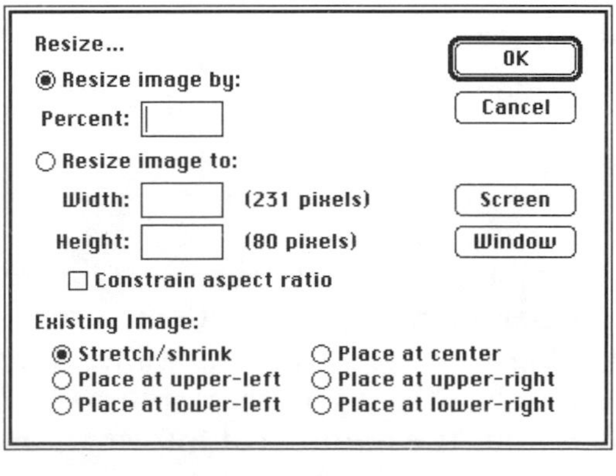

Figure 6-175   The Resize dialog

▼ **Tip:** Remember, the interpolation method chosen in the Preferences dialog affects the image-rendering quality of the Resize command.

You can specify an overall percentage, choose to resize the image to the current screen or window size, or enter arbitrary width and height values. To resize to the current window or screen size, click on the Screen or Window buttons. The corresponding values are automatically entered into the arbitrary resize fields.

▼ **Tip:** When you use the Window button to specify a new size, the values used are the absolute height and width sizes of the window at a 1:1 magnification ratio. If you are looking at an image in a reduction mode and click the Window button, you won't get the relative values of the entire window at the current reduction or magnification level, just the 1:1 size.

Constrain Aspect Ratio forces the image to maintain the proper aspect ratio, and to resize without any distortion. When selected, Photoshop will automatically decide to modify either the width or height value, depending on the orientation of the image and the entered resizing factor.

Note that the arbitrary width and height fields display the current size immediately to the right of the number fields.

The Existing Image options determine whether you are resizing the image or just the current canvas. The default selection is Stretch/Shrink, which resizes the image and the corresponding working canvas. The other options (Place at center, Place at upper left, etc.) allow you to place the unresized image in a specific location in the resized working canvas.

Resampling

Resampling involves bumping up the resolution of an image using interpolation: Photoshop inserts a new pixel with an intermediate value in between two existing pixels. At the same time, the size of the pixel is reduced accordingly. When you resample an image, its printed size doesn't change, but the amount of information in the image increases.

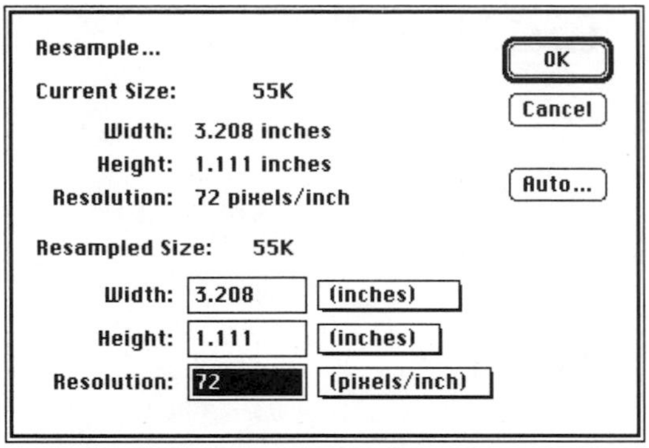

```
┌─────────────────────────────────────────────┐
│  Resample...                      ┌─────────┐ │
│  Current Size:      55K           │   OK    │ │
│       Width:   3.208 inches       └─────────┘ │
│      Height:   1.111 inches       ┌─────────┐ │
│  Resolution:   72 pixels/inch     │ Cancel  │ │
│                                   └─────────┘ │
│  Resampled Size:    55K           ┌─────────┐ │
│       Width: [3.208]  [(inches)]  │ Auto... │ │
│      Height: [1.111]  [(inches)]  └─────────┘ │
│  Resolution: [72   ]  [(pixels/inch)]         │
└─────────────────────────────────────────────┘
```

Figure 6–176   Resample dialog

You can see the results of a resample by clicking on the size indicator in the lower left-hand corner of a document window immediately before and after resampling. The actual output size of the image doesn't change, but the disk/RAM size of the document increases (evident in the numerical size indicator).

▼ **Tip:** When using resampling, keep an original version of a high-res scan on the disk and resample the image as necessary for output. If you resample an image down in resolution, and then resample it back up again, there is data loss, resulting in decreased overall image quality.

Another way to see the effect of resampling is to zoom in on an image after resampling. You'll note that the 1:1 magnification mode appears to be a zoomed view of the image. On a 300–DPI image, the 4:1 reduction mode actually displays the image onscreen at the size at which it will be output.

The Resample command is located in the Image menu. Its dialog allows you to control how the image is resampled (Figure 6-176).

The dialog shows the current image measurements, size, and resolution. You can type in new width and height values, or more often, you'll just type in a new desired resolution, without changing the width and height measurements. When you enter a new resolution, you should note that Photoshop guesses the size of the new image and displays it as the Resample size (located above the Width field).

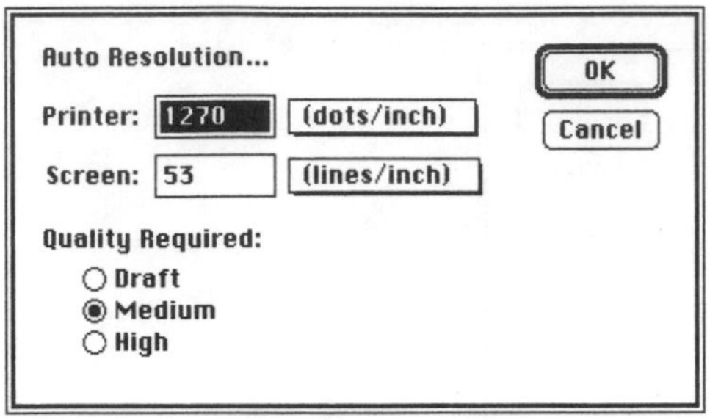

Figure 6–177   The Auto resample dialog

The Auto button takes you to a secondary dialog, which allows you to specify the resolution of the output device, the desired linescreen frequency, and the desired output rendering quality (Figure 6-177).

The formula used is as follows:

—High quality: resolution is screen frequency times two.

—Medium quality: resolution is screen frequency times 1.5.

—Draft quality: resolution is screen frequency times 1 (with 72 DPI the lowest resolution).

After you enter the desired Auto quality and click the OK button, you're brought back to the main resample dialog, with the new resolution entered in the resolution field.

7

Advanced Photoshop Techniques

In the time that we've been working with Photoshop, we've come up with a number of tips and tricks that we thought many of you would find interesting and useful for your own work. As with any creative graphics program, you can discover many arcane and not-very-obvious effects by haphazardly playing around with different combinations of commands and controls. In this chapter we'll explain:

- Creating basic shapes

- Multichannel special effects

- Creative uses of the alpha channels

- Soft dropshadows

- Glowing objects

- Life, the Universe, and Everything (sorry, Mr. Adams!)

This chapter assumes that you already know how to use many of Photoshop's basic features. You should be familiar with Photoshop's menus and commands and where they are located; we don't take the time to explain where each command is, and how to find a certain filter.

Creating Basic Shapes

Even though Photoshop doesn't have basic primitive shape tools, it's possible to create boxes, circles, and polygons filled with any solid color or gradient. The Fill command can be used to fill a selected area.

1. Create a new document.
2. Click on the Marquee tool and select a portion of the white background in the document.
3. Choose the Fill command from the Edit menu.
4. Press the OK button.
5. The selected area will be filled with the current foreground color (Figure 7–1).

Try the same technique using the gradient tool.

1. Set the foreground and background colors to the desired values.
2. Select an area with the circular Marquee.
3. Click on the Gradient tool in the tool palette.
4. Drag the gradient indicator line in the direction that you want the gradient to follow.
5. Release the mouse button (Figure 7–2).

Figure 7–1   Rectangular selection before and after fill

Figure 7-2   Circular selection before and after gradient fill

By using the Option key and the Lasso, irregular polygonal areas can be filled with solid colors or gradients.

▼ **Tip:** One of the drawbacks of this technique is that the rectangular and circular Marquees are always anti-aliased. If you want to create nonanti-aliased basic shapes, you should:

—Create an alpha channel for the whole image (Select All and Selection → Alpha).
—Set the background of the alpha channel to black and the foreground color to white.
—Create the desired shape and fill with the white foreground.
—Open the Brightness/Contrast control, and slide the contrast slider to the right, increasing the contrast. This will take the gray anti-aliasing away from the shape.
—Apply the alpha channel to the selection and use as desired.

Suppose you want to create a shape that has no fill but is simply an outline.

1. Follow the same steps as above up to the point of filling the selection.
2. Choose Fringe from the Selection menu.
3. In the window that pops up, you can enter the weight of the outline by choosing the width of the fringe. This will give the selection only the outside edge.
4. Now do the fill and the result is an outlined shape with no fill (Figure 7-3).

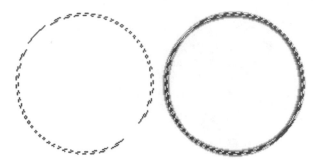

Figure 7–3   Fringe selection before and after fill

The Molten Metal Effect

By using a combination of filters, you can take just about any detailed image and turn it into what looks like stamped or molten metal. While this technique works especially well with scanned, highly detailed black-and-white line art, you can use it on many different types of color or grayscale images.

1. Open the desired image, and apply a Gaussian Blur with a variable radius of 4 to the entire image (we've had success using values between 3 and 6) (Figure 7–4).
2. Apply the Find Edges filter to the entire image (Figure 7–5).
3. Invert the image (Figure 7–6).

Figure 7–4   Blurred image

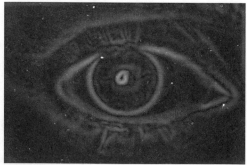

Figure 7–5   Find edges filtered

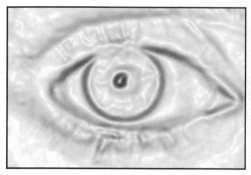 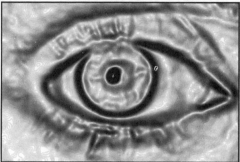

Figure 7–6 Inverted image   **Figure 7–7** Final image

4. You might want to try using the Levels control to bring out the detail in the newly filtered image. You can also try using the Equalize command to balance the brightness in the image (Figure 7–7).

If you are applying this effect to a color RGB image, you can enhance the effect by the following procedure.

1. Copy the color image to the clipboard before applying the Gaussian Blur.
2. Do the filtering process.
3. Once the image is "metallized," paste the color image back on top, open the Paste controls, and apply the pasted image with Color Only.

This colorizes the metallic version with the original image colors (Figure 7–8 in color pages).

If you are applying this effect to a grayscale image, you might want to try different types of "metal" by converting the grayscale image to RGB and using the Hue/Saturation control with the Colorize option turned on to tint the image with various solid colors. You can easily create gold, bronze, and copper metal effects with this technique (Figure 7–9 in color pages).

Special Effects with the HSB and HSL Display Modes

The HSB and HSL display modes are useful for creating special effects that can't be created easily in the RGB display mode. As discussed elsewhere in this book, the HSB and HSL display modes show an image broken down into its Hue, Saturation, and Brightness (or Luminance, in the case of HSL) components. Although the Photoshop manual describes the difference between these modes, we've found them to be very similar.

Normally, you would convert an RGB image into HSB or HSL to adjust the brightness without disturbing the hue or saturation values; we've found that you can get some interesting effects by manipulating the Hue component of an image, and then converting it back to RGB. For example

- Try applying different filters, such as Find Edges, Median, Facet, Twirl, and Wave to the Hue component of an image. This technique allows you to dramatically shift and distort the color of an image without changing the details made up by the brightness and saturation components. You can use the Sharpen and Unsharpen Mask filter to apply sharpening to the brightness and/or saturation component without disturbing the colors of an image.

- Invert the Hue component of an image. This will give you negatives of the colors while leaving the main detail of an image positive—very unusual and fun (Figure 7–10 in color pages).

Alpha Channel Tricks

The alpha channel capabilities of Photoshop are an endless source of special effects. Here are some techniques for getting the most out of the alpha channels.

Creating Smooth Crossfaded Images

By using gradient fills in the alpha channel, you can create smooth "crossfades" between images.

1. Take two images of approximately the same size (it's best for the images to be exactly the same size).

2. Select All of one of the images, and choose the Selection → Alpha command under the Select menu, or make a New Channel.

3. When the alpha channel appears, choose the Select All command.

4. Making sure that the foreground color is black and the background white, double-click on the gradient tool and choose linear gradient.

5. Create a linear gradient from one side of the alpha channel to the other. The window will be filled with a linear gradient (Figure 7–11).

6. Choose Selection → Alpha from the Select menu.

7. The alpha channel will appear over the RGB/color image , with the lighter side of the gradient selected (Figure 7–12).

8. Click on the window of the other document, select the entire image, and copy it.

9. Making the other (alpha-selected) image active, choose the Paste Into command from the Edit menu. The clipboard image is pasted "through" the gradient alpha channel into the first color image. The result is a horizontal crossfade (Figure 7–13).

Figure 7–11 Alpha channel with blend

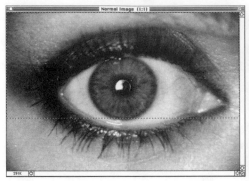

Figure 7–12 Alpha channel overlayed onto main image

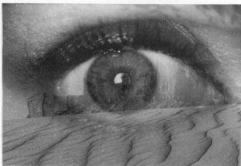

Figure 7–13 Final crossfade image

The same technique can also be used to crossfade between different modified versions of the same image, and between color and black-and-white versions of the same image (Figures 7–14, 7–15; Figure 7–16 in color pages).

Alpha Channel Gradient and Filters

A variation of the previous technique can be used for the selective application of filters to an image.

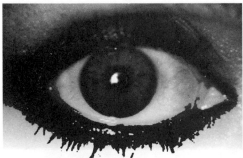

Figure 7–14 Crossfade between normal and thresholded image

Figure 7–15 –Crossfade between normal/heavily screened bitmap image

1. Starting with a color or grayscale image, create an alpha channel of the same size (Select All, and Selection → Alpha), and fill it with a linear black-to-white gradient.
2. Choose the Selection→Alpha command.
3. When the alpha channel appears over the RGB/grayscale image, choose the Gaussian Blur filter.
4. Type in a value of 5. Press OK.

This effect (Figure 7–17) also works quite well when the radial gradient is used.

1. Repeat the previous example, but instead of using a linear gradient fill in the alpha channel, try a radial gradient fill with the outer edges in white and the center in black (Figure 7–18).
2. Apply the Gaussian Blur to the image (Figure 7–19).

This is a perfect simulation of the classic "vaseline on a UV filter" photographic effect.

This technique, combined with other filters and image processing commands, opens the door for some very bizarre effects.

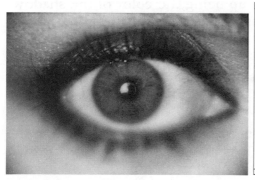

Figure 7–17 Alpha channel with Gaussian Blur

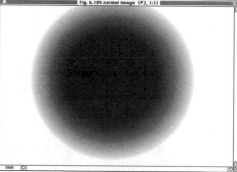

Figure 7–18 Alpha channel with radial blend

Figure 7–19 Final image with Gaussian Blur applied through radial blend alpha channel

Creating Smooth Dropshadows for Text and Graphics

One of the most over-used effects in the graphics design world is the dropshadow. Using the alpha channels and filters, you can create perfectly realistic dropshadows for any object or type. The difference with these dropshadows is that they are soft and natural, displaying the characteristics associated with natural light dissipation of shadows.

Let's try this technique with some text. Before beginning, make sure that you have ATM installed and specify solid black as the foreground color (this will end up being the color of the shadow, so if you want a colored dropshadow, change the foreground color to the desired shadow color).

1. Select a background (either a picture or a texture) that the type will be in front of (the shadow will fall on top of this background).

2. Select the entire image (using the Select All command from the Select menu), and copy it into an alpha channel by choosing Selection → Alpha from the Selection menu.

3. With the alpha channel displayed on screen, use the type tool to create some type. Use the anti-aliased option in the text creation dialog.

Figure 7-20   Selected text

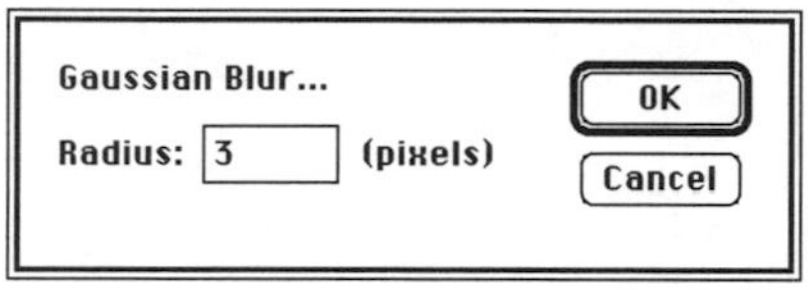

Figure 7-21   Gaussian blur dialog

4. Position the type where you want it in relation to the background image in the original RGB window.

5. Once the type is in the desired location, deselect it.

6. Using the rectangular Marquee, select the type and a small area around the type (Figure 7-20).

7. Choose the Gaussian Blur command from the Filters menu selection (Figure 7-21).

8. Type in a blur factor of 3.

9. Select the entire alpha channel and Invert it. This makes the blurred type the mask (Figure 7-22).

Figure 7-22   Blurred inverted text in alpha channel

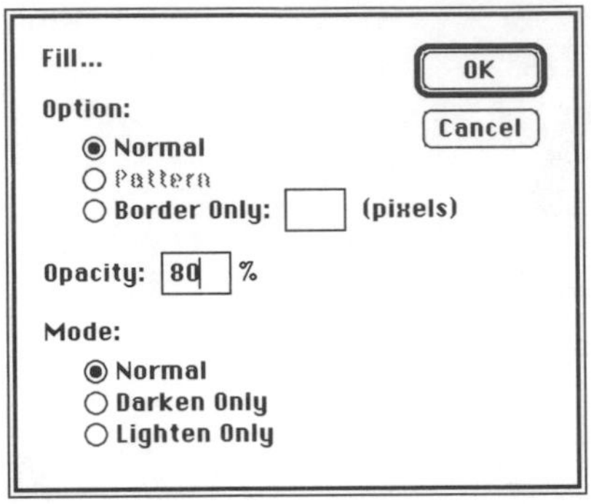

```
Fill...                          ┌─ OK ─┐
Option:                          ┌ Cancel ┐
    ⦿ Normal
    ○ Pattern
    ○ Border Only:  [    ]  (pixels)
Opacity: [ 80] %
Mode:
    ⦿ Normal
    ○ Darken Only
    ○ Lighten Only
```

Figure 7–23

10. Choose the Alpha → Selection command.

11. When the RGB image window appears (with the blurred type mask visible as "marching ants"), choose the Fill... command from the Edit menu.

12. Choose "Normal" fill, with 80% opacity. Press OK (Figure 7-23).

13. The Fill command is applied through the blurred text mask, while still allowing part of the background texture to show through (Figure 7-24).

14. Change foreground color (if you started this exercise with a foreground color of black, make it red now).

15. Click the type tool on the screen and, using the default entries (which are the same used for the dropshadow), click OK.

Figure 7–24 Blurred text mask with background texture showing

Figure 7–25   Final type in place above dropshadow

Figure 7–26   Sample image of object with dropshadow

16. Place the colored type on top of and slightly to the side of the dropshadow (in the exercise, we'll place the type above and to the left of the dropshadow) (Figure 7–25).

This technique is also very useful for creating shadows for objects (Figure 7–26). You can also use the Brightness/Contrast or Level commands instead of the Fill command to darken the shadow area instead of filling it.

Glow Effect Around Text or Objects

Making objects and text glow is an attractive technique that goes a long way; some higher-end computer graphics systems have specialized commands for creating this effect. In Photoshop, you can get this popular effect by combining the Fringe and Feather commands.

Figure 7-27 Simple shape

Let's start by adding a glow to a simple object on a solid, dark background.

1. Set the background color to a dark gray or black.
2. Make a simple shape using the circular selection Marquee; fill it with a medium-to-dark gray (or an equivalent color value, such as a darker red or blue) (Figure 7-27).
3. Copy the object to the clipboard.
4. With the object still selected, choose the Fringe command.
5. Type in a value of 16. Press OK (Figure 7-28).
6. Choose the Feather command, and type in a value of 8. Press OK (Figure 7-29).

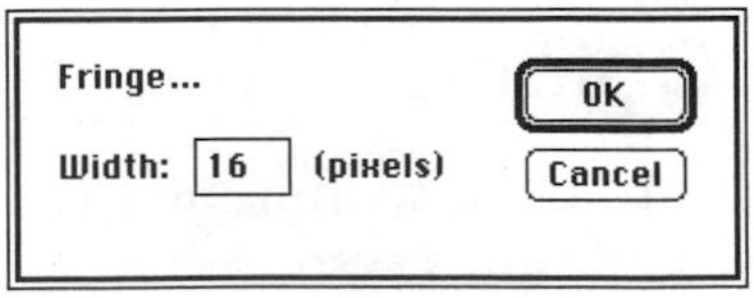

```
Fringe...                    OK
Width: 16   (pixels)       Cancel
```

Figure 7-28 Fringe

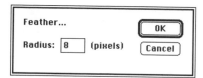

Figure 7–29 Feathered fringe

▼ **Tip:** When using this technique, the size of the fringe determines the range of the glow; lower numbers result in a less glaring or "bright" glow. We've found that the optimum Feather value is usually half that of the Fringe value; a fringe of 16 requires a feather value of 8. You can experiment with these values to achieve more exaggerated glow effects.

7. Choose a light gray as the foreground color, and Fill the selected area with that shade (Figure 7-30).

8. Paste the clipboard image into the document, and move it into the correct position (Figure 7-31).

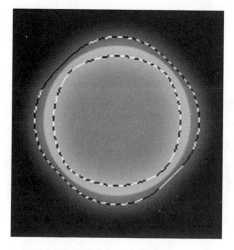

Figure 7–30 The halo of the glow

Figure 7–31 Final image positioned above glow

Figure 7-32 Object with glow against complex background

You can use this same technique with any object that you either Lasso by hand or select with the Magic Wand tool. In the previous example, we added a glow to an object on a solid background; the technique also works well with objects against more complex backgrounds (Figure 7-32).

The glow technique also works extremely well with type.

1. With ATM installed, and a medium-to-dark gray selected as the foreground color, make some large (70+ point) type (Figure 7-33). Make sure the type is anti-aliased.
2. Copy the still selected type to the clipboard.
3. Choose the Fringe command, and type in a value of 12 (assuming the type size is 70 point).
4. Choose the Feather command, and type in a value of 6.
5. Choose a lighter gray as the foreground color, choose the Fill command, and click OK with the default value (normal fill, 100% opacity).
6. Paste the type back onto the image, and move it into place over the glow (Figure 7-34).

```
╔═══════════════ Type ═══════════════╗
  Font: │ Goudy                    │     ┌─────────┐
                                          │   OK    │
  Size: │ 70│  │ point │                  └─────────┘
                                          ┌─────────┐
Leading: │        │                       │ Cancel  │
                                          └─────────┘
Spacing: │        │

Style:                          Alignment:
   ☒ Bold      ☐ Outline        ● Left
   ☐ Italic    ☐ Shadow         ○ Center
   ☐ Underline ☒ Anti-aliased   ○ Right

  │ ERIKA                                        │
  │                                              │
  │                                              │
  │                                              │
  │                                              │
```

Figure 7–33   Choosing type for glow effect

Figure 7–34   Final type over glow

Custom Contour Fills

A talented Photoshop artist we know, Thomas Cushwa, turned us on to a technique he developed for using the selection tools (primarily the Lasso), the Feather command, and the Paintbucket for creating custom contour fills. The technique is extremely useful in giving a three-dimensional look to shapes that have rounded edges.

Type is a great example of this technique. Usually type is made to look three-dimensional by simply adding depth. This technique, however, will give type the look of liquid—a shape with no hard, sharp edges.

Compare the two effects shown in Figures 7–35 and 7–36. Figure 7–35 is using the usually applied effect to get the three-dimensional

Figure 7–35 Traditional 3D Text

Figure 7–36 Contoured 3D Effect

quality. Figure 7-36, however, has more dimensionality—a far more realistic and original approach to the same problem.

The exercise here is done in grayscale, but it works just as well and is more vibrant in color.

1. Start a new file.
2. Select a light gray tone in the Foreground color box.
3. Select the type tool (Figure 7-37).
4. Select a rounded font. In the image created for this book, Souvenir Demi was used.
5. Set the size to 250 points.
6. Set style to Bold and Anti-aliased.

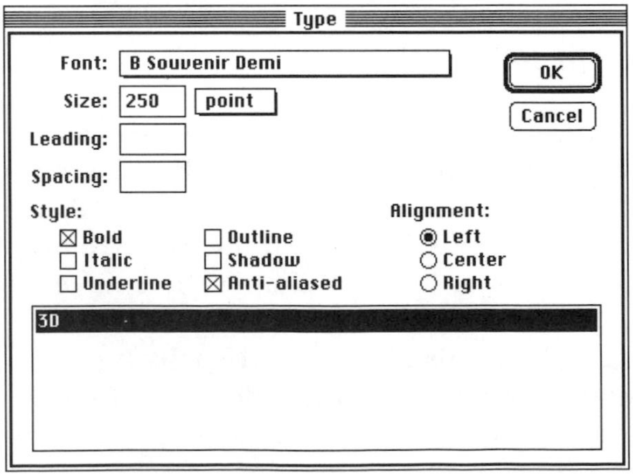

Figure 7–37 Text Entry dialog

Figure 7–38 Text appears on screen

7. Type in the letters "3D" (Figure 7–38).
8. The text will appear on the screen.
9. Double-click the Lasso selection tool.
10. The Feather window appears. Enter a low value (Figure 7–39).

This will make any selection made with the Lasso automatically feathered at the edges. Remember that the higher the feather value, the softer the edge. If you require the object to have just a slight curve to the edges as in this type, a low number is best.

11. Select the edges of the type. Be sure to select a good portion of the white surrounding the type edges (Figure 7–40).

▼ **Tip:** Keep in mind that light hits a curved edge in different ways. By taking an actual three-dimensional, smooth-edged object and holding it up to a light, you can study the effects of real light on the edges and have a real model to work from.

12. Select a black or dark color for the Foreground color.
13. Select the Bucket tool.

Feather...	
	OK
Radius: 3 (pixels)	Cancel

Figure 7–39 Feather dialog box

Figure 7-40   Selected portions of type to receive shading

14. With the Bucket, click within the gray portion of the letters in the selection (Figure 7-41).

   While the white of the page is also selected, the fill will hit the outside edge of the type and not venture into the white. The portion of the gray into the letters gets a soft transition of the black to the gray due to the feather.

▼ **Tip:** Even though the selected portions of the letters are not connected, filling one selected area will sometimes automatically fill the others.

   For a little extra realism, a highlight should be added.

15. Choose the Airbrush tool with a small size.
16. Spray a soft line that follows the edge opposite the one with the shadow (Figure 7-42).

   The end result is the image at the beginning of this exercise (Figure 7-36).

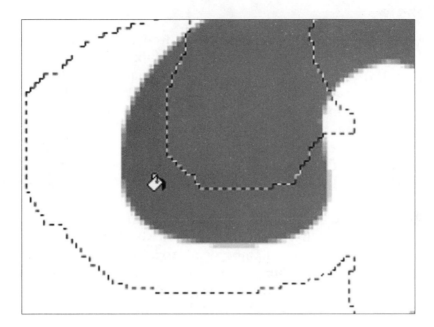

Figure 7–41   Bucket tool fills selected area

Figure 7–42   Close-up of highlight

Glass Sphere

There is an effect that up to now required the talents of either a photographic setup or an extremely skillful illustrator—a glass sphere. If it stands on its own on a solid surface, then it is simply a matter of painting a circle with a few highlights in it. If, however, the sphere is in a setting with other objects and different light sources, the matter becomes quite complicated (Figure 7–43).

The glass sphere in the image "sphere chamber," which is also in this book's "Photoshop Gallery" color pages, was entirely created using the Circle selection tool, filters, and the Brightness/Contrast control.

The portals in the chamber were done by hand. They are simply geometric shapes that have been filled with color. The Add Noise filter was applied to the chamber walls to add the stonelike texture. In alpha channels, gradients were used to create the shadows. The chamber was darkened through the gradients in the alpha channels.

The sunset visible through the arches is a scan.

Figure 7–43   Sphere chamber

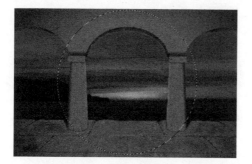

Figure 7–44 Overall selection

The image you start with can be anything. To add a glass sphere, follow these simple steps.

1. With the Circle selection tool, select a circular area encompassing most of the image or the area that will be reflected in the sphere (Figure 7–44).

2. Copy the selection into the clipboard, then deselect.

3. With the Circle selection tool, this time select a circular area where the sphere is to be placed (in this image, that area is dead center).

Note: Since many modifications will be done to this area, it is vital to not deselect the sphere until the end of this exercise.

4. Choose the Brightness/Contrast control under the Adjust submenu of the Image menu (Figure 7–45).

5. Slide the Brightness slider to the right to lighten the selection. Click OK.

6. Choose the Spherize filter from the Filters submenu under the Image menu.

This will make the background showing through the glass look as if the glass is in fact a sphere rather than flat.

Now that the sphere is created, it is necessary to give it reflections. The sphere should still be selected.

7. Choose Paste Into under the Edit menu.

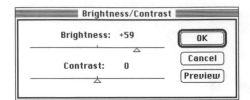

Figure 7–45   Brightness/Contrast dialog box

The large circle selected at the beginning of the exercise should now appear within the smaller sphere. Notice that the actual dimensions of the selection are displayed by the "crawling ants."

8. Choose Paste Controls from the Edit menu (Figure 7–46).
9. Bring the opacity down to 30%.
    This will make the pasted-in image look transparent.

▼ **Tip:** Hitting the Preview button will let you see the effects without making them permanent. If 30% is not enough, give it more; once the image is right, click OK.

10. Select Stretch from the Effects submenu found under the Image menu.

Four handles will appear at the corners of the large circular selection.

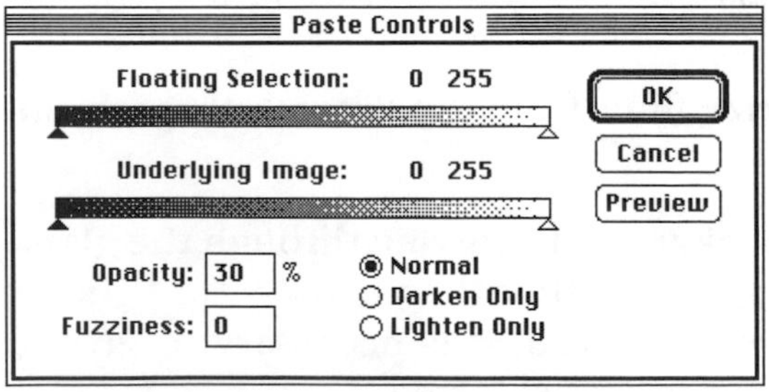

Figure 7–46   Paste controls dialog box

Figure 7–47 Pasted image resized to fit small ball

11. While pressing the Option button on the keyboard, click on and drag each of the handles until they form a square around the glass sphere (Figure 7–47).

12. Choose the Spherize filter from the Filters submenu under the Image menu.

This will make the reflection showing on the glass look as if it is following the contour of the sphere.

The highlights on the ground below and in front of the sphere were created with the Lasso selection tool. The shapes of the reflections were selected and Feathered. Brightness/Contrast setting were played with to get shadows and highlight effects within the selections.

Custom Patterns As Halftone Screens

The Custom Pattern capability of Photoshop is normally used in order to create custom fill patterns for use with the Fill command. Hidden in the Photoshop User Manual is a technique which describes how to use custom fill patterns as halftone screens. These come into play when you convert a grayscale image into a black-and-white bitmap. The following exercise uses a scanned stone texture as the custom pattern — you should also try different textures, such as noise patterns and other natural organic textures (wood, marble, or anything with a dense, chaotic pattern). You

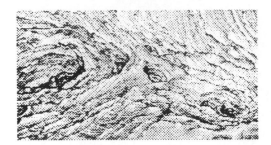

Figure 7–48   Scanned stone texture

need only grayscale textures—the color information of an image is ignored when creating custom patterns for use as halftone screens.

1. We'll start with a scanned stone texture (Figure 7–48).

2. Select the entire pattern, and choose Define Pattern from the Edit menu. You can now close the stone texture document.

3. Open an image document to be processed through the stone (you might want to try an image close in size to the custom pattern.) If the image is a color RGB file, convert it to grayscale mode. We'll try it on our trusty eye.

4. Choose the Bitmap mode from the Mode menu. Select the Custom Pattern option at the bottom of the dialog (Figure 7–49).

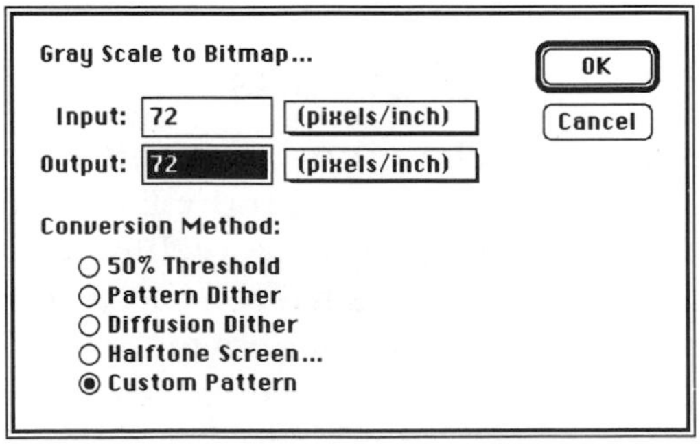

```
 Gray Scale to Bitmap...                          ( OK )

   Input:  72      (pixels/inch)                  [ Cancel ]
  Output:  72      (pixels/inch)

  Conversion Method:
     ○ 50% Threshold
     ○ Pattern Dither
     ○ Diffusion Dither
     ○ Halftone Screen...
     ◉ Custom Pattern
```

Figure 7–49   Grayscale to Bitmap dialog, Custom Pattern selected

Figure 7–50 Final image

The image is now processed through the custom pattern. An amazingly versatile technique is now at your command (Figure 7-50).

The Calculate Commands

Photoshop's abilities to manipulate individual channels of an image are extended by using the commands in the Calculate hierarchical menu. Essentially, the Calculate commands allow you to perform operations on one or more channels at a time. Typically, the brightness values of channels are compared, and the specific command determines what will happen to the resulting operation. For example, the Subtract command subtracts the brightness value of the pixels in one channel from the brightness values of the pixels of another channel, and puts the resulting pixels in yet another channel. While this seems esoteric, it's actually quite useful for complex layering of individual elements.

The Photoshop User Guide has an extensive technical discussion of these commands, down to the actual mathematical formulas that these commands employ. The problem with the user manual discussion of the Calculate commands is that the examples of the functionality of these commands are sparse—we've found that in actual everyday use, some of the Calculate commands are more immediately useful than others.

Here are some practical applications of some of the Calculate commands:

Duplicate: Creating a Separate Multichannel Document

When an alpha channel is created for an image with the Selection → Alpha command, the resulting alpha channel is added as a new channel to the color image document. While this is OK, there are times when you might not want to place the alpha channel into the color document, but instead, you might want to create a separate multichannel, grayscale document containing just the alpha channels that you define. This is especially true if the color image is a large, high-resolution file, which is probably already quite large. The Duplicate command is the ticket.

1. Starting with the desired color image (saved to the disk with the name "Color Image"), select a portion of the image (using any of the selection tools) for which you want to make an alpha channel.

2. Open the Duplicate command in the Calculate hierarchical menu (Figure 7-51).

3. The Source file is the document from which you are creating the alpha channel. Beneath it, you'll see the current channel as RGB. We don't want to create the alpha channel out of the whole RGB image, just what's selected in that image. Press the mouse button on RGB, and choose Selection from the pop-up menu.

4. Leave the Destination and channel as the defaults—both say *New*. Press OK.

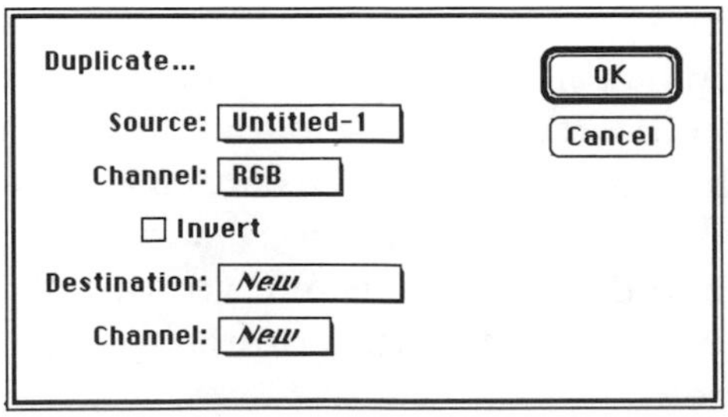

Figure 7–51   The Duplicate dialog

5. You now have a new untitled document open on the screen, showing the alpha channel created with the selection from the original RGB image. Save file to disk, naming it "Color Image Masks."

6. Go back to the original RGB image, select another area from which to make an alpha channel, and open the Duplicate command.

7. This time, you'll want to add this new alpha channel to the existing "Color Image Masks" file. The Source image is still "Color Image"; make sure that selection is the selected Source channel. Choose "Color Image Masks" as the Destination file, and "New" as the destination channel. Press OK (Figure 7–52).

8. You'll now have two alpha channels in the "Color Image Masks" file. These alpha channels can be overlayed onto the original color image, even though the alpha channels are in a different document.

9. Select the alpha channel you wish to overlay onto the "Color Image" document, and choose the Duplicate command again.

10. Make sure that the "Color Image Mask" file is the source (the name appears truncated in the pop-up field name, as you can see in Figure 7–53). The Source channel is the alpha channel selected from step 9. The Destination is the "Color Image" document, and the channel that you want to overlay the alpha onto is the selection. (While you might think that the destina-

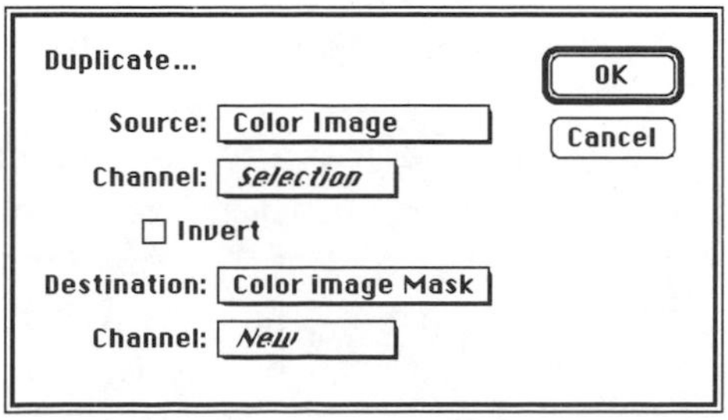

Figure 7–52 The Duplicate dialog, copying the new alpha into the existing "Color Image Mask" file as a new channel

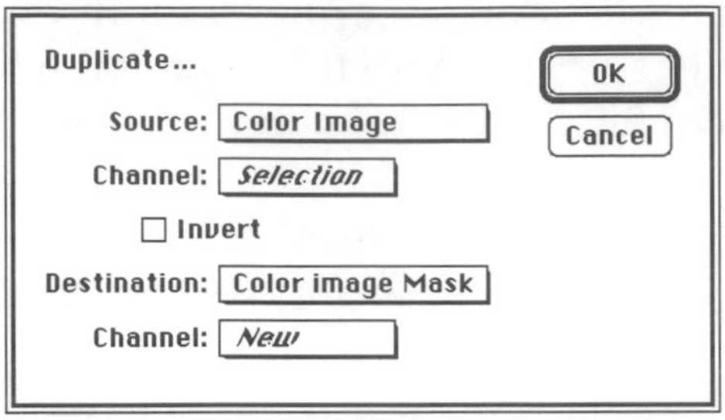

```
┌──────────────────────────────────────────────┐
│  Duplicate...                    ┌──────────┐  │
│                                  │    OK    │  │
│        Source: │ Color Image │   └──────────┘  │
│                                  ┌──────────┐  │
│       Channel: │ Selection  │    │  Cancel  │  │
│                                  └──────────┘  │
│              □ Invert                          │
│                                                │
│   Destination: │ Color image Mask │            │
│                                                │
│       Channel: │ New       │                   │
└──────────────────────────────────────────────┘
```

Figure 7–53   Duplicating a mask from the mask file into the color
image, with the mask coming in as a selection area

tion channel should be the RGB channel, this is wrong;
duplicating the alpha to the RGB channel in the destination
image would completely replace the color image with the alpha
channel. Remember that when you normally overlay an alpha
channel onto the RGB image, you use the Alpha → Selection
command, even though nothing is selected in the RGB image.
Yes, it's a bit confusing, but you'll soon get the hang of it).

Tip: The whole point of this technique is that you can create alpha
channel documents that aren't part of the actual main image; this
allows you to keep the size of your main image relatively smaller
than it would be if you had all of the image's alpha channels stored
with it.

Warning: You'll run into problems if you resize the main image in
any way after creating a separate corresponding alpha channel document. If you do this, the alpha channels can no longer be superimposed onto the main image. This is true for any of the Calculate
commands that involve more than one channel/document. The sizes
of the images can't be changed, because the registration between the
main images and alpha channels is lost. This is one of the reasons that
you might sometimes want to store the alpha channels with the
actual image: Any resizing to any of the channels of the document
will resize all of the document's channels accordingly, in order to
retain exact registration between the channels.

11. You'll now see the Color Image with the alpha channel overlaid and selected, even though that alpha channel isn't actually in the "Color Image" document. You can now apply any command or filter to the image through the superimposed alpha channel.

Subtract: Extracting Layers from Existing Graphics

The Subtract command is useful when you've defined a number of alpha channels and discover that you need to make modifications to an alpha channel of a masked image that lies behind an overlapping image placed with another image mask. An example:

1. Create a heavily feathered circular selection against a complex RGB image, and select the Selection → Alpha command. This will make an alpha channel of the area of the feathered circular selection.

2. Create a new channel, and place some type into the channel. Make sure that you place the type on the screen such that there is some overlap between the area occupied by the type and the feathered circular selection created in the previous steps.

3. Overlay the text alpha channel onto the image, fill with a solid color.

4. Overlay the feathered circle onto the image, fill with a different solid color. It should overlap and obscure part of the colored text created in Step 3.

Now let's say that you decide that you want to change the color of the type, without disturbing the colored feathered circle in the foreground. One way to do this would be to apply the feathered circle alpha again, copy the contents to the clipboard, apply the text alpha again, change the color of the text, apply the circle alpha again, and then paste the clipboard into the circle alpha selection. Wheeww! And that's only assuming that you have two alpha layers: If you have more than a single alpha layer in the foreground, this can become a scary nightmare quite rapidly. An easier way to do this is to subtract the feathered circle alpha away from the text alpha, resulting in another alpha channel or overlay that contains the text without the feathered circle overlap.

5. Select the Subtract command from the Calculate hierarchical menu. The Source files are the image documents that contain the alpha channels to be manipulated. In this case, both alpha channels are coming from the same document.

   Specify Source 1 as the Text alpha channel and Source 2 as the feathered circle. You'll want to apply the results to the actual color image, so choose the origin document as the destination, and the Selection as the destination channel. Press OK.

6. You're brought back to the RGB image, and the text not underneath the feathered circle is selected. Any command or filter you run will now be applied only to the selected text area, with the smooth feathered border of the overlapping circle treated properly—any change will follow the smooth edge of the overlap.

▼ **Tip:** While this is a very basic application of the Subtract command that only dealt with two alpha channels, you can use Subtract to create more complex differential composite masks by placing the results of the calculations into new alpha channels, instead of automatically overlaying them onto the target color image as in the example above. You'll also notice that the Subtract command has a field for a Scale and Offset value—these are used as compensation factors in much more complex subtract calculations that we have yet to utilize. Read the description in the User Manual for a detailed discussion of the mathematics behind the Subtract command.

Subtract: Creating a Raised Shadow Effect

Another use for the Subtract command is to add a perfect raised pseudo-shadow effect to a complex image. For example, let's say that you had a scanned image or some scanned type, and you wanted to give it a dropshadow that would perfectly conform to the shape of the image or text. The trick is to create two alpha channels—one with the actual shape, and one with an offset version of the shape— and subtract the first alpha channel from the second alpha channel.

Shadow Shadow

Figure 7-54   Image without raised background and with it

The result is a perfectly contoured, raised background effect that conforms to the shape of the image (Figure 7-54).

Add: Combining Multiple Alpha Channels into One

The Add command is useful for combining multiple alpha channels into a single channel. When you use Add, you can select two alpha channels and make them into a single alpha channel, in which overlapping white areas from the two channels remain pure white (transparent), while the luminosity values of overlapping gray areas are added together. You can continue adding more alpha channels to the results of the first addition, in order to create a single channel consisting of the contents of many alpha channels. Let's say that you create two separate alpha channels for two objects, in order to process each one separately through two different filters. After filtering the two images, you decide that you want to apply a color correction or increase in brightness to both of the objects. The long way to do this would be to reapply the two alpha channels individually to the main RGB image, doing the color correction or brightness change twice, once for each alpha channel. The easier way would be to combine both of the separate alpha masks into one, and then apply this new combination alpha to the main RGB image and make the desired color correction or brightness change, which would affect both of the objects at once.

The Constant Command

The Constant command is useful for placing a solid gray value (from 0 to 255) into a channel. It's almost exactly the same as filling a channel with a solid shade of gray—the only real difference is that you can specify the shade of gray numerically, ensuring absolute precision and consistency in selection of the grayshade.

The Composite Command

The Composite command is used in order to overlay an image with an alpha channel onto a complex background, while maintaining smooth anti-aliased edges between the image and the background. While you can essentially do this by simply selecting an image through its alpha channel and copying and pasting this image onto a background, this process may become problematic if the image and the background are large, high-resolution files (in which case the Copy and Paste commands might take a long time and a large chunk of hard disk space in order to work). The Composite command does the same job without the lengthy waits involved in copying and pasting large, high-resolution images.

Here's a simple example of the Composite command:

1. Let's start with two images of exactly the same document size: One is a complex background, the other a distinct object with an alpha channel mask of itself (Figure 7–55).
2. With both documents open simultaneously, choose the Composite command.
3. Here's what we want to do: Choose the RGB channel of the object document as the Foreground channel and document, choose the alpha channel of the object document as the mask, choose the RGB channel of the background document as the background, and choose the RGB channel of the Background document as the Destination. This should all look like Figure 7–56. Press OK.
4. You'll now have the object composited onto the background with anti-aliased edges (Figure 7–57).

The drawback of using the Composite command is that all documents to be composited must be exactly the same size.

The Multiply and Screen Commands

The Multiply and Screen commands are different, but related. Multiply is comparable to taking two lithographs and laying them on a light table: The common light areas are light, overlapping dark and light areas result in darks areas, and overlapping dark areas result in dark areas. Screen has the opposite effect: It's like projecting two slides onto a wall. So what does this mean? Let's take a look at an example where we want to "place" a black-to-white gradient inside of some antialiased type to create the final effect of text that fades into a background.

Figure 7–55 Background document and image document with alpha mask

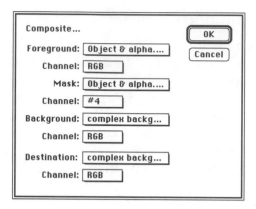

Figure 7–56 The Composite dialog with the proper selections for this exercise

1. Start with a complex RGB image. Select All, and create two alpha channels for the image.

2. In the first alpha channel (#4 in the channel list), create some anti-aliased text that covers most of the alpha channel. Do this by using the Stretch command to resize some large text created with the text tool. Make sure that the text is white against a black background (the text is the live area of the mask).

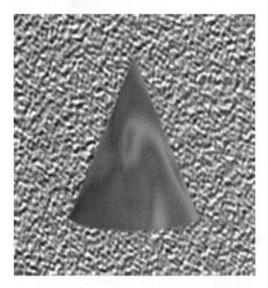

Figure 7–57 Final composited image

What we want to do here is to place the gradient "inside" of the text, while retaining the anti-aliased edges of the text characters so that we can get smooth edges when we layer the text onto the RGB image. You might think that a way to do this would be to select the black background in the text alpha channel with the Magic Wand tool, use Select Inverse in order to isolate the white text characters, and then use the Gradient tool to fill the selected text. The problem with this is that you'll lose the anti-aliased edges of the text. Read on!

3. In the second alpha channel (#5), create a black-to-white gradient that covers the whole area of the channel.

4. Select the Multiply command.

5. Set the two sources to the main document (the only choice available), one source channel to the text alpha channel, the other source channel to the gradient alpha, specifying Destination as the main document, and channel as either New (to create a new channel with the composite effect) or Selection (to overlay the result directly onto the RGB image, without creating a new alpha channel with the results of the Composite command). The Multiply dialog should look like Figure 7–58.

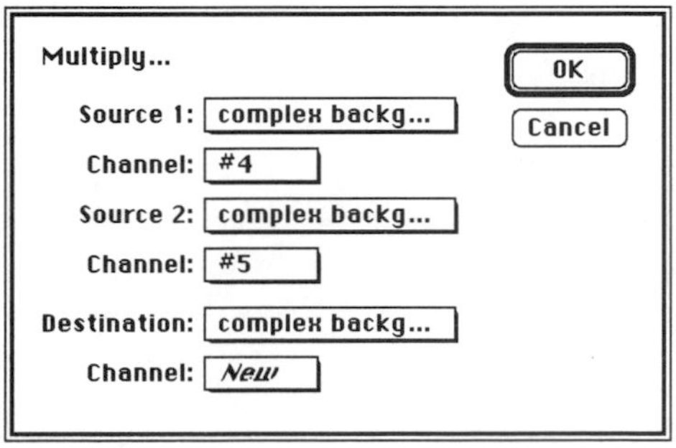

Figure 7–58 The Multiply dialog with the appropriate values for this exercise

Figure 7-59 Final image created with Multiply command

6. Overlay the new alpha onto the RGB image, and try filling with a solid color, or pressing the Backspace/Delete key (Figure 7-59).

As you practice using the Calculate menu items, you'll soon discover a world of new multichannel effects. These commands are the single most complicated aspect of using Photoshop, so don't be discouraged if things don't immediately make sense. Work on these examples, experiment with some exercises of your own, and you'll soon get the hang of it.

8

Output

Once you create your masterpiece in Photoshop, the last thing you'll need to do is to get the image off of the screen and onto paper. You can:

- Print black-and-white halftones on a LaserWriter.

- Print color proofs directly to a color printer.

- Separate color images into four-color process separations.

- Import a Photoshop image into a page layout or illustration program, combine it with text and object graphics, and separate the entire finished document.

This chapter will discuss the issues of printing images from within Photoshop, calibration of the screen, the halftoning controls, and producing color separations.

Color and Quality

Before we talk about how to get things out of Photoshop, we'd just like to take a moment to discuss the issue of *quality*.

Quality has been, and will always be, a subjective hot potato. Quality is gauged by your past experiences, what you've come to expect of the tools and methods at hand, and the nature (and expectations) of your audience. Too often, when reading about desktop publishing and production of color separations with microcomputer technology, we run across references to *quality* without proper *context*: the quality standards of an in-house report are different from those used to produce four-color glossy national and international magazines, though that statement wouldn't necessarily be true for some companies and corporations. Too often, quality is a term used objectively to create an artificial level of expectation without the consideration of practical issues of the situation. In other words, if it ain't broke, it will probably work, unless you're in a black hole, where physics doesn't work as you might expect.

Quality and Technology

The final quality of whatever you produce in Photoshop is directly affected by the technology used to acquire and print images used to create your work. There is a very real qualitative difference between images scanned from a newspaper with a handheld scanner and those scanned from large color transparencies and carefully developed 35mm slides on professional prepress laser drum scanners-not to mention the amount of money you would spend doing it both ways. Remember, today the "traditional" method of creating high-quality color separations actually involves high-end laser drum scanners and custom computer hardware and software. You're essentially recreating the process with Photoshop and much cheaper hardware, but the basic techniques used are fairly similar. General rule of thumb: the more money you can spend on the scanner and output device, the better the overall final quality of your work—software and creative expertise being equal.

Color Calibration

Another key issue that arises in the discussion of quality is calibration: original artwork, the scanned artwork viewed on the computer screen, and a color proof print will all probably end up looking slightly different, in terms of color saturation and consistency. Light reflecting off of an image and light being used to draw an image on a cathode ray tube are perceived by the eye to be very different beasts. One of the largest problems facing desktop color publishers is the calibration of color and brightness between the various stages of the production process. While there are devices that allow you to calibrate a color monitor, we haven't had the experience of using any of them. (Various companies, including Radius and SuperMac, sell color calibration devices, but for some reason these companies did not respond to our requests for test units. We'll have to let you draw your own conclusions regarding the reliability and accuracy of these devices.)

Color is a science, one that requires years of hard work, experience, and pain to master. While programs such as Photoshop dramatically increase the abilities of amateur color publishers, you should expect to spend time experimenting with and learning about the intricacies of color. It takes more than a day and less than a lifetime to get the hang of it. We're still learning the ropes ourselves.

Separation Setup in Preferences

In the standard Photoshop Preferences dialog, you'll find a button that leads you to a secondary Separation Setup window (Figure 8-1).

This dialog allows you to control

—Monitor Gamma
—Screen color calibration
—Black generation

• Monitor Gamma: Each different monitor has a predefined brightness balance factor, called Gamma. The gamma factor of

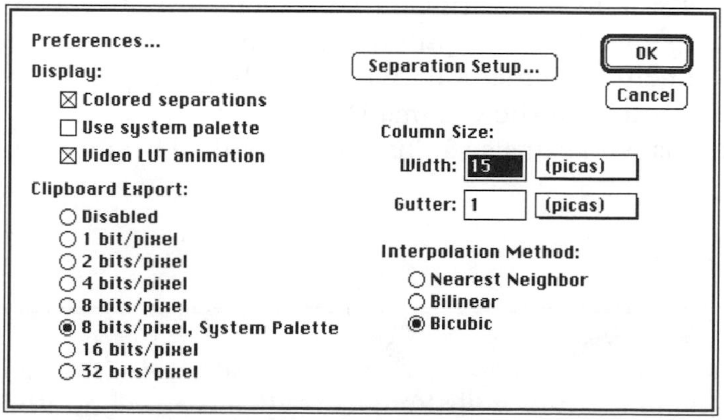

Figure 8-1 Preferences dialog, and Separation Setup window

▼ **Tip:** Any of the combination of settings that you make can be saved as a template by using the Load and Save buttons in the upper right side of the Separation Setup dialog.

a monitor is a predetermined value (even though there is a degree of difference in the gamma values of two monitors of the same manufacturer and model, though this difference is usually quite small). The default value in this field is 1.4, the Apple-specified gamma of the Apple 13-inch RGB color monitor. If you are using another size and brand of monitor, you should consult with the documentation or directly with the manufacturer for the optimum gamma setting for that monitor, and enter that number into the gamma field in the Separation Setup window.

With the shipping version of Photoshop 1.0.7, a new INIT/CDEV called Gamma is included with the package. This INIT/CDEV allows you to precisely set the gamma levels of any monitors you have attached to your Macintosh—for optimum screen brightness calibration in Photoshop and any other applications. It can also be used to calibrate monitors among various people so that each can work the same color images, with consistent color representation from screen to screen.

By adjusting the Gamma adjustment slider so that the gray bars above the adjustment slider appear to be equal, you can "normalize" the monitor gamma to its optimum setting. Please refer to the Gamma documentation included with the Photoshop 1.0.7 update for a full description of the Gamma INIT/CDEV.

Using Gamma, you can also adjust the individual brightness of the

Gamma actually refers to the midtone values in an image; different gamma values will affect the balance of the midtones, without any effect on pure black and white.

> Gamma effectively replaces the need for calibrating the screen as described in Chapter 20 of the Adobe Photoshop User Guide.

RGB guns in the monitor, allowing you to "preview" duotone effects, even though Photoshop doesn't inherently have the ability to create true duotones (look for this ability in future versions of Photoshop).

- The color swatches in the Separation Setup dialog are for matching the screen representation of color to a printed version of the color swatches: By printing a sample of the displayed colors on the desired color output device, you can effectively calibrate the screen representations of the colors with the printed colors. This calibration must be done separately for each different output device you intend on using (including different printers of the same make and model), and you can save each calibration session for later use by using the Load and Save buttons in the Separation Setup dialog.

In order to adjust the color swatches, simply click on them, which brings up a standard Apple color picker wheel. Select the closest matched color to the printed swatch, and click the OK button. Do this for cyan, magenta and yellow swatches (the top row). Note that you can also specify saturation percentages of each of the swatches by typing the desired number in the field underneath the color swatch.

- The Black Generation control refers to the way that Photoshop will create the black printing plate. When you convert an RGB image to CMYK mode, Photoshop analyzes the image and calculates a black layer, based on a certain threshold value. The black generation control allows you to determine the threshold. By changing this setting, the black plate can be made heavier or lighter. For example, if you set the black generation to light, and the printed proof image doesn't have enough detail in the shadow areas, you might want to try setting the black generation to medium or a darker value, and reseparating the image (the black generation is called into play specifically when converting an image from RGB to CMYK). Please refer to the discussion in the Photoshop User manual regarding Black Generation and Undercolor removal (page 370–374 in the User manual). You can also load them into the Separation preferences dialog using the Custom Map command found in the Black generation hierarchical menu.

Page Setup

The Page Setup dialog is accessed via the Page Setup command, found under the File menu. It is in this window that all the parameters for the final output of the image are set (Figure 8–2).

The top portion of the dialog is the standard LaserWriter Page Setup, giving the paper size selection, scaling, orientation, and effects. For further detailed information on these commands, refer to the LaserWriter manual. It is the section below the dotted line that we will concentrate on in this section.

There is a collection of buttons and options available at the bottom of this dialog. These commands give Photoshop the capability for output of the color image and separations with precise control.

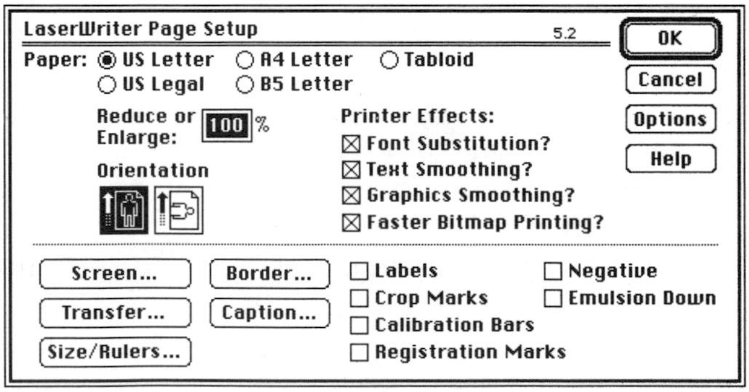

Figure 8–2   The Page Setup Dialog

Screens

Any photograph, illustration, or scene that consists of a wide range of tones or gradation of tones is called "continuous-tone." In letterpress and offset lithography, tones cannot be reproduced by varying the amounts of ink. A printing press can only lay solid ink for image areas and no ink for non-image or white areas. To reproduce gradients or different tones within an image, it is necessary to convert the image into what is known as a halftone.

The halftone principle is an optical illusion where patterns of small dots of different sizes are printed with ink of uniform density. Halftoning is the process by which varying tones are converted into these patterns of clearly defined dots of various sizes.

The size of the dots determine the tonal values. For instance, a cluster of large dots where the dots are so large that they leave little white space between each other will reproduce an area that is dark. On the other hand, an area composed of tiny dots where the white area is stronger will produce a light gray area. If the dot sizes are varied, the result will be a reproduction of any gradients within the image (see Figure 8–3).

Traditionally, halftones are created photographically using screens. These screens consist of two sheets of glass, each ruled by precision equipment with a given number of lines per linear inch. The lines are equal in width to the spaces between them. The two sheets of glass are cemented together at right angles to each other, thus forming a screen. The screen is placed a short distance from the film in the camera, which is negative film. This camera is used

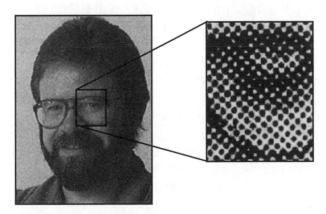

Figure 8–3   Halftone screen close-ups

to create a negative film from the original art, which is then used to create the plate for the printing press. When exposed, the light transmitted from the image is projected through the transparent spaces of the screen. The spaces act as pinhole lenses that produce dots on the film proportional in size to the amount of light reflected from the art. The light areas reflect a lot of light and produce large dots on the film. Dark areas give off little light, thus producing smaller dots.

Digitally produced halftones and screens are essentially equivalent to traditional screens, with the major difference being that the computer digitally simulates the analog screen extraction process. The results are very close (if not better, in some cases) to what is produced with analog methods. The fact is that most of the "traditional" color separation work going on in the world uses high-end computers, and it isn't unreasonable to project into the future and come up with a world where all halftoning and screening is done digitally (we're sure that some hardcore purists who happen to read this might call us up and angrily disagree, but notice what happened to the typesetting world with the development of desktop publishing and high-resolution PostScript laser imaging devices).

Different screens have varying degrees of resolution, or lines per inch, in order to create the different screen requirements for the different forms of printing. Newspapers, for instance, require a coarse dot screen. Newsprint paper is very absorbent and cannot reproduce screens that are too dense; the ink will spread and mix together, thus muddying the images. Coated or glossy stock such as the ones used on slick magazines can hold a small tight dot without the ink spread, thus attaining much finer detail in reproduction. This spreading of the ink is known as dot gain.

The screens of dots are set at different angles. In black-and-white, you are dealing with only one screen, black, so the angle can be set to any degree. In color separations these angles are crucial. Without the correct configuration, you run the danger of getting what is known as moiré patterns (pronounced mwa–ray). These are patterns that interfere with the appearance of the image. The size of the moiré patterns depends on how off the screen angles are. These moiré patterns appear as checkerboard patterns over the image. Using a proper screen angle will avoid these annoying patterns. A minimum pattern is formed when an angle of 30° between screens is used. Since halftone screens consist of line rulings at 90° to each other, there is room for only three 30° angles before they repeat. In four-color printing, two of the colors must be printed at the same angle or must be separated by other than 30°.

A typical angle configuration used is black, 45°; magenta, 75°; yellow, 90°; and cyan, 105°. The default settings in Photoshop are 108.39° for cyan, 161.59° for magenta, 90° for yellow, and 45° for black. These settings typically allow enough room for accurate color reproduction. An error of as little as 0.1° between screen angles can cause a moiré in areas where three and four colors mix.

Moirés can also be caused by poor registration on the part of the printer. The screens are positioned at precise locations on the film to properly interact with each other (Figure 8–4). Register marks are used to insure the proper alignment of the four plates; if they do not align, a moiré results. If the registration is off dramatically, it can also result in a color shift. This is an effect that makes one of the colors seem to appear as a ghost or double image. Let's say the red plate is off—the image will have on one of its sides a red halo. If the image is a grayscale image, activating the Screens button will pop up the Halftone Screen window with only one input for Frequency and Angle.

Besides the frequency and angle of the screens, Photoshop gives you control over the shape of the dots. The shape can be the traditional circular dot, which is the default shape. The dot can be elongated or elliptical in shape. The dot can be replaced by a square. For a totally different effect, lines or crosshatching can be used to emulate the tones. In this case, the line weights and the space

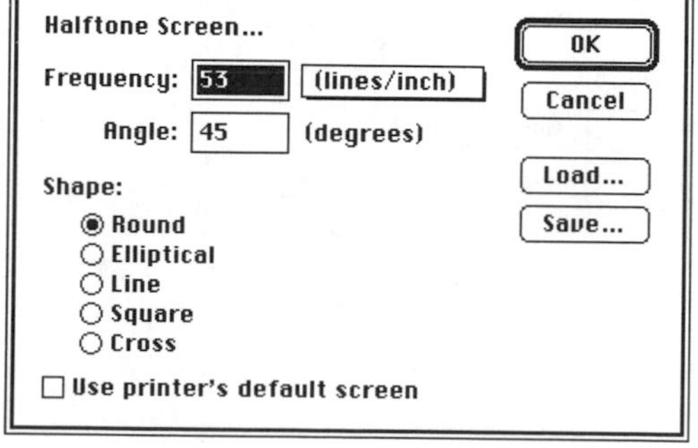

Figure 8–4 The black-and-white Screens window

between them will determine the tonal value much the same way that the size of the dot does. The direction of the lines is determined by the screen angle. The size of the dots or lines can be further controlled by adjusting the resolution. Modifying the shape will add special touches and effects to the printed image.

When all the settings have been established, they can be set to be the default. When the default button is used, all the new settings will then apply to every new document started.

When the image is a color image, the frequency and angle, as mentioned earlier, have to be set for each plate individually (Figure 8-5). Notice that in this window, there are inputs for all four colors.

On the right side of the window there is an Auto button (Figure 8-6). In this window you enter the resolution of the printer being used for output and the screen necessary for final output.

The screen in this case is dependent on the needs of the particular printing press and paper being used. Your printer will give you that information.

The screen is the amount of lines per inch and is also known in the industry as the screen ruling. Some common screen rulings are 65- to 85-line for newspaper by letterpress, 100-, 120-, and 133-line for offset, 133- and 150-line for slick magazines, commercial letterpress, or offset lithography.

Any change in this window will reset the Frequencies and Angles in the Halftone Screen window. Photoshop will automatically cal-

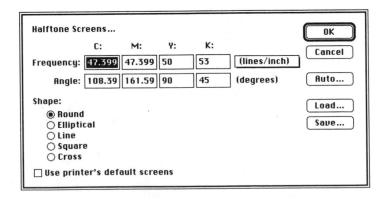

Figure 8–5   Color Halftone Screen window

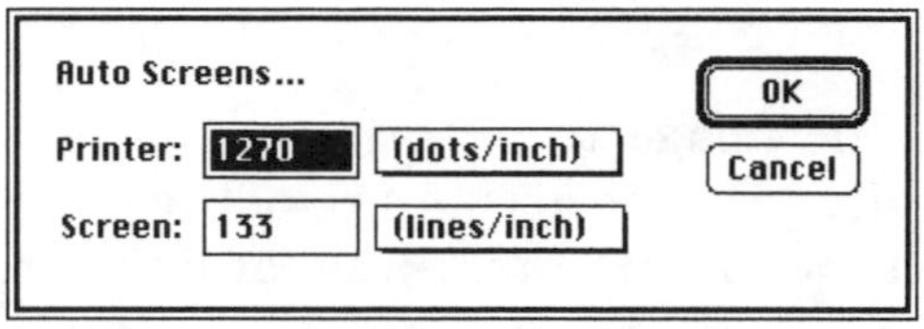

```
┌─────────────────────────────────────────────┐
│  Auto Screens...              ┌──────────┐   │
│                               │    OK    │   │
│  Printer: │ 1270 │ (dots/inch)└──────────┘   │
│                               ┌──────────┐   │
│  Screen:  │ 133  │ (lines/inch)│  Cancel │   │
│                               └──────────┘   │
└─────────────────────────────────────────────┘
```

Figure 8–6 Auto Screens window

culate the best possible configuration for output based on all the information fed into it.

Transfer

In the Transfer Function window, the image output can be modified to compensate for dot gain. As mentioned before, different types of paper will absorb ink differently. Newsprint is one of the most absorbent. When ink hits it, it spreads out forming a much larger dot than the size of the dot on the original screen. It is necessary to have a meeting with your printer to fully understand the expected results based on the complexity of the images and the type of press and paper to be used.

The Transfer Function basically operates as a lookup table. When printing, Photoshop looks at the density of the dots and puts them into one of five levels. These levels consist of highlights, 1/4 tones, midtones, 3/4 tones, and shadows. Which level is assigned depends on the color value or grayscale value of a pixel. White pixels have a value of 255 and so are classified as highlights. The black pixels have a value of 0 and are thus considered shadows. All the colors or values in between are considered 1/4 tones, etc.

Any adjustments in the transfer functions are based on a printed page. Careful study of the way tones are being represented will determine the settings.

If an image is printing too dark, then it is necessary to lower the value in the areas of excessive darkness. The opposite is true for light areas.

Size/Rulers

The size and resolution of the image to be printed can be set for printing purposes without affecting the actual size of the image. The height is set to inches, centimeters, points, picas, or columns. The width can be set by inches, centimeters, points, or picas. The resolution can be specified in pixels per inch or pixels per centimeter.

Borders

A border can be used to frame the printed image. By pressing the Border button you get a window that allows you to enter the thickness of the border in either inches, millimeters, or points

Caption

A caption can be set to print with the image. Pressing the Caption button will pop up the caption entry box. The box employs standard text editing functions but does not allow the specification of font, style, or size. All captions print in 9-point Helvetica.

On the right-hand portion of the Page Setup window opposite the five buttons discussed above are six boxes for additional functions.

Labels

When Labels is activated, the document name and the name of the particular channel being printed are printed with the page.

Crop Marks

With this option checked, crop marks will print at the edges of the image. Crop marks are used to show the edge on which the printed page is to be trimmed.

Calibration Bars

Calibration bars are an 11-step grayscale bar that represents the transition in density from 0 to 100% in increments of 10%. This bar is used with a densitometer to determine the appropriate Transfer Functions.

The bar appears only on the black plate when printing four-color separations. The cyan, magenta, yellow, and black are represented in what is called a progressive color bar appearing on both sides of the printed image. These bars are used to calibrate monitors.

Registration Marks

With this option activated, registration marks and star targets are printed. These are used to line up the four individual plates to ensure that they will print in register, to avoid any moiré patterns or ghosting colors.

Negative

If you are printing separations directly to film, it is advisable to print in negative. This process will give you the best results. This is something that should be discussed with your printer to verify their particular requirements. If you are printing to paper, then positive is best.

When the Negative option is used, the printed image is inverted. The screen image will remain in positive form.

Emulsion Down

The emulsion side of the film or paper is the side that is sensitive to light. This is the side that will record the image. When the emulsion is up, any type on the image is readable when the emulsion side faces you. Emulsion down is the opposite; the text reads as a mirror image. This is the preferred format when printing to film.

Photoshop and Illustrator

Often you may need to incorporate some sharp-edged objects with a photograph. You may also need to have a photo cropped within an irregular shape with a clean edge.

Illustrator has the ability to create the objects. Photoshop has the ability to import those Illustrator EPS files. The one problem is that when the objects come into Photoshop, they lose their clean edges.

The answer is to reverse the process—bring Photoshop images into Illustrator.

When an image has been modified in Photoshop, separated into CMYK, and then saved as an EPS file, it can be placed into an Illustrator file. That Illustrator file can have text, objects, and most importantly, objects that act as masks to trap the Photoshop image. When the file is complete, it can be run through Adobe Separator or Quark XPress to create the four-color separations for printing.

Case Study

The following case study demonstrates many of the features of both Photoshop and Illustrator, while showing the procedure for integrating the two to create a final piece of art and four-color separations.

The assignment was to create a comp for a book on the planet Mars.

- In Photoshop, a scanned image of a desert was opened (Figure 8-7).

- The blue sky was selected with the Magic Wand selection tool.

- The selection was brought into an alpha channel (Figure 8-8).

- The alpha was brought back to selection.

- A bright red was selected as the Foreground color.

- A yellow was selected as the Background color.

- With the Blend tool, a gradient was applied to the sky.

- The sand in the foreground was selected with the Lasso tool.

- The selection was brought into an alpha channel (Figure 8-9).

- The alpha was brought back to selection.

- The Levels control was activated from the Adjust submenu to the Image menu (Figure 8-10).

- The light tones to the right were brought in to lighten the sand.

Figure 8–7   Desert scan

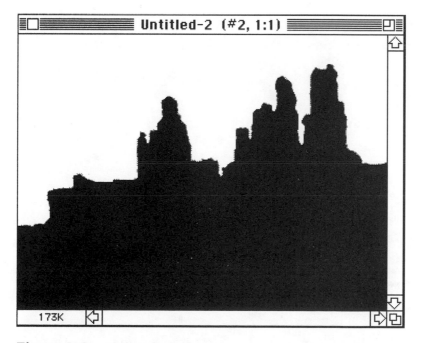

Figure 8–8   Alpha channel

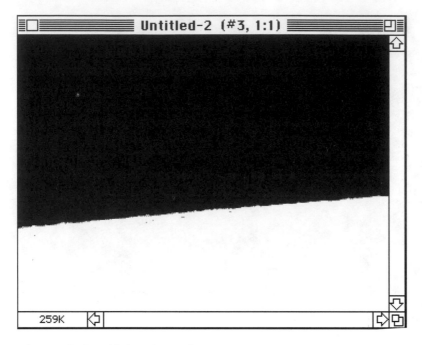

Figure 8–9   Alpha channel

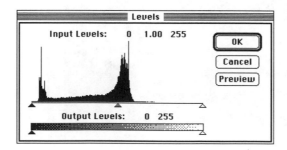

Figure 8–10   Levels window

- The dark and middle tones were adjusted to bring out the details in the sand.

It was now necessary to create an alpha channel for the rocks. Since channels existed for the other two areas of the image, this task was simple.

- The Composite command was activated from the Calculate submenu to the Image menu (Figure 8-11).
- The first alpha channel (4) was made Foreground Channel.
- The second alpha channel (5) was made Background Channel.
- The Destination was set to the existing image with New for its Channel.

This created a new alpha channel that was a composite of the two other alpha channels. Applying an Invert to this new channel turned it to an alpha of the rocks (Figure 8-12).

- This new alpha channel was brought into the image, and once again the Levels control was used to modify the image.
- The image was separated into CMYK by making the CMYK choice under the Mode menu.

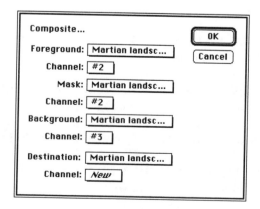

Figure 8–11 Composite window

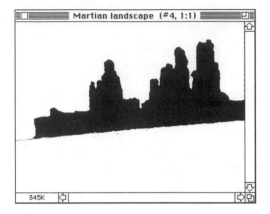

Figure 8–12   Alpha channel

- The image was saved as an EPS file with an 8–bit preview file attached.

- Adobe Illustrator was opened.

> The remainder of this example assumes that the reader has a working knowledge of Adobe Illustrator.

- A New file was started.

- A large rectangle was created using the Rectangle tool to form the outside dimension of the book.

- In the Paint window, a Fill of hot red was created by selecting Processed Colors and entering 100% magenta and 90% yellow.

- In the Preferences dialog, the Corner Radius was set to .25 inch.

- With the Option button depressed to draw from the center out, a second rectangle was made within the original.

- Its fill was set to 20% magenta and 40% yellow, making it a warm yellow.

- The title "MARS" was typed in the Adobe font FrizQuadrata.
- In the Paint window, with the type selected, a Fill of hot red was created as before, by selecting Processed Colors and entering 100% magenta and 90% yellow.

Illustrator 3.0 has the ability to create an outline of any Type 1 font typed out on the screen.

- An outline was created.
- The right downstroke of the "M" and the top portion were extended to form a stylized logo of the word.
- The balance of the type was created, and put into place, and made black.
- Using the Circle tool, a large circle was created in the center of the book cover.
- In the Paint window for this object, No Fill, No Stroke, and Mask were selected.
- With the Rectangle tool, a large square was created to cover the entire circle; it was set at 50% black.
- With the Option button depressed, a narrow rectangle was created in the center of the square with the top and bottom equal.
- It was filled with a 15% black.
- With the Blend tool the square and the rectangle were blended.
- The resulting blend was rotated at a 45° angle.
- The blend and the masked circle were grouped.
- A small 65% black circle was created.
- A smaller circle about one third the size of the first was created and assigned 10% black. It was placed inside the first to the upper left.
- The two circles were blended.
- The blended circle was duplicated over the inside edge of the large masked circle, about half the diameter of the bolt in

distance to the outside circle, to form what appears to be bolts around a porthole.

- From the center out, a new circle was made just large enough so that it formed an inside border equidistant from the outside circle and the little bolts.
- This new circle was assigned No Fill, No Stroke, and Mask.
- Place EPS was selected from the Edit menu.
- The Photoshop EPS file was selected.
- The file came in with its Bounding box.
- The Bounding box was centered within the last circle.
- The EPS file's Bounding box was selected and the last circle was created as a mask. They were then grouped.
- Preview Illustration from the View menu was chosen.

The entire image could then be viewed in full color.

- Adobe Separator was opened.
- The file was separated using the default settings in Separator.

The finished illustration appears as Figure 8–13 in the color pages.

This same basic technique works with Quark Xpress—if you save an image from within the CMYK display mode in Photoshop as an EPS file with DCS/5 file format selected, that image can be imported into XPress and separated with other elements on a page. Refer to the Quark XPress documentation, which discusses specific techniques for separating pages from within XPress.

The Trap Control

Current printing technology, although quite good, still can't insure perfect registration. The colors in a printed image are composed of rosettes, or combinations of the cyan, magenta, yellow, and black. There are instances where one or more colors are not present in a part of an image or two areas of solid distinct colors butt up against each other. A plate shift will cause these areas where colors butt to leave a gap between the colors. To avoid this discrepancy, a slight overlap is typically created to prevent these gaps from appearing.

The preparation of these overlaps is called Trapping. Traditionally, print shops used methods called choking and spreading to overexpose an image in the film process in order to create the necessary overlaps. Photoshop prints directly to film, thereby making these former processes impossible. The trapping in Photoshop is controlled with the Trap command.

> The Trap command works only in the CMYK mode—it's only relevant when color separating an image, and has no effect on onscreen image editing.

When an image has been converted to CMYK, the Trap command found under the Image menu becomes active. When selected, the Trap dialog box appears.

The pop-up menu next to the text box allows you to choose the unit of measure in either pixels, points, or millimeters.

To use the Trap command, simply enter the value to compensate for misregistration. You can specify the amount of trapping in pixels, points, or millimeters. Your print shop will be able to supply the necessary numbers based on their particular equipment, as they know (through experience) the amount of misregistration that can be expected from their presses.

9

Animation

During the time that we've been working with Photoshop, we've found that its usefulness extends into the rather demanding task of creating animation and multimedia. In fact, most of the graphics production tasks for animation projects that we've produced over the past couple of years have been done exclusively with Photoshop. While the program was designed primarily to be a print production tool, its screen dithering capabilities and special effects put it into the category of Essential Multimedia Production Tool. Every Macintosh animator and multimedia production staff should make Photoshop part of their standard repertoire. (Short story: The spinning cars technique described later in this chapter was seen by John Sculley, CEO of Apple Computer, and declared as "undoable"— read on and learn how you can do that which can't be done.)

This chapter includes a number of techniques (in capsule form) that describe how to use many of Photoshop's capabilities to achieve unique and lovely special effects animations. There is virtually no way to accomplish them without Photoshop.

Some of the animation effects possible using Photoshop include

- Custom animated filter effects

- Complicated reveals and wipes

- Smooth rotation and spinning effects

- Alpha channel mask/layer animation

One of the main considerations for creating animation effects is the issue of the playback medium. Animation meant for Macintosh screen playback (with either MacroMind Director, Paracomp Filmmaker, or any other current or future animation package) is typically created with an 8-bit color palette, while animation created by dumping PICT files to videotape is usually done with RGB files saved as 16- or 24-bit PICT files.

▼ **Tip:** Normally, the relative lack of resolution of standard NTSC video is a drawback in terms of quality, but for creating animation files using the standard Macintosh II system palette, the softening effects of NTSC actually contribute to improving overall image quality. If you wish to optimize hard disk space when creating lengthy animation sequences, you can get away with 8-bit system palettes, especially when using low-to-medium end video output peripherals (such as the RaserOps 364, Truevision NuVista +, and other video output cards or devices). If you're using an RGB Technologies or Lyon Lamb scan converter/ouput device, the difference between 8- and 16-bit files becomes much more noticeable.

NTSC video typically uses only 12 bits of color information, so that 16-bit PICT files provide a full, substantial color range; 24-bit files are only useful if you are planning on creating video with a top-quality analog videotape format (such as Betacam SP) or full digital format, such as the current industry standard D1 and D2 digital video formats. The actual live size of an NTSC video frame is less than that of a Macintosh 13-inch monitor; the monitor size is 640 x 480 pixels, but the edges of this frame will be cropped if the output is to NTSC video. For video output, you'll want to work with images that are approximately 580 x 420 pixels. You should experiment with the particular video card and tape deck you plan to use for output to fine-tune the size of the active frame.

▼ **Tip:** If you plan on dumping your Photoshop/PICT images out to videotape using a video deck controller board such as the Diaquest animation controller, you have to be aware of numbering schemes of filenames; for example, the Diaquest software, Animaq, expects you to

—Name files in ascending numerical order.
—Start the filename with an alphanumeric character or characters.

—Follow the initial characters with a space.
—Put the number of the file after the space.

If you don't stick to this numbering scheme, the Animaq software will confuse the proper order of the files, and you'll have to do the tape dump again—which can become a nuisance when you are creating animation sequences consisting of a lot of PICT files. We suggest that you determine the necessary filenaming and numbering requirements before you begin production work.

Some of you might be wondering about the feasibility of creating 24–bit animations for use on accelerated 24–bit display cards . While it can be done, remember that a 24–bit image requires three times the RAM and disk space of a comparable 8–bit image, limiting the length of your accelerated 24–bit animations. At some point in the near future, 4–megabyte SIMMs, 32 megabytes of RAM, and hundreds of megabytes of free hard disk space will be a feasible fantasy; when that day arrives, we can talk about 24–bit real time Macintosh animation.

When creating any kind of animation effects using Photoshop, you'll want to apply all effects to 24–bit versions of the images, even if you've imported 8–bit indexed images into Photoshop for processing. This will insure maximum final image quality.

Photoshop and MacroMind Director

While there are a variety of animation programs for the Macintosh, we've done most of our Photoshop animation work with the Video-Works/Director line of products produced by MacroMind. Director is a two-dimensional sprite-animation program; sprites are independent objects that can have individual motion attributes. With Director, you have up to 24 layers, or channels, of independent movable objects on the screen at once, as well as simultaneous sound effects. Director 2.0 also has a rather extensive HyperTalk-like programming language, Lingo, which allows you to create fairly elaborate interactive presentations that control external devices such as laserdisk players and CD-ROM drives. VideoWorks is a cheaper, less powerful version of Director that lacks many of the advanced animation features, powerful painting tools, and Lingo programming language found in Director.

Director can import PICT files and scrapbooks, which are both useful for importing images (and sequences of images) created in Photoshop. One of the most important issues to consider when creating graphics for VW/Director is color palettes. VideoWorks only works with the standard Macintosh II system palette, while Director has facilities for handling multiple different color palettes. If you are using Director, you have the ability to import images with custom or adaptive color palettes.

▼ **Tip:** When you convert an RGB Photoshop file to indexed color, you can specify the number of bits per color—anywhere from 2 bits/black-and-white to 8 bits/color. While you'll typically want to use 8 bits for images ending up in Director, it's sometimes useful to convert images to 6 or 7 bits if you want to reserve color palette positions for consistent or recurring color objects in the Director animation (such as control buttons for interactive presentations that are always the same color). Additionally, you can convert 24-bit color images to a usable format for a standard 4-bit/16-color Apple video card (in fact, when running VW/Director with the monitors control set to 16 colors, you can get accelerated animation speeds without any additional hardware or technical tricks).

PICT images and Scrapbooks are imported into Director through the Import command found in Director's File menu (Figure 9-1).

If you are importing a Scrapbook file into Director, you might want to use the Centered command in the Import dialog; this will assure that incoming images are centered around a central axis. (Fine print: This axis is defined as the center of the image's bounding box.)

▼ **Tip:** You should import images into Director in the order in which they're meant to play back—import the first image first and the last image last.

When importing images with adaptive palettes, you'll be asked to either adapt the image to a palette that already exists in Director (not desirable), or import the incoming palette into Director as a new castmember (Figure 9-2).

Once you have imported the sequence of PICT files or the desired scrapbook into Director, you select the images in the Cast window by clicking on the first one, holding down the Shift key, clicking on

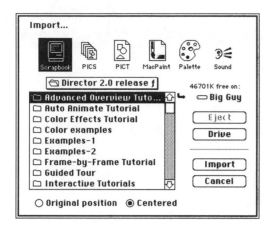

Figure 9–1   Import dialog in Director

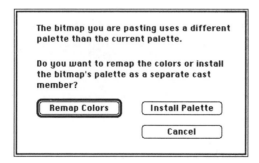

Figure 9–2   Director Palette importation dialog

the last image in the sequence, and choosing Cast to Time from the Score menu (Figure 9–3).

This places all of the images, in their proper order, onto the main screen, or Stage (in Directorese). At this point, you can play the movie by pressing Command-A, or by pressing the Play command in the Transport controls/Panel dialog (you can open and close this dialog by pressing Command-2) (Figure 9–4).

Figure 9-3 Cast window with selected image sequence

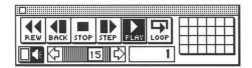

Figure 9-4 The Panel dialog with the Play button selected

If you have imported more than 64 images, you have to repeat the above Cast to Time process to place all of the imported images into the Score.

Animated Filter Effects

While Photoshop's special effects filters do wonders with still images, they truly come to life when you use them to create animated special effects. Filters that have adjustable parameters are the most useful ones for this purpose—the main concept is to gradually modify an image over time by processing it multiple times through a filter, increasing (or decreasing) the parameter increments with each pass.

The general flow of the process is as follows:

1. Make sure that you're in RGB mode.
2. Select and crop the desired image.
3. Save the cropped image to disk.

4. Determine the increments you will use for the filter (we'll describe exactly what increments to use in the specific filter examples that follow).

5. Choose the desired filter from the Image menu (you don't have to select the whole image explicitly with the Select All command in the Select menu; if nothing is selected, then the filter is applied to the entire image).

6. Enter the desired parameter values in the filter dialog.

7. Click the OK button in the filter dialog.

8. Once the filter effect has been applied to the image, convert the image into an indexed image by selecting the Indexed display command from the Mode menu and choose the appropriate options from the RGB-Indexed conversion dialog (most of the time you'll probably want to use the system palette and the diffusion dither).

9. Select the Save As... command from the File menu.

10. Name the file (we tend to use the original filename with an extension that reflects the number or numbers typed into the filter parameters) and choose the PICT format from the Format Pop-up menu.

11. After the file is saved, choose the Revert command from the File menu. Click the OK button in the Revert dialog. This restores the image to the original RGB version you saved at the beginning of the process.

12. Apply the next filter pass, and repeat the conversion and saving process.

This is generally the process you'll follow. Note that we are using the standard Mac II system palette, instead of converting each image to an Adaptive palette. Why? Many times, when you apply filters in varying degrees to a specific image, each filter pass will yield a distinct range of colors. If you were to convert each of the passes to an adaptive palette, chances are that each image would have a slightly different 256–color palette. Once imported into MacroMind Director, you would have to have palette transitions between many of the frames, which would drastically slow down the overall flow of the animation, as well as use up valuable castmember positions. Converting each image to the system palette ensures that each iteration of the filtered image has the same color palette going into Director.

Our choice of the Diffusion dither is meant to provide the smoothest 256-color system palette image possible. You could use the other two dithering settings (None and Pattern) instead of the Diffusion dither; the resulting images would look rougher, or more quantized than the diffusion-dithered alternative.

▼ **Tip:** If you decide that you like the pattern dither, you can take a shortcut around some of the steps in the process desribed above. When you are working on an 8-bit display, the RGB mode is automatically displayed using a pattern dither. If you save the filtered images as PICT files directly from the RGB mode, the pattern dither is automatically applied to the saved image. Once the filtered image is saved, you can simply select the Undo command, which will de-apply the filter, and you can then apply the next iteration of the filter. This process saves you the mode conversion and revert steps. The drawback of this technique is that the palette dither doesn't look quite as smooth as the diffusion dither used in the more lengthy version of the process.

Filter Animation

Gaussian Blur Dissolves

By taking advantage of the programmability of the Gaussian Blur filter, you can create a stunning animated "blur-on" effect that is distinctly different from the various dissolve transitions found in Director. Different amounts are entered into the Radius factor in the Gaussian Blur filter dialog (Figure 9-5).

Start by determining the number of steps for the dissolve—we usually go for 5-10 frames, starting at a Gaussian Blur setting of between 20 and 30, and in increments of 4-5, gradually decreasing the blur factor until the image is normal (0 Gaussian Blur, the original image saved as an Indexed PICT file). Notice that we start from the end and move backwards—you can go either way and end up with the same results. Move into Director and simmer until ready.

Figure 9-5 Gaussian Blur dialog

Mosaic Filter

Another favorite. Starting with the normal image, gradually increase the mosaic effect—you'll find that incrementing the mosaic factor by a single step on each pass (4, 5, 6, etc.) yields the best results (Figure 9-6). A common computer transition effect is now available on the Macintosh.

Twirl

Down the drain! Use increments of 10-40 in this dialog, and take it all the way to 999. The effect is quite dramatic and unique. The more increments you use, the smoother the overall effect, though it's easy to go overboard on this one. If you're really in a creative mood, try touching up the edges of the image so that it appears that the borders of the image are following the main image.

Another fun way to use twirl filter is to reverse the sequence: Create an animation that starts with a fully twirled image, and end up with the original untwirled image. You can take this further by gradually building up the brightness or transparency of the twirling image as it unfurls—words can twirl onto the screen out of a misty background. Reverse twirl is a fun way to put a logo on the screen.

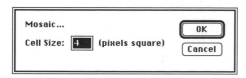

Figure 9-6 Mosaic filter dialog

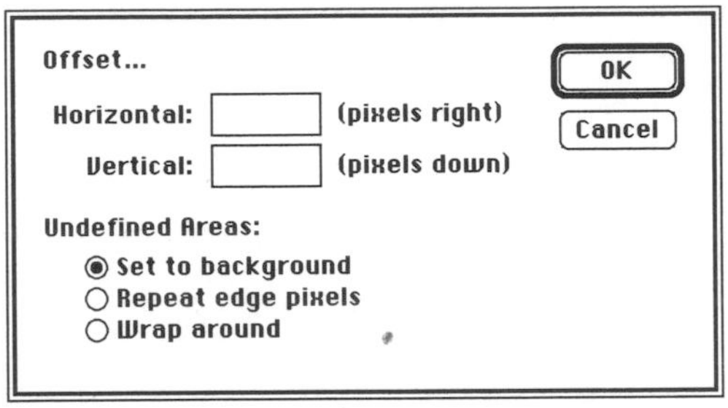

Figure 9–7   Offset filter dialog

Offset

By selecting the "Wrap around" option in this filter, you can spin a portion of an image around while the rest of the image stays still. Very effective and unique (Figure 9–7).

Something to remember about this filter: Offset moves an image within the selected area—it won't actually move a selected image smoothly across the screen. Why would you want to do this in Photoshop when you can just as easily do it automatically in Director? Well, if you want to move an image against a complex background, and have the edges of the foreground image anti-aliased against that background, you'll have to do it in Photoshop. Anti-aliasing is a feature to look for in some future release of Director.

Motion Blur

With a name like "Motion Blur" it's easy imagine this filter being used for animation purposes. Motion blurring is the effect that you see when something moves right past you at high speed—instead of a solid detailed image, you see a blur. The Motion Blur filter allows you to determine the angle and distance of the blur effect (Figure 9–8).

The longer the distance, the more of a "trail" is left behind the moving object. The angle relates to the motion of the object—if the

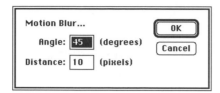

Figure 9–8 Motion Blur dialog

object is moving at a 45–degree angle with respect to the horizontal plane, then the blur should also be at 45 degrees.

Alpha Channel Animation

The alpha channel and masking abilities of Photoshop are key for creating very complex layered image effects. The techniques for creating alpha channel animation are labor-intensive, but the results are well worth the effort.

One of the most basic alpha channel animation techniques involves moving an object "inside" of an alpha selected area. For example, you might want to fill some type with a moving picture, so that the picture appears only within the type.

1. Select an image to animate inside of some type and copy it to the clipboard. Try to use an image that's at least twice the size of the text mask that you want it to move within.

2. Create a blank RGB image, Select All, and copy the Selection → Alpha.

3. With the alpha channel onscreen, make the background black and create some bold type using white as the foreground color.

4. Save the image to disk.

5. With the text in the desired location on the screen, select Selection→Alpha.

6. Paste the image with the Paste Into command. It will appear centered inside of the type.

7. Using the Offset filter with the "Wrap around" option selected, shift the image horizontally by about 2–5 pixels.

8. Without leaving RGB display mode, save the resulting image as an 8–bit PICT image.

9. Select Selection→Alpha (which repeats step 5 without explicitly starting off in the alpha channel), and paste in the clipboard image again.

10. Repeat the Offset, but this time use double the offset amount specified in step 7. Repeat step 8 by saving the image in PICT format.

As you keep doubling the offset amount, the result is that the image gradually "spins" around inside of the text selection mask. Once you have a full rotation of the image (in the horizontal offset example above, the number of required steps will be equal to the horizontal size of the animated clipboard image divided by the number of pixels that you specify in the horizontal offset field), import the sequence of PICTs into Director and animate. Voilà! Spinning images inside of a text logo!

There are many variations to this technique—you could use the above process with more complex filtering and a combination of gradual filtering and alpha channel reveals to create highly complex dissolves. We also took the easy way out by saving the images as PICTs directly from within RGB display mode—you can get better final image quality by converting each individual step of the process to a diffusion-dithered indexed image before saving the PICTs. For example, one interactive kiosk project that we created for Knoll International (a large furniture and office systems manufacturer) utilized a variation of this technique to make the Knoll logo gradually fade onto a complex background made up of a "molecular" field. It was done using the Fill command and the Gaussian Blur filter.

We determined that we wanted the text to appear in full-saturation red (the Knoll corporate logo color) in five steps. This meant that we would fill the text with 20% increments of the solid red with the Fill command, and would gradually blur the molecular background behind the type in increments of six pixels with the Gaussian Blur filter. Because we were increasing both the fill and the blurriness of the area within the text, the last image in the sequence wouldn't even need the specified 30–pixel Gaussian Blur, so we skipped that final filtering effect for the last image.

Here's how we did it, and how you can do it:

1. Starting with a full-screen image of the molecule field, create an alpha channel for the whole screen and put the text into the alpha channel. (Instead of creating the text in Photoshop, we pasted a scanned version of the text logo into the alpha channel and inverted the whole channel. This resulted in a white logo against a black background.) Save the image to disk.

2. Superimpose the logo with Selection→Alpha. Blur the alpha selection with a 6-pixel Gaussian Blur, and then use the Fill command to fill the alpha selection with a 20% opacity fill of the red color (specified as the current foreground color).

3. Convert the image to an 8-bit system palette indexed image, using a Diffusion dither.

4. Save the image to disk as an 8-bit PICT file.

5. Revert the image to the last saved version. Select Alpha →Selection, apply a Gaussian Blur of 12 pixels, and then use the Fill command to fill the alpha selection with a 40% opacity. Repeat steps 3 and 4.

6. Revert the image, increase the Gaussian Blur to 18 pixels, the Fill to 60% opacity. Repeat steps 3 and 4.

The final image is a full 100% red opaque text logo with no Gaussian Blur filter (as the text was filled with a solid color at this point, the effects of the Gaussian Blur would've been lost). Import into Director, and animate. A unique effect, and doable only with Photoshop (Figure 9-9).

There is a more sophisticated variation on this technique for creating special effects reveals. Using the Zigzag filter, for example, you can create a unique dissolve between two images. This is done by combining the incremental filter effect on one image with a threshold mask of the same effect, using this threshold mask as an alpha channel, into which the second image is pasted. Here goes:

1. Select two images, optimally of the same (or similar) size. Create a blank alpha channel for the first image. Save the image to disk.

2. Create a five-step sequence that ends with a filter value of 300, with a fixed Zigzag increment of 60. That means that every step

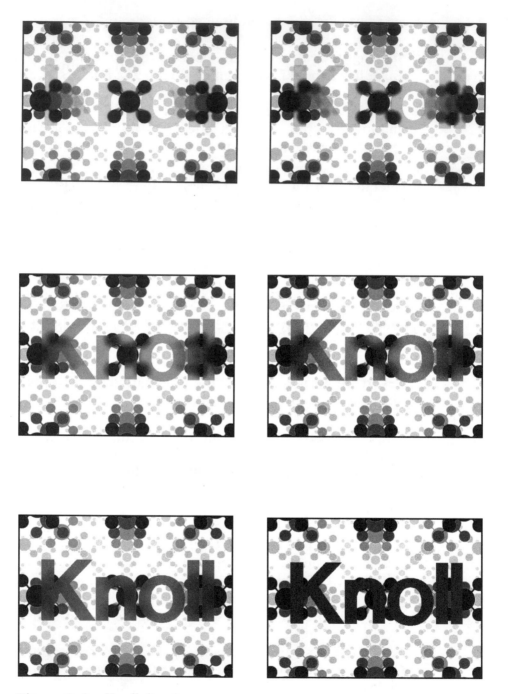

Figure 9–9   Knoll dissolve-on sequence

of the animation increases the Zigzag filter by 60. Apply the first pass of the Zigzag filter to the first image with a value of 60.

3. Select the whole image, copy, and paste it into the alpha channel.

4. Select the entire second image from its window and copy. Click on the first image window to make it active.

5. Create a threshold mask for the first pass of the Zigzag filter. The threshold crossover point should increase along with the zigzag effect, with the final threshold mask being predominantly white (so that most of the pasted second image can show through). Open the threshold control and manipulate the slider until you have a predominantly black image with some white details. Click OK.

6. Select the Selection→Alpha command. You'll be brought back to the RGB mode, with the threshold mask superimposed. Select Paste Into from the Edit menu.

7. Save the image as an 8–bit PICT file; name it "dissolve 1".

8. Revert the first image to the saved version.

9. Apply the same Zigzag filter, but with a value of 120. Repeat steps 3 and 4.

10. Repeat step 5, increasing the threshold slider to introduce more white details into the threshold mask. Repeat steps 4, 5, 6, 7, and 8.

11. Repeat the above sequence, increasing the Zigzag filter by 60 each pass and changing the threshold mask to gradually turn white. You can see the effect as you create each step.

This process can be applied using many different filters and with more intermediate steps for smoother transitions. We've barely scratched the surface of the creative potential of this technique. We expect that you'll discover other variations of this process that are much more exotic and wonderful. Enjoy!

Soft Explosions

This technique is especially useful for video: Using the selection tools and the feathering command, you can create a gradually growing soft-edged "burst" from any portion of the screen. The trick is to make an increasing centered selection, with an increasing soft feather, and fill the feathered selection with a solid color. As the selection increases, you could even increase or decrease the brightness and saturation of the color to enhance the effect. While you might want to try this effect for Mac screen playback, you'll find that the larger burst frames will slow down the animation speed and increase the "screen tearing" effect. (See Figure 9–10.)

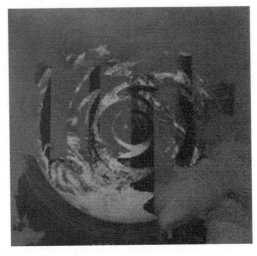
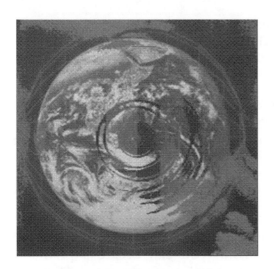
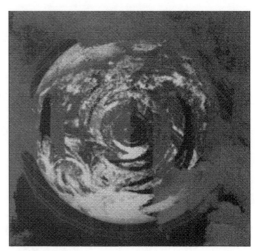

Figure 9–10   Threshold mask animation sequence

Figure 9–10   Threshold mask animation sequence *(continued)*

One of the problems you may run into with this effect is that as the feathered selection grows toward the edges of the document, it becomes "flattened out" or restrained by the document boundaries. You can avoid this problem by creating a larger canvas size (using the Resize command to enlarge the current image area without changing the actual image size, and placing the image in the center of the resized document), with the final document area masked in an alpha channel. The burst can grow beyond the edges of the active area of the document, and the feather won't be distorted in any way.

Dynamic Effects — Stretch, Perspective, and Distort

Creating smooth movement in animation is usually a long laborious process. Three-dimensional objects can be created using one of the various 3–D programs available. The objects can then be rotated at single-degree increments and each movement captured as an individual frame for the animation. A problem that occurs quite often is how to change the viewing angle of a two-dimensional image. Some examples are the turning of a page in a book with a picture on it or spinning a plate with an image mapped onto its side. In this case, the image must go through a series of distortions to appear as if it is moving in three-dimensional space.

A kiosk that we created for the Oldsmobile division of General Motors required the visual effect of a rotating plate of glass that had a picture of a car on the face. With each revolution of the plate a different car had to appear on the opposite side.

To insure a smooth movement of the plate of glass, a rectangular object of a narrow thickness was created using a 3-D program. On the vertical axis, the plate was rotated at 15-degree increments. Each movement was recorded. Twenty-one of the movements were at an angle in which a car would be visible. A file was created in Photoshop that contained the 21 movements of the plate.

The original images of the cars were scanned from 4 x 5 color chromes on a Howtek color scanner. The images were saved as 24-bit color Photoshop files.

1. Using the Marquee selection tool, the image of a car was selected and copied into the clipboard.
2. In the plate movement file, the car was pasted.
3. Using the Distort feature under the Effects choice of the Image menu, the image of the car was affixed to each plate.

When the Distort feature is activated, four handles appear at the corners of the selection. Placing the cursor at any of the four handles will convert the cursor to an arrow cursor. Clicking and dragging the cursor in any direction will move the handle in that direction. This action will distort the rectangular selection, and the image will distort to fit the new shape.

4. Each corner of the scanned car image was matched up to a corner of the 3-D plate.

In developing this animation technique before the appearance of Photoshop, we experimented with variations of this technique using a variety of 8-bit paint programs. In all cases, when the images were animated, the results were unacceptable. One typical gremlin was the appearance of white pixels along the light edges of the fender of the car at certain angles. When animated, the white pixels gave the impression of a sudden electric shock to the fender. The colors on the body of the car were inconsistent from frame to frame, which completely ruined the desired effect.

▼ **Tip:** When creating these effects in Photoshop, you'll always want to start working in RGB mode, with 24 bits of data. When you apply a dynamic effect to a selected image, the result is smooth, with maximum optmization of image quality. Remember, the interpolation method selected in Photoshop's Preferences dialog will affect the quality of the resulting animation: Nearest Neighbor interpolation yields the lowest quality effect (with the fastest processing speed), while Bicubic interpolation gives you the most bang for your money.

With Photoshop, when each of the 21 movements were put together in Director , the result was a smooth transition. The plate seemed like a single object moving around in three-dimensional space.

In the animation, the plate was suspended over a field of Oldsmobile logos with a blue sky above. Since the plate was supposed to be made of glass, the edge had to be reflective and continue the sensation of movement. To achieve this the following steps were employed:

1. A portion of the background was copied into the clipboard.
2. The edge of each plate was selected.
3. Paste Into was applied. This pasted the contents of the clipboard into the selected areas only.
4. The pasted background was shifted slightly for each plate so that it would be different on each. When animated this gave the impression that the plate was in fact moving within the environment over which it was suspended.

To add further dimensionality, using the airbrush tool, a glare was placed on the edge of the plate. This gave the impression that a light source somewhere was being picked up as the plate turned.

5. A white or light shade of any color was selected as a foreground color for the airbrush to use.

6. While the edge of each plate was still selected, after the paste into of the background, a simple pass of the tool over the edge created the glare.

7. The position of the glare was offset on each plate so that when the plate moved, the glare would seem to travel up the side as would a real reflection on a moving object. These small details help to add life and realism to an animation.

The final animation files were assembled in Director, accelerated with MacroMind Accelerator, and played back from within Hypercard with the Director Player software.

You can use any of the dynamic effects to create smooth transforming images—text in perspective rolling in from the background, images mapped onto the sides of flying shapes, smooth camera moves around two-dimensional images, and more. As long as you're patient, a whole new world of animated special effects is at your fingertips.

10

Color Publishing and Retouching

Photo retouching is considered an art form in itself, requiring a highly tuned artistic skill. Illustration skills come into play to add elements or to enhance an image. Some images, however, require a minimum of alteration to increase their quality or change the look.

Once you understand the basic Photoshop tools, you can handle basic alterations without professional illustration or retouching skills.

Up to this point, we've shown Photoshop to be a powerful tool for color production. In this chapter, we'll look at case studies that have put it into actual working situations. These situations make use of all the tools and effects available in the program. These case studies can serve as models for your own work.

The images used in these case studies were purposely created under poor conditions. In a graphic design studio or ad agency, the conditions can be better controlled for a higher quality starting image.

Comp Production

Paint box systems are used extensively in ad agencies and graphic design studios for the preparation of comprehensives for presentations. These comprehensives, or comps, as they are referred to in the industry, are a close facsimile of a finished ad. The comp will have all the images and text in position. Production costs in time and money are high, so it is important that clients have a clear understanding of the look and effectiveness of the campaign. With the comp, the clients get to see the ad as it will look in finished form so that they can make changes where necessary and subsequently give their approval.

Comps can be simple marker renderings. There are clients who require a more realistic representation. Some ad budgets are so high that they demand a much cleaner presentation. To achieve this realistic approach, stock photos and rub-down lettering is used, thus giving the comp a more polished look. In some cases, the agencies will go to the expense of hiring photographers to shoot the campaign and typesetting for the text, and present a finished comp with actual elements in place.

With advertising budgets being what they are today, the latter form of comp is becoming the norm. It is for this reason that agencies and studios are turning to computer systems to develop the comps. Large investments have been made to outfit departments with paint box systems.

Desktop publishing on the Macintosh computer brought down the cost of typesetting and increased the ease of use to the artist. Visuals, however, still required expensive paint box systems and high production costs. Photoshop brings the power of the high-end systems down to the Macintosh level. With a Polaroid camera and a little imagination coupled with a few Photoshop techniques, finished-quality comps are a snap.

Case Study 1: An Album Cover

In this job we created a comp for an album cover.

To start, we selected a drab image of a domed structure. (See color pages—"Case Study 1, Chapter 10.") The photo was taken under cloudy conditions. The sky and the structure are too monotoned, and the trees have no luster. This image, however, is perfect for use as the cover for a record album entitled *ROMA: Italian Love Songs*.

The assignment:

- Change color of the structure's domed cap to gold.

- Make trees rich green color.

- Gradate sky from dark blue at top to bright blue at bottom.

- Second version of sky has a sunset with clouds.

- Add title of album "ROMA" in metallic gold letters.

- Add caption "Italian Love Songs" in vibrant red letters.

Studying the work to be done on this image, we carefully considered which tools would create the effects required. All of the modifications were to be applied to entire sections of the image. This made the Magic Wand selection tool the best for the task at hand.

- First, the color of the dome had to be changed from the muted blue of the original to a rich golden color.

- Using the Magic Wand tool, we clicked within the area of the dome. This allowed us to search out the edges of the colors that made up the dome and selected the entire area of the dome.

- With the dome selected, we brought up the Hue and Saturation controls.

These controls are found under the Adjust choice of the Image menu. By clicking on the Adjust choice under the Image menu and keeping the mouse button depressed, an additional menu will drop down showing the Hue and Saturation modifier. Releasing the mouse button over the Hue and Saturation choice brings up its control window. This window employs the use of sliding handles represented by the little triangles under a line for each of the two controls.

- With the Colorize option selected, we brought the Hue slider left to the 36 position. We dragged the Saturation right to 78, producing a reddish golden color (Figure 10–1).

- At this point we saved the document under a different name to preserve the original.

We then got to work on making the trees brighter green.

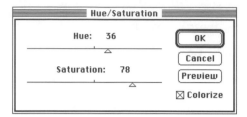

Figure 10–1   Hue/Saturation dialog

We selected the Magic Wand once again. Using it, we clicked within the area of the trees to select them.

The archway, however, had some of the same values of color as the trees. These additional areas had to be deselected because the green alteration applied to the trees alone. To deselect these areas, the Lasso tool was used.

• With the Command button depressed, we circled the areas of the archway to be deselected. Since this was a deselection process, it was important to accurately trace out the edges of the trees where the overlap took place in order to leave the trees selected.

• Certain lighter tones of the trees might not have been selected since their color value was beyond the range selected for the wand. To select these areas, we depressed the Shift key and surrounded the areas with the Lasso tool.

• Once the trees were totally selected, under the Image menu, we selected Adjust and, from the additional menu which pops down from Adjust, selected Color Balance (Figure 10–2).

The Color Balance control dialog works in the same fashion as the levels dialog, the only difference being that the modifications are applied to highlights, midtones, and shadows separately. Clicking

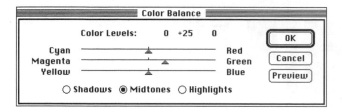

Figure 10–2 Color Balance dialog

in the radial buttons for each will apply the modifications to each separately.

- We created green for the trees by sliding the middle of the three bars toward the Green to plus 25 for the highlights, plus 30 for the midtones, and plus 25 for the shadows.

After each adjustment, we saved our work. At this point, saving was essential, because the next step was to have two versions.

The colors of the sky were to be replaced by a much richer deep blue gradient. These colors now had to be determined. The background and foreground colors were displayed at the bottom of the tool palette.

The foreground color is the small box within a larger one. The larger one represents the background color. When the program is first opened, the foreground uses black as the default; white is the default for the background. Clicking once on the foreground color box brings up the foreground color selector box. The box shows a ramp of red from white to black. Along the right side there is a bar which, since black is currently selected, displays only black. Click within the red area of the color box; this will show a gradation of

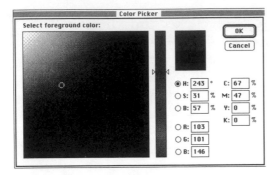

Figure 10–3   Foreground Color dialog

the color ranges within the bar to the right. Click on the blue range within the bar and the color box will display a ramp for blue tones.

Clicking within the ramp on the desired color selects it—or the value can be typed in the boxes to the far right of this window (Figure 10–3).

- We then created a light blue by entering a 67% for cyan and a 47% for magenta. We clicked OK to leave the color selector window, and the foreground color box displayed the new light blue.

Since the alteration to the sky required a gradient, it was necessary to alter the background color. If the background is not changed from white, the gradient will be from the light blue to white. A darker blue was required here.

- We clicked once within the background color indicator to bring up the background color selector. As before, we selected a blue color range within the bar and this time entered 100% cyan, 98% magenta, and 25% yellow to get a much darker blue.
- We selected the Magic Wand tool.

- With the Magic Wand, we clicked anywhere within the sky area. This searched out the edges of the colors that made up the sky and selected the entire area of the sky.

  - We then used the Blend tool to add the gradient to the sky.

  - We clicked and dragged from bottom to top of the selected sky area. The foreground color was applied where the first click of the mouse was placed, with the background color applied to the end of the mouse drag and button release.

This step created a blue gradient sky much richer than the original.

Since there is an alternate sky for this image, it was saved at this point as a separate file.

  - To create the alternate version with a sunset, we opened the last version saved prior to adding the gradient sky.

  - With the Magic Wand, we selected the sky area as before.

  - Going to Open under the File menu, we opened a file that had a large sky area such as a sunset or clouds.

  - Once opened, we used the Marquee selection tool to select the sky area of the new image and copied it into the clipboard.

  - Closing the new document, we returned to the original.

Even though a new file had been opened and manipulated, the program remembered the selected area of the original file and kept it selected.

  - Under the Edit menu there is a choice called Paste Into; this allowed us to paste the image of the sunset into the selected area.

The sky in the clipboard fell within the selected area. The outside perimeter of the new sky was visible with the crawling ants of the Marquee tool; however, only within the selected area could the actual image be seen. Since the new image was still selected, it could be altered. One typical alteration is to stretch or resize the image to fill an area or to reposition it. Often, two images might not be equal in size or proportion, thus requiring alterations.

The end result of this job was two images completely different from the parent image. (See color pages—"Case Study 1, Chapter 10.")

Now that the image had been altered, we needed to create a title for the record album. The assignment called for golden letters. To get clean anti-aliased type, it was necessary to have the Adobe Type Manager installed (see ATM section in Chapter 4).

- In the foreground color, we selected a bright orange consisting of 100% yellow and 56% magenta.

- The Type tool was selected, and clicked in the area where the type was to be displayed. In the case of the album cover, the upper right was the spot. A text entry and specifications window popped up. In it, Goudy Bold was selected and set at 36 points and Anti-aliased. In the text entry box we typed the title of the album: "ROMA."

- The type came in as a selected element. It was repositioned by using the mouse to drag the type to the position desired.

- From the Image/Effects menus, we selected the effect Stretch. Small handles (white boxes) appeared at the four corners of the type as shown in Figure 10-4.

- Grabbing the handle on the lower left, we clicked and dragged it downward to elongate the type.

- The assignment called for metallic gold, so a highlight had to be added to give the metallic effect. Since the type was still selected, it acted as a mask.

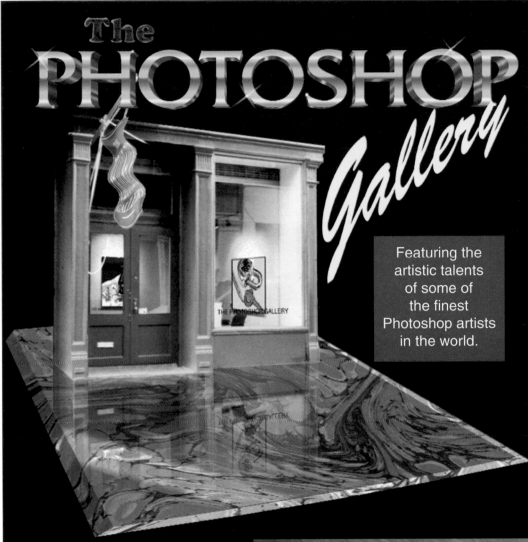

The PHOTOSHOP *Gallery*

Featuring the artistic talents of some of the finest Photoshop artists in the world.

Gallery Intro
Bert Monroy
Manipulated scans and original art.

brush on ledge
Bert Monroy
Drawn from life. A detailed description of the creation process is found in chapter 11.

lock

Bert Monroy. Painted from life. A detailed description of the creation process is found in chapter 11.

Sam's

Bert Monroy. Painted from reference photos. No scans were used.

objects on cloth

Bert Monroy
Painted from life. A detailed description of the creation process is found in chapter 11.

Height's Deli

Bert Monroy. Painted from reference photos. No scans were used.

Earth EyeLight

David Biedny

Tin Robot
Tom Cushwa, NYC

jif
Tom Cushwa

Marilyn Monroe
Tom Cushwa

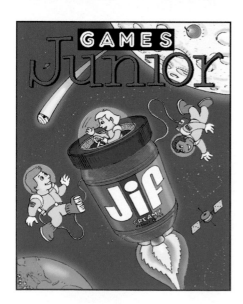

Ghosts
Tom Cushwa, NYC

Tiger Art Final
Nick Fain, San Fransisco

jungle
Gordon Baker, CA

Night Airport
Yusei Uesugi, CA

Expirer
J.M. Casey, NYC
and
John Knoll, CA

Dollar Eye
J.M. Casey

Streetcar 6
Nick Fain

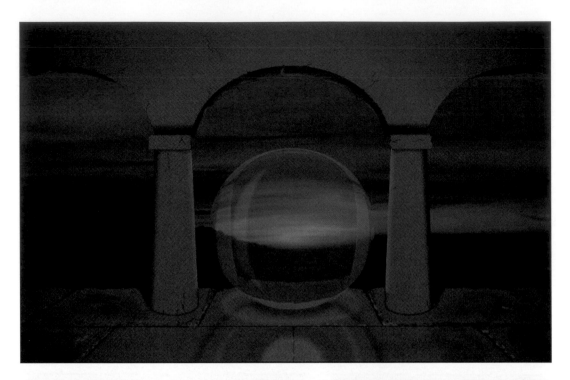

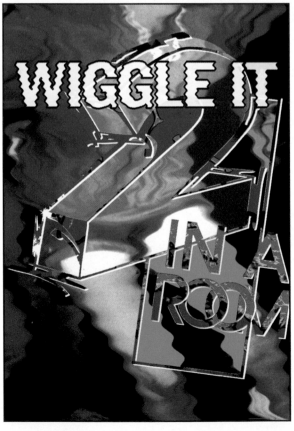

sphere chamber
Bert Monroy

Wiggle It
Ron Meckler, Re:Design, NYC

Oger Graphics
Dave Laymon, Anchorage, Alaska

Figure 10–4 Type with Stretch handles

- A lighter version of the gold color had to be created in the foreground color; this time we created a yellow consisting of 64% yellow, 4% magenta, and 4% cyan.
- We double-clicked on the airbrush tool, and the Options window appeared.

- We selected the largest circular size.
- Using the airbrush, we sprayed the type at a 45-degree angle with the sprays at different positions to give the impression that light is being reflected from different angles.

It was now time to add the caption "Italian Love Songs." The assignment called for a bright red.

- In the foreground color, we created a bright red made up of 100% magenta, 9% cyan, and 97% yellow.
- The Type tool was selected again and this time clicked at the lower left portion of the image.
- We chose a Goudy italic at 28 points and typed the caption.
- The type appeared as before and could be positioned. It was placed inside the dark reflection of the trees in the water.

The comp was now ready for presentation. (See color pages— "Case Study 1, Chapter 10.")

Case Study 2: Comp for Liquor Ad

In this assignment, we transformed a photo of a brandy bottle and a glass into a finished comp. (For a comparison of the original and finished comp in color, see color pages—"Case Study 2, Chapter 10.") We purposely shot the original photo under poor conditions to show the effectiveness of Photoshop in producing a high-quality comp. We didn't even clean the glass. The lighting consisted of removing the lampshade from a table lamp and the natural light coming from a window.

To begin with, we placed the brandy bottle and the glass on a pool table to provide a setting. We photographed the subject with Polaroid film. We then scanned the picture on a Microtek MSF-300Z color scanner at 300 dpi and 24-bit color.

Studying the shot, we complied a list of refinements. We prepared the list in the same fashion in which an art director would outline the necessary work for an artist or retoucher. It read as follows:

- Remove the glares and reflections from the bottle; make smoother in tone.

- Polish the glass and remove the glares at center.

- Tone down glare on left edge of glass.

- Add liquid to the glass.

- The label on the bottle has to be made legible; remove the hot spot, which is obliterating some of the type.

- Move the glass in to the right to slightly overlap the bottle.

- The background is too busy—it conflicts with the headline. Replace with dark fall-off in tones to match bottle.

- Add headline in same tone as the liquid.

- Crop off half of the foreground.

We then studied the process we'd use to achieve the desired results. When textures are involved, such as clouds, water, skin, and so on, the process is far more complicated. In these cases, it is necessary to duplicate the texture in order to get realistic results. Since all the elements in this picture were smooth, it was quite an easy task.

The bottle and glass could be completely reprocessed with only the selection tools and four modifying tools, the Paintbrush, the Smudge tool, Pickup Dropper, and the Water Drop.

- We eliminated the glares and reflections around the label of the bottle by smearing the dark areas over the light ones using the Smudge tool.

- We double-clicked on the Smudge tool to bring up its Options dialog box (Figure 10-5).

- The bottle and glass had large areas to cover. We set the tool to the largest circular size; the pressure at 80%. The higher the percentage, the farther a tone could be dragged.

- Each glare had a dark tone surrounding it. We placed the Smudge tool over one of these dark areas and then dragged over the light. This process smeared the dark tone over the glares thus eliminating them (Figure 10-6).

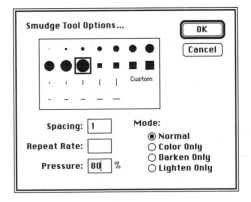

Figure 10-5 Smudge Tool Options dialog box

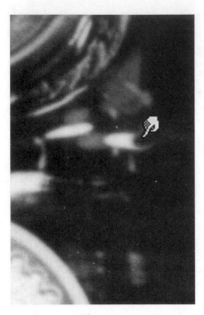

Figure 10-6   Smudge tool eliminating unwanted glares

This technique is demonstrated in the section of this chapter entitled "Case Study 4: Eyelash Creation Exercise."

In tight, crucial areas like the ones around the seal, we made the size of the tool smaller for more control. This technique was of particular use in the elimination of the scratches on the glass, and in cleaning up the stem of the glass as well.

- We repaired a small crack on the seal, at the three o'clock position, using the same technique.

- For larger areas, we employed the Paintbrush.

- The Pickup Dropper came into play for selecting the color to be used. With this tool, we clicked on he color desired for fill-in with the brush foreground color.

- Once that color was selected, we used the Paintbrush to paint over the areas.

The large brown area in the center of the glass and on the right side of the bottle are good examples of where this technique was applied.

To tone down the hot spot on the left side of the glass, caused by the harsh lighting, we used a different technique.

- First of all, we cleaned up and defined the area using the Smudge tool technique.

- We then used the Magic Wand selection tool to select the area.

- When we clicked in within the desired color region, this tool sought out the edges of that color and selected the entire area where that color existed.

- Once that area was selected, we called up the Brightness/Contrast controls (Figure 10–7).

- We reduced the brightness to –20, softening the white hot spot down to a softer gray.

Adding liquid to the glass was not as difficult as one might think.

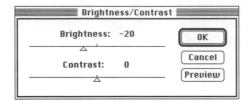

Figure 10–7   Brightness/Contrast controls dialog

- With the Elliptical selection tool, we selected a long flat ellipse from edge to edge within the glass; it served as the surface of the liquid (Figure 10–8).

- With the selection made, we brought up the Hue/Saturation controls.

These controls are found under the Adjust choice of the Image menu. This dialog employs the use of sliding handles represented by the little triangles under a line for each of the two controls.

- With the Colorize option selected, we adjusted the color until the desired tint of brown was created (Figure 10–9).

- Once this was done, we copied with the liquid surface (still selected) into the clipboard.

- Next we had to color the bottom of the liquid. We employed the Lasso to trace out the area at the bottom of the glass up to the surface area.

Figure 10–8   Selected portion inside glass to be converted to the surface of liquid

- We brought up the Hue/Saturation controls again, and this time attained a slightly darker version of the brown. (Playing with the Saturation control will give you varying degrees of color richness.)

- With this completed, we initiated a Paste, bringing the liquid surface back to place over the original one to cover up the overlap caused when the bottom of the liquid was created.

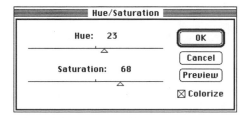

Figure 10–9   Hue and Saturation dialog

Figure 10–10   Hot spot on label

Repairing the labels required a little more skill and steadiness than had been employed up until now. In the neck label the edge motif and the letters had been burned out by the hot spot (Figure 10–10).

- Using the Eye Dropper, we selected the color of the motif closest to the lost area (Figure 10–11).

Figure 10–11   Pickup Dropper selecting color on undamaged portion of label

Figure 10–12   Paintbrush repairing motif

- With a small paint brush, we drew in the missing motif (Figure 10–12).

- We replaced the missing letters in the same manner.

The large "N" in the word "AND" was handled differently.

- The left stem of the letter was intact, so we selected it using the Lasso. We made a copy by holding down the option key and clicking and dragging the stem over to the missing stem.

- We then flipped the stem horizontally.

- We then rotated the stem to follow the angle of the rest of the lettering. This was all done by eye at a close zoom-in position. With the stem still selected, we employed the Arbitrary Rotate feature from the Image menu.

- We then created the cross stem with the paint brush. We clicked on one corner, then holding down the Shift key, clicked on the other corner, and the line connected (Figure 10–13).

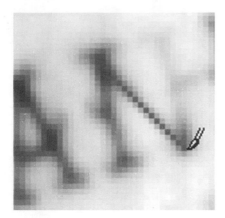

Figure 10–13   Stem of letter is created.

- Moving the glass over was a question of proper selection techniques. Using the Magic Wand, we selected the right edges of the glass.

- We then used the Lasso (with the shift button depressed for multiple selections) to add the other sections of the glass and background.

- The tabletop was a fairly consistent color, making it easy to duplicate. There was a slight shadow being cast by the glass in front of it; the shadow also had to be selected.

- The background to the left of the glass was selected as well.

- With all the elements selected, we held down the Option key to duplicate the selected image, then dragged it to the right until the desired overlap was achieved.

- We used the Blur tool with a small setting to soften the edge of the glass where the overlap occurred, as well as any rough edges on the tabletop.

- The Smudge tool technique was used to smooth out the background to the left of the glass.

- The overall background consisted of out-of-focus bookcases, which according to the outline of changes had to be turned into a smooth backdrop with fall-off. To accomplish this, we selected the entire background with the help of the Magic Wand and the Lasso. Since many of the tones in the bottle and the background were similar, clicking on a tone in the background selected parts of the bottle as well. These areas were then deselected with the Lasso by depressing the Command key and surrounding the areas to be deselected.

- With the entire background selected, we created a color ramp. With the Eye Dropper tool, we selected the color of the liquid as a foreground color.

- Clicking on the background color box over in the tools palette brings up the color selector box. In this box we chose a very dark version of the brown. This created a deep brown fall-off from dark to light.

- We then used the Blend tool to add a blend to the background.

We were then ready to add the headline to the comp.

- With the Type tool we clicked in the area where the type was to appear. This action brought up the type entry and specification box.

Here, We selected Belwe Light as a font with 18 points for size and Anti-aliased for smooth edges. We typed in the headline and clicked OK (Figure 10–14).

Last, we needed to crop the foreground area. The Crop tool makes this a question of simply selecting the size and clicking. This tool functions in the same manner as the Marquee selection tool.

We started the selection from one corner and dragged the tool to the opposite corner to make a selection rectangle.

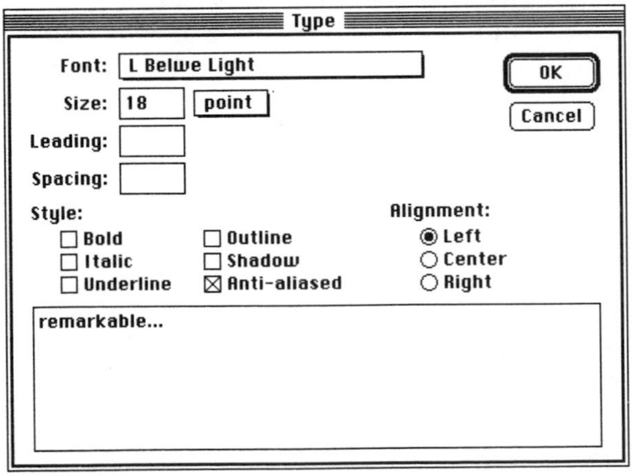

Figure 10–14   Type dialog

> The selection area has handles at the four corners. These handles allow you to redefine the selection.

When the area had been defined, we clicked within the selection and the area was cropped, eliminating all the elements of the image outside of the selection.

The result was a comp of professional quality from humble beginnings.

Case Study 3: Retouching

As beautiful as a model may be, or however good the photographer and make-up artist are, very few shots make it into a magazine without some degree of retouching. For a still life, it is easy to set up lighting to make it as perfect as possible; but shooting people is a very different situation. People move, and in the case of fashion photography, constant movement is necessary to add life to a shot.

We have come across many shots where the garment is perfect but the face is wrong or vice versa. It is easier to fix the face than it is a garment. A photographer will usually shoot a few rolls of film to attain one good shot. You can't know the right shot until you see them all. The editing process weeds out the bad ones, and you're left with two to five possible shots from which to choose.

From these finals the client and art director will weigh the pros and cons to narrow the choice of the shot to use. The camera is usually very unforgiving. The lights can pick up blemishes or cast undesirable shadows.

In this situation, we took a poor shot of a woman's face and completely changed its appearance. (Of course, this is an extreme case, undertaken primarily to demonstrate the retouching power of Photoshop! See color pages—"Case Study 3 and 5, Chapter 10.") The assignment read as follows:

- Clean up blemishes.

- Add strong eyeshadow.

- Open up eyes.

- Add more eyelashes.

- Close mouth.

- Make lips fuller.

- Change lip color to warmer red.

- Remove earrings.

- Raise jaw line.

- Change garment color to pastel green.

- Make hair golden blond.

To start with, a shot was done in harsh daylight, which casts strong shadows. Little make-up was applied, and no attempt was made to hide blemishes.

The first step was to eliminate the blemish just to the left (viewer's left) of the lips (Figure 10–15).

When retouching images that have a texture, it is important to maintain that texture. It is easier to use the Smudge tool and smear the right color over the blemish, but the result will be a blurred area that stands out from the rest. To use the texture itself to paint with, the simplest tool is the Rubber Stamp in Clone mode.

- With the Rubber Stamp, with the Option key depressed, we clicked in the skin area next to the area to be covered. This keyed the Rubber Stamp tool to the area from which we wished

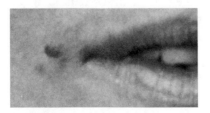

Figure 10–15 Blemish to the left of the lips

to clone (Selecting an area close to the damaged area is vital in order to maintain the same color and angle).

- Releasing the Option button then allowed us to paint over the blemish with the skin tone previously selected.

> This process is very useful in retouching. It is important to copy small areas at a time. In the case of, say, removing a boat from the water, using small areas of the water at a time will ensure the randomness of the waves. If the same area is used over and over, the eye will pick up the pattern in the image, thus taking away the realism the retouching is suppose to achieve.

- The next step was to add eyeshadow to the upper eyelid.

- We needed to zoom in on the area of the eye to achieve greater accuracy. The best thing to do in such a situation is to create another window in which to view the results of your work.

Under the Window menu, there is the New window choice; this will create a second window for the same file. Position the two windows so that both are visible. Set one at actual size, the other as the zoomed-in work window. When modifications are done in the work window, they will be viewed in the actual size window, making it easy to avoid mistakes.

- Getting back to the retouching, there was a little make-up visible just below the eye. It was necessary for the make-up color to be consistent, so using the Pickup Dropper tool, we picked up the color of the make-up.

- Clicking the Eye Dropper over a color will select that color as the foreground color. We selected the color just below the eye.

> Note: Clicking the Eye Dropper over a color with the Option key depressed will select that color as the background color.

- Using the Lasso selection tool, we then selected the area of the eyelid.

Since eyeshadow is usually a smooth blend at the edges, the Feather option was brought into play.

- Under the Select menu, we chose the Feather option. This option allows the creation of vignettes with the fade-out controlled by the radius entered by the user. The higher the radius, the further the fade-out. In this case, we used the vignette as a mask with soft edges (Figure 10–16).

- The Feather control dialog pops up when the feature is selected. In this window we entered a radius of five. This created an edge smooth enough for the eyeshadow.

Figure 10–16   Feather window

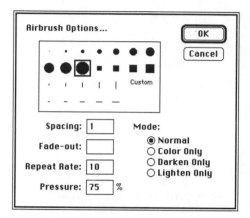

Figure 10–17 Airbrush Options dialog

- Now we switched to the Airbrush tool. Double-clicking on it brought up its settings dialog (Figure 10-17).

- Here we selected the largest size, and increased the pressure to 75%.

- Spraying within the selected area produced a soft haze of eye shadow in the color previously selected.

- Once the color had been laid down, some additional smoothing was required.

- We deselected the lid and switched to the Blur tool which here came in handy to soften any rough edges and to lighten certain areas that would pick up light. A typical area that would pick up light on the eyelid is a small circular area just above the eyeball.

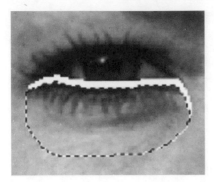

Figure 10–18   Eyelid dragged downward to open eye

Opening the eye was a bit more complicated and required some special techniques.

- Using the Lasso, we outlined the bottom lid just along its top edge and far enough below to capture skin texture. Once it was selected, we dragged it downward a slight bit (Figure 10–18).

- Using the Lasso, we outlined the bottom lid just along its top edge and far enough below to capture skin texture. Once it was selected, we dragged it downward a slight bit. We kept the modification very slight, for fear that our model might end up looking like a cartoon character.

This action exposed some white area below the eyeball. It was in this area that the eye needed to be extended.

- Double-clicking on the Smudge tool, we brought up the settings window (Figure 10–19).

- With this window we selected the third smallest size (the size chosen here was small because the area to be fixed was tight).

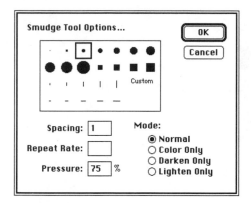

Figure 10–19   Smudge Tool Options dialog

- We zoomed into the eye for a better working view, and with the Smudge tool, slowly and with small strokes, pushed the eyeball colors down to fill the gap.

- The curvature of the iris had to be maintained. Pushing the edges of the iris in the same direction in which they follow will fulfill the curve.

- Employing the smallest Blur brush, we run the tool along the edge where the bottom lid was separated and the finishing touch was to be done.

- Using the technique described in Case Study 4 in this chapter, we created additional eyelashes for a fuller look.

- With a small Smudge tool setting, we pushed up the dark tone of the existing lashes in order to create new ones. They had to be pushed out in the same direction as their neighbors and at different lengths. If the lengths had not been varied, the result would have looked like fake eyelashes.

Closing the mouth was handled in much the same manner in which the eye was opened but, naturally, in reverse.

- Using the Lasso, we selected the bottom lip and part of the skin below it (Figure 10–20).

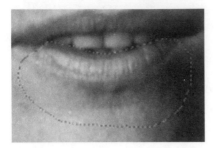

Figure 10–20 Lip selected

- Holding down the Option key, we moved the lip up a slight amount until it just covered the tips of the teeth. The Option key makes a duplicate while you drag so that the skin texture is repeated, thus eliminating the need to retouch a gap as in the eye.

- We made upper and lower lips fuller, closing the gap between them.

- Then we brought a small-size Smudge tool back into play (Figure 10–21).

Using the natural lines of the lips as a guide, we dragged the colors downward from the upper lip to close the mouth and make the lips

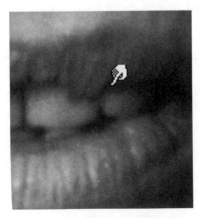

Figure 10–21 Smudge Tool Options window

fuller. It was also necessary to drag some of the color from the lower lip up. When the mouth was open, there was a curve to the bottom lip. With the mouth closed, the separation of the lips was almost straight.

- Using the Magic Wand tool, we selected the lip color. (Where there are a few variations of color, it may be necessary to evoke the Grow command under the Select menu. This option forces the selection to look for the next value of the selected color and selects it as well.)

- Once the entire lip was selected, we brought up the color balance controls. These controls are found under the Adjust choice of the Image menu. Here the tones for the shadows, midtones, and highlights were adjusted to give a warmer red hue to the lips (Figure 10-22).

As the bars are manipulated, hitting the Preview button will allow you to see the effects of the change against the rest of the image. Once the desired tone is accomplished, pressing OK will confirm the changes to the original.

- We again used the Smudge tool to remove the earrings. Following the flow of the hair, we pushed the strands upward to cover the earrings. We used small strokes to maintain the fluid look of hair. Long strokes would have made the hair look too rigid, therefore unrealistic.

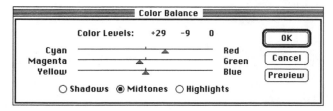

Figure 10-22   Color Balance dialog

We raised the jaw line with the same technique used to move the lower lip.

- With the Lasso, we selected and duplicated upward the entire jaw line plus a small area of neck. This movement was done by eye and had to be carefully adjusted to avoid the look of a deformed lower jaw.

- We then used the Water Drop tool, with a small size setting, to clean up the seams created by the move. We didn't drag the water drop over the area, but simply clicked over specific spots that showed the seam. Dragging will produce a smear which will loosen the skin texture and look abnormal.

Changing the garment color was the next task.

- With the Magic Wand, we selected the small section of the collar.

- We then changed the color with the Hue and Saturation controls found under the Adjust choice of the Image menu (Figure 10-23).

- With the Colorize option selected, we moved the Hue bar until a desired color was attained; we moved the saturation bar until we reached the desired intensity of the color.

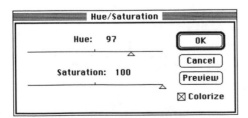

Figure 10-23   Hue and Saturation dialog

Changing the hair color was a little more difficult. The selection process required careful attention.

- With the Magic Wand, we selected a midtone of the hair. Holding down the Shift key for multiple selection, we selected highlight, then a shadow.

- With these three tones selected, we chose Similar under the Select menu. This scanned the rest of the image and selected all the tones that matched the ones selected.

When the Similar function is used, many times the selected tones appear in areas that are not desired. In the case of the girl's face, the hair tones also appeared in portions of her face.

- Switching to the Lasso with the Command key depressed, we surrounded the undesired areas. This deselected those areas.

- With the hair entirely selected, we again brought up the color balance control.

- This time we adjusted the colors to add yellow to the gray, thus satisfying the request for golden blonde hair.

The end result was a much more radiant image than the original. (See color pages—"Case Study 3 and 5, Chapter 10.")

Case Study 4: Eyelash Creation Exercise

In the course of retouching photographs, certain problems make it necessary to create elements that are not there. One common situation is the extension or addition of eyelashes to an eye, as in Case Study 3 in this chapter.

In a case like this, the Pencil and the Paintbrush produce a harsh line with little or no control over the thickness variance within the stroke.

Let's follow a short, step-by-step exercise to develop the skill necessary for this technique.

1. Start with a New file.
2. Select the magnification tool.

Figure 10–24   Small arc

3.   Click twice in the window. This will bring you into zoomed-in view close enough to properly see the effect of the strokes.
4.   Select the Paintbrush.
5.   Paint a small arc similar to the one shown in Figure 10–24.

This arc will serve as our eyelid. In the case of an actual photograph, the tones from which to extend the lashes would be present. Notice the dark tones along the edge of the eyelid in Figure 10–25. The lashes already visible on the lids can serve as a guide for creating new ones. In the case of this tutorial, however, you have no scan of an eye to work from. The arc you created is to be the lid.

6.   Double-click on the Smudge tool.
This will bring up the options window for the tool (Figure 10–26).
7.   Set the size to the third smallest from the right in the top row and set the pressure at 80. Click OK.

Figure 10–25   Eye

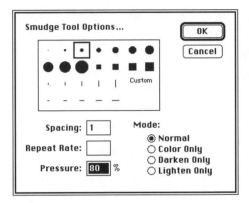

Figure 10–26   Smudge Tool Options dialog

8. Placing the tip of the finger cursor on the black stroke you created with the brush, click and drag the mouse so that the finger moves at a small arc away from the stroke as in Figure 10-27

As the finger moves, it will slowly lighten the color saturation. How far the stroke carries color is controlled by the amount of pressure you have entered in the options window. In this case the pressure is set at 80.

In a real eyelash retouching situation, the lashes would not be uniform but rather a series of random lengths as in Figure 10-28.

Pulling strokes at various lengths will produce a more realistic look.

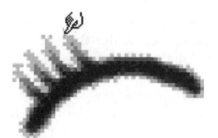

Figure 10–27   Smudge tool creates lashes

Figure 10–28   Eye with new lashes

Case Study 5: Aging a Face

The image of the blonde girl in Case Study 3 was retouched to make her look better. (See color pages—"Case Study 3 and 5, Chapter 10.") What if the opposite is desired? Many things can be done. Horns can be added, a third eye perhaps. A multitude of effects can be attained. In this case study, forty years will be added to the young girl's face. Adding such details as wrinkles requires some illustrative skills.

To further enhance the effect of an aged face, we discarded the color information by turning the image into grayscale. We accomplished this by selecting the Grayscale option under the Mode menu.

After the image was converted to grayscale, the shadow cast from the nose appeared too dark; it needed to be lightened.

- Using the Magic Wand, we selected the shadow tone (Figure 10-29).

- We then modified brightness and contrast by choosing Brightness/Contrast from the Adjust choice under the Image menu, which brought up the control dialog (Figure 10-30).

In this dialog, we raised the Brightness level to lighten the shadow. Pushing the Preview button allows a check of the effect of your manipulation.

- When we arrived at the desired tone, we clicked OK.

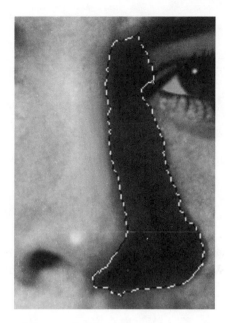

Figure 10–29   Nose shadow selected

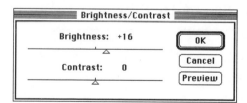

Figure 10–30   Brightness/Contrast dialog

We also lightened the nostril that was within the shadow area. It had to be returned to a tone to match the other nostril.

- Using the Eye Dropper tool, we selected the tone of the darker nostril by clicking within the center of the darkest area of the interior of the nostril (Figure 10–31).

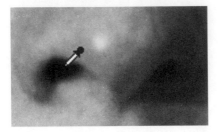

Figure 10–31   Selecting the color of the nostril

- Using a small paintbrush, we traced the interior of the lightened nostril as in Figure 10–32. We then softened the edges to match the darker nostril.

- We then applied a small Blur tool to the edges (Figure 10–33).

We then turned our attention to the eyebrows, which had to be thinned out with white hairs sprinkled through.

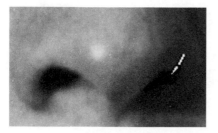

Figure 10–32   Paintbrush restoring the original color of the nostril

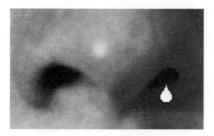

Figure 10–33 Water Drop being applied to the paint stroke in nostril

- We used the second smallest Smudge tool to push the light skin color into the brows. The small size of the tool created lines equal to the thickness of the brow hairs. The tones were pushed in the direction of the natural hairs. One or two of the hairs can break direction to add a natural look to the white hairs that sometimes normally break the flow.

- The eyelashes also had to be thinned out. The same process was used. A small Smudge tool pushed the skin tones into the lashes. These strokes were done at varying lengths.

Wrinkles will age the face tremendously. Studying images of aging people will give you a knowledge of the way that wrinkles form on the face and body.

The first obvious place is around the eyes. Crow's feet or laugh lines, as they are sometimes called, start at the outside corners of the eyes. Under the eyes, bags form. The mouth gets outlined by deep creases. The lips shrivel. The cheeks sag and develop wrinkles that travel in vertical lines starting at the cheekbones. The forehead also develops its own system of lines.

To create this maze of lines, three tools were utilized—the Airbrush, Paintbrush, and the Smudge.

A tone had to be chosen. This tone was slightly darker than the actual skin tone. It was supposed to give the effect that light was casting shadows in the crevices formed by the wrinkles. Too dark, and it would seem like the lines were painted on the face. A good formula is to double the intensity of a tone—i.e., a facial tone of 20% has a wrinkle tone of 40%.

- Once the tone was selected, we double-clicked the Airbrush tool to bring up its settings dialog. We selected the second smallest size and a pressure in the range of 50 to 75. The higher the pressure, the darker the first spray.

- Using short quick bursts of the Airbrush, we created lines that followed the contours and direction that the facial lines naturally took (Figure 10–34).

- The same technique was used with the Paintbrush, but the Paintbrush was used in tighter areas, as in the bags under and above the eyes.

- The Paintbrush was also used to create new lines on the lips.

Figure 10–34   Eye wrinkles

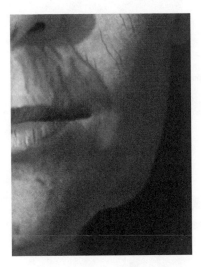

Figure 10–35 Jowls

- After creating lines throughout the face, we put the Smudge tool into action. With a small setting and a pressure similar to the brush tools, we smeared out smaller wrinkles from the tips of the main ones forming little forks.

The cheeks had to be puffed up and dropped. The Finger tool was used here.

- We set the size at the largest circle.

- The tone that outlines the outside edge of the cheeks was pushed out to form the puffed cheeks. We created an indent in the cheek at its base to form what is referred to as a jowl. We placed additional creases where the jowls meet the chin to accent their existence. We added additional wrinkles from under the jowls upward toward the cheeks (Figure 10-35).

If the tones have been carefully administered, the end result is the accurate depiction of an elderly individual. (For the results, see color pages—"Case Study 3 and 5, Chapter 10.")

11

Fine Art

This chapter will deal with Photoshop as a system for creative exploration. No boundaries are set here. There is no client to appease—no corners to be cut.

Fine art has many interpretations. Some say it is a reflection of humanity and its times. Some say it is a playground for creative people. Some artists, in fact, communicate the political stirrings of their time. Others simply capture the beauty they might see in their minds or surroundings so that others may share them.

Dreams, imagination, and environment are the inspiration for all artists to enter realms that enhance everyday life. Artists tap their skills to create images that mesmerize viewers and force them to face certain realities, or perhaps, let them escape reality for a moment.

Whatever the definition, computer-generated visuals have only recently been accepted as a medium for creative expression. Thanks to the efforts of pioneers like Yoichiro Kawaguchi, whose bizarre landscapes lift you away from the confines of this world, computers have become an acceptable medium. Many studios, such as Industrial Light and Magic, have also been instrumental in bringing the power and beauty of computer graphics to the public eye with images that were once only the stuff of dreams.

The artist will use many different mediums to achieve certain effects. The computer combines many of these mediums—airbrushes, paint brushes, 3-D modeling for sculpting, and a vast array of others all in one convenient little box.

Photoshop perfects many of these tools, and in conjunction with other programs opens avenues never before available in a microcomputer. The exercises here will give you only a fraction of the effects possible within Photoshop. The rest is up to you, the user, and the limits of your own imagination.

Case Study 1: Still Life of Glass Objects on a Cloth

The first of these case studies uses Photoshop purely as a painting tool. The multitude of filters and special effects were not employed here, only some of the time-saving features. Applying years of experience with traditional brushes, this image was created. (See Gallery color pages—"Objects on Cloth.")

Why in Photoshop and not with traditional brushes?

Photoshop does make the process cleaner and more efficient. Being able to zoom in for certain detail work is one good reason. The ability to try different colors or undo the last stroke of the brush makes the creative process much more interactive.

The creation of most images, especially photorealistic ones, requires some preliminary sketching to establish the form and relationship between different objects. For this purpose, Adobe Illustrator 88 or 3.0 is enlisted to first generate an outline or sketch. If you have a photograph that you wish to use as reference, it can be scanned in to be used as a template for tracing. Refer to the Illustrator documentation for further details on this process.

The image of the bottle and glass balls, however, was drawn from life. As in any still-life drawing, the objects were placed in the desirable setting and then sketched by eye. If you have ever attended a drawing class, you will find this procedure quite familiar.

If you have not had such training, then it is necessary to train yourself to draw from life. It is simply a matter of training your hand to follow the angles and spatial relationships that the eye is seeing. The power of observation plays a critical part in this process. It is through visual interpretation of all the elements that the subject can be accurately captured. A subject can be simplified by eliminating certain parts, leaving only the basics necessary to depict the essence; or every detail can be captured to give the image true realism. This concept can be compared to the difference between a portrait of a person and a caricature. The portrait will be detailed whereas the caricature will use only the basic elements that make up the person's look—for example, a large nose and sloping forehead.

Mastering Illustrator for this purpose is no easy task for most people, but when you have accomplished it, you will never again resort to the use of pencils and paper. That's because following the angles of objects can be done so easily. Once a line has been created, it can easily be moved into the right position. Spatial relationships are also a snap. When a particular object has been completed, it can be resized and repositioned to interact with the other elements in the image.

Since the Illustrator file is to be simply an outline or guide for use in Photoshop, it is essential to keep it simple. Let the details be attained in Photoshop. This process is similar to the use of a charcoal sketch for an oil painting—too much charcoal and it gets messy.

Here's how we created our painting:

- Once the outline had been completed, we made a screen dump was made of the art in Artwork Only mode (Figure 11–1).

Sure, the image could have been brought in as an EPS file; but if you observe an image in Illustrator while in Preview mode, you will notice that the line thickens at certain angles and joints. This thickening is due to the way the screen's resolution handles that particular line weight. This is also important when you consider that the outline might be for a light-colored area and you have to deal with that build-up of unwanted color in the outline. In Artwork Only

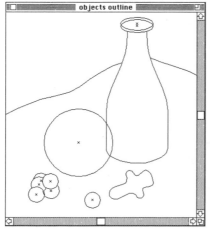

Figure 11–1 Screen dump from Illustrator

mode all lines are a single-pixel weight, making their use as an outline far more efficient. The only way to take a file into another program in this mode is via a screen dump.

It is advisable to have installed one of the various applications that allow you to make a screen dump to a PICT file. If, however, you do not have one, then switching your Mac to black-and-white or 2–bit mode and executing a Command-Shift-3 will give you a Mac-Paint screen dump. Photoshop does accept MacPaint format, so all is not lost.

- Once the screen dump was made, we switched to Photoshop.

- We saved the Illustrator file in case we needed it later.

- In Photoshop, we selected Open... from the File menu.

The standard open dialog box appeared (Figure 11–2).

- We searched for the file of the screen dump. Unlike some paint programs which require that the format be selected before you can see the listing of available files, Photoshop will see all files and inform you as to their format at the bottom of the window.

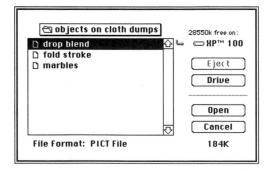

Figure 11–2 Open dialog box

- Using the Crop tool, we selected the area of the outline and cropped. Clicking and dragging with the Crop tool causes it to act as a Marquee. Once the desired area was outlined, we moved the cursor within it and the cursor was transformed into a scissor. We clicked within the area with the scissor and the area was cropped. This got rid of the menu bar, tool palette, and other unwanted elements.

Now we were ready to start the painting process. Again, the power of observation was crucial here. We were recreating on the screen what was being viewed in life.

The cloth on which the objects had been placed had a series of folds, which captured light in different ways. Studying these folds, we noticed that they were in fact shapes of different tones. (It is important to think of them as shapes. These shapes are outlined by an interplay of different tonal values. If the material has no printed pattern, then how effectively these shapes are interpreted will determine how real the cloth will appear.)

▼ **Tip:** If the cloth does have a printed pattern, it is vital to distort the patterns into the folds. One great example of this technique is the work of Maxfield Parrish. He created a lot of work in which intricately patterned cloth was ruffled.

To create these tonal values it was necessary to create a palette of colors.

- We clicked in the Foreground color box.

- In the Foreground color window, we selected a tone that closely matched the darkest value of the fold. This was done by eye.

Once the color was selected, we stored it for later use. By choosing Show Palette from the Window menu the palette appeared. With the Bucket tool, we clicked in one of the available boxes on the lower left portion of the palette, and the color filled the box.

- We then selected the Paintbrush.

- Double-clicking on the tool brought up the Options dialog (Figure 11–3).

- Here, we selected a size that best fit the need.

If the pressure is set at 100%, the stroke will lay down an opaque coat of the color. The lower the percentage of pressure, the more translucency the stroke will have.

- In the same manner in which pigment paints would be laid down, we applied a stroke of the color following the shape of a fold (Figure 11–4).

- We selected the Blur tool, and again applying traditional techniques, the stroke was softened and blended into the background to get the soft quality of cloth (Figure 11–5).

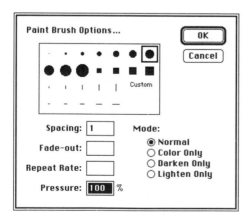

Figure 11–3 Paintbrush Options dialog

Figure 11–4   Folds of cloth

For larger areas it was better to use the Blend tool instead of the Paintbrush.

- With the Lasso, we selected the area to be filled.
- We selected a starting color in the Foreground color window as before.

Figure 11–5   Water Drop applied to edges for smooth finish

- We selected an ending color in the background color. This was achieved in the same manner except the Background color box was clicked.

- With the Blend tool, we clicked and dragged in the direction in which the shade had to travel. A blend was created.

- As before, the edges were softened with the Blur tool.

▼ **Tip:** In this method of applying a tone, there is an alternative technique for softening the edges. When the selection is first made, Feathering the edges will soften them equally, thus eliminating the need to use the Blur tool.

Since all of the objects in the still life were made of glass, light travelled through them casting colorful shadows. The folds in the cloth that picked up these tones were handled in the same manner as above, but with the appropriate color.

The blue marbles in the foreground were a series of blue shapes.

- Using the Magic Wand, we selected the inside area of each marble and kept it selected until it was completely rendered (Figure 11–6).

- We then selected a blue tone that encompassed the overall color of the marble.

Figure 11–6   Marble selected

- We applied a fill by selecting Fill from the Edit menu.

- We created a darker blue value that added the reflection within.

- Again using the technique we used on the cloth folds, we applied and blended strokes.

▼ **Tip:** Since the marble is selected, it is masked from the rest of the image, making it easy to stay within the lines. Strokes can be applied more liberally without the worry of maintaining the shape, as one would with traditional painting.

The one thing that differentiated the marbles from the cloth was their texture. The marbles were made of a glass that was highly reflective. In observing the actual marbles we noticed that the light source cast a reflection on them in the form of a sharp highlight.

- Using a small Paintbrush and a near-white color, we applied a stroke to the top of each marble (Figure 11–7).

The larger crystal ball presented a new problem. It had details that had to be duplicated. The ball acted as a magnifying glass, creating within it a pattern caused by the weaving in the cloth beneath it. The ball also had a larger area, which made reflection and distortion more discernible.

Figure 11–7   Highlights on marbles

▼ **Tip:** The concept of seeing everything as a series of patterns that relate to each other simplifies the task of achieving photorealism. In photo retouching, when it is necessary to add elements to the photograph there is one method that works well. An example of how this method works is duplicating someone's signature. If you look at the signature and try to copy it, you are too aware of the way the other person renders letters. If the signature is turned upside down, you see it as a series of lines, making it much easier to duplicate. Likewise in photographs, if you enlarge an area until it is just a series of tonal shapes, it is easier to replicate the photo.

- We selected the crystal ball in order to mask it.

Using brushes, airbrushes, and blending tools, we added detail to the ball.

We rendered the bottle in the same fashion: selected, painted, and so on. The neck area, however, allowed us to use one of the features of Photoshop. Since the neck was a straight surface, all highlights were straight lines. The following technique works with the paint brush, airbrush, pencil, and the rubber stamp as well as with the eraser, smudge, and water drop.

- We selected a color lighter than the dark blue of the bottle.

- With a large airbrush, we held down the shift key and clicked at the top of the bottle neck.

- Still depressing the shift key, we clicked at the bottom of the neck.

The result was a connecting line between the two points.

▼ **Tip:** Continuous clicking of the tools with the shift key depressed will create a continuous line connecting the clicks.

With all the images created, the backdrop was all that was left to create. In this case a simple fall-off (dark-to-light area) was deemed best in order to not draw attention away from the subject.

- With the Magic Wand, we selected the background area.

- We selected a very dark blue as the foreground color.

- We chose a brown as the background color.

- Using the Blend tool, we dropped in the fall-off by clicking and dragging from the top down.

- Finally, all the outlines had to be softened or removed.

- We double-clicked on the Blur tool to pop up its Options window. We selected the second smallest Water Drop size and traced all the edges.

This blended and anti-aliased the edges, making the image look smooth. The result can be seen in the Gallery color pages—"Objects on Cloth."

Case Study 2: Still Life of Different Textured Objects

As in Case Study 1, the image of the lock was painted from life. (See Gallery color pages—"Lock.") A few more features of Photoshop were brought into play for this image.

We once again created the outline in Adobe Illustrator (Figure 11-8). Notice that actual type was used as a guide to be later transformed to the actual type appearing on the pencil and lock. In Illustrator, type can be skewed and rotated to follow the contours of the objects.

Once in Photoshop, we selected and worked on each shape individually. The wood section of the pencil point required a few special techniques for realism.

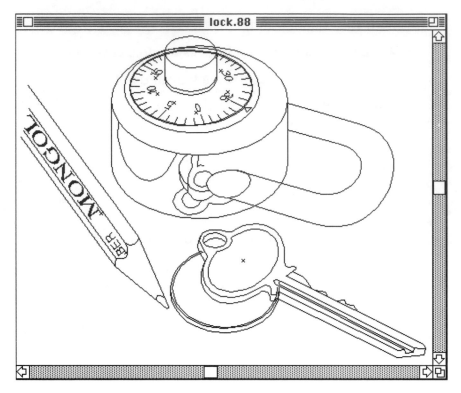

Figure 11–8   Screen dump from Illustrator

- Using the Magic Wand, we selected the pencil point.

- We selected a beige tone for overall value.

- We filled the selected point using fill from the Edit menu.

- We then selected a darker version of the beige.

Using the airbrush, we darkened the lower edge of the point to give it the depth of a cone shape rather than that of a simple triangular shape.

- With the airbrush and the shift key depressed, we clicked on one end of the point, then on the other. The tone flowed along the edge.

Figure 11–9   Pencil point with wood grain

- We then selected a reddish tone equal to that of the wood grain.

- With a small airbrush, we rendered the grains (Figure 11–9).

Study the point of any wooden pencil and you will notice a slight glistening quality to the wood after it's been through a pencil sharpener. To get this effect, we used a filter.

- With the pencil point still selected, we went up to the Image menu and held down the Filters option. An additional menu dropped, displaying the filters available. We chose Add Noise.

A window popped up (Figure 11-10). We then determined the amount and distribution. (For further details of the functions, refer to the filters section of this book.)

The pencil point required little noise, just enough to provide a texture.

- We entered a value of 10 with a Uniform distribution.

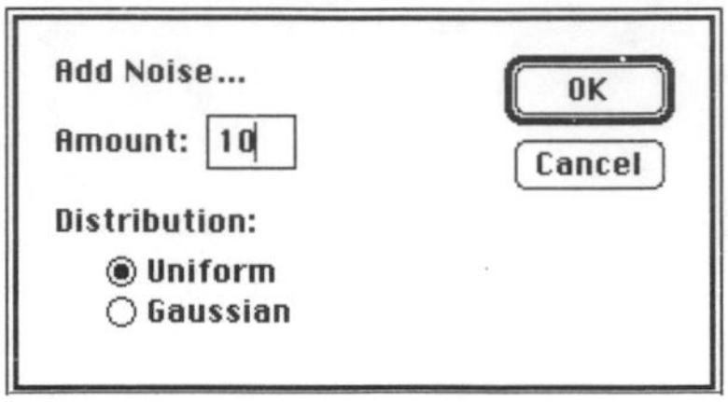

```
┌─────────────────────────────────────┐
│ ╔═══════════════════════════════════╗│
│ ║                                   ║│
│ ║ Add Noise...          ┌──────────┐║│
│ ║                       │    OK    │║│
│ ║ Amount: │10│          └──────────┘║│
│ ║                       ┌──────────┐ ║│
│ ║ Distribution:         │ Cancel   │ ║│
│ ║   ◉ Uniform           └──────────┘ ║│
│ ║   ○ Gaussian                      ║│
│ ║                                   ║│
│ ╚═══════════════════════════════════╝│
└─────────────────────────────────────┘
```

Figure 11–10   Add Noise dialog

The result was a slight sheen to the wood grain. This completed the rendering of the point, so it was deselected.

The graphite tip of the pencil was next.

- We selected it with the Magic Wand.

- We Filled it with a dark gray.

- We Airbrushed a darker tone along the bottom edge.

- We added a very light gray highlight at the tip to show the reflection of light.

The outside portion of the pencil was made up of flat planes. Each plane was colored individually.

- We added a different yellow tone to each plane. Darker tones were used as the edges moved away from the light source.

- For added realism, we added nicks and bite marks to the surface of the planes.

- We added shapes of the bites with a small airbrush and a light tone.

- With a very small airbrush and a dark tone, we added a shadow to the edge against the light, which gave the effect of depth to the nicks (Figure 11–11).

- With a black airbrush, we rendered the lettering on the side of the pencil.

Figure 11–11   Nicks and bite marks on pencil

- With the type created in Illustrator as a guide, we rendered the new letters to match those that actually appeared on the pencil (Figure 11-12).

- The only thing left to finish the pencil was to eliminate the black outlines of the Illustrator file. With the line tool, we traced over these lines.

Figure 11–12   Type on pencil

- With the Eye Dropper, we picked up the color of each of the pencil's edges.

- With the color, we drew a line over the black outline.
- We did the same on the pencil point with the tones of the wood.

This technique used for the lettering on the pencil was also applied to the dial portion of the lock.

- We selected the lock dial (Figure 11–13).
- We went to the Image menu and clicked on the Map choice to see its submenu. Under the submenu we found Invert. We chose Invert.

The lock dial reversed in color leaving the numbers white on a black field.

- With a small Paintbrush and the shift key depressed, we filled in each of the lines (Figure 11–14).
- We also cleaned up the numbers.

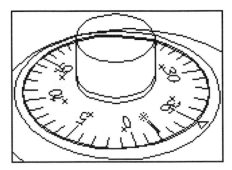

Figure 11–13 Lock dial

Figure 11–14 Strokes applied to the dial

- With the dial still selected, we generated a gray tone to match a light reflection on the dial.

- With a larger Airbrush, we sprayed the tone over the dial (Figure 11–15).

▼ **Tip:** Another method for applying highlights is to select the area for the highlight and to lighten it with either the Levels control or the Brightness/Contrast controls found under the Image menu's Adjust submenu.

The knob portion of the dial had ridges. These ridges were defined by highlights.

Figure 11–15 Highlights applied to the dial

Figure 11–16   Dial knob with grips

- We selected the knob.

- Holding down the shift key, we applied vertical strokes with a small paint brush. Since the knob was selected, it was masked. We started each stroke by clicking outside of the mask area. This ensured a uniformity of the stroke (Figure 11–16).

To add dimensionality, we decided to differ the values used for the vertical strokes, darkening them slightly at two-stroke intervals.

The key, having so many distinct areas, made individual selections a must. Being a metallic object, it reflected everything. In this case we brushed the metal flat, making the reflections colors rather than details.

▼ **Tip:** Sometimes in making something look real, a little "Artistic License" is advisable. In reality the key looked a little dull. To duplicate it as such would not have given the effect of metal. A few additional highlights here and there added realism that was not there in reality.

- All of the tones within the key's edges were added with different size airbrushes and different tones of brown and yellow.

- We selected the flat panel at the holding portion of the key.

- We then applied a fill.

- We added reflections with an airbrush.

- We employed the Add Noise filter to add a little texture.

- We then selected the face of the coin underneath the key.

Being a polished metal, the reflections on the coin are sharper in detail than on the key.

- We selected and filled an overall tone.

- With an airbrush and a tone similar to that of the key, we traced the contour of the key to create a reflection of it on the coin.

- With a dark airbrush, we traced the contour of the key against the edge of the key to create a shadow under it (Figure 11–17).

- We sprayed different tones over the surface of the coin to form additional shadows and highlights.

- With a small light-colored airbrush, we created the hint of an imprint on the coin.

The lock's surface was a highly polished metal, which acted as a mirror to all the other objects around it. Here, the power of observation came into play.

Figure 11–17 Reflection and shadow of key on coin

On the lock, all the reflections appeared as shapes of color. We observed that the pencil's reflection was simply a series of gray and yellow concentric circles.

With each of the objects completed, the surface on which they were placed was last to be rendered. Unlike the first exercise, where the cloth was filled with intricate details of its own, this surface was flat.

- Using the Magic Wand, we selected the background. With the shift key depressed for multiple selecting, we also selected the background areas within the key's ring hole and the lock's bolt.

- We chose a light gray for the foreground color.

- We chose a lighter gray for the background color.

- With the Blend tool, we applied a gradient from the upper left corner to the lower right corner.

Since the background is still selected, it was masked it from the elements. This made it easy to add the shadows necessary to place the objects on the surface and add depth to the overall image.

- We chose a dark gray for the foreground color.

- With the airbrush set at the largest size and 100% pressure, we sprayed on the shadows.

- To get the straight lines of shadow as under the key and pencil, we used the shift-click method. The other areas were done by tracing the part of the element casting the shadow.

- With the tones and shadows done, we needed a texture to give the surface some life.

- Since the background area was still selected, the Add Noise filter worked perfectly once more.

The final result for this process can be seen in the Gallery color pages—"Lock."

Case Study 3: Still Life of an Airbrush

This third case study used many of the same techniques as the first two, with some additional filter uses and a scanned image. The subject was somewhat of a tribute to the old days. It was simply an airbrush sitting on a ledge. (See Gallery color pages—"Brush an Ledge.")

The image of the airbrush was drawn from life in Illustrator. You, of course, can set up your own subject and create an outline from scratch or scan an image to trace for an outline.

- We selected each section individually with the Magic Wand for rendering (Figure 11-18).

- We used a large airbrush with a dark gray tone; we sprayed straight lines across the surfaces of the airbrush to get the metallic effect. It is important to vary the grays and stroke sizes to get the circular feel of the tool.

- We selected the air hose and filled it with an overall red tone. Fill is found under the Edit menu.

- With the hose still selected, we simulated more roundness by adding darker tones of the red to the edges.

Figure 11-18 Shafts of airbrush rendered

- We applied light tones with a small airbrush at specific spots on the hose to act as highlights or reflections from a light source.

- We opened a new file separate from the airbrush to work on the background.

The one feature of this image that was different from the first two exercises was the use of a scanned image. The stone ledge on which the airbrush sits was a scan. This particular scan was of a paper that had a gray splatter pattern printed on it. Using a Howtek color scanner, the paper texture was brought into Photoshop (Figure 11-19).

The two green textures that seem to be beyond the ledge were created from the same gray texture.

- We divided the texture into three sections as they appear in the image.

- We opened the scan three times and saved it as three different new textures.

▼ **Tip:** Photoshop allows you to open multiple files. This makes it possible to have the airbrush file plus all three texture files opened simultaneously.

Figure 11-19   Scanned texture

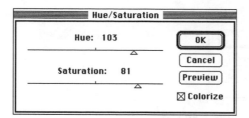

Figure 11–20   Hue/Saturation dialog

- The two files that made up the two sections on the top were put through a Hue/Saturation change to turn the gray into a green (Figure 11–20).

The Hue/Saturation control is in the submenu to Adjust under the Image menu.

The file which made up the upper right side of the image was modified further with filters.

- Going up to the Filters under Image, we applied the Motion Blur filter (Figure 11–21).

- In the Options dialog, we set the angle value to 45°. The distance was set to –20. We clicked OK.

- We brought up the Brightness/Contrast from Adjust in the Image menu (Figure 11–22).

- We then increased the brightness to lighten the texture.

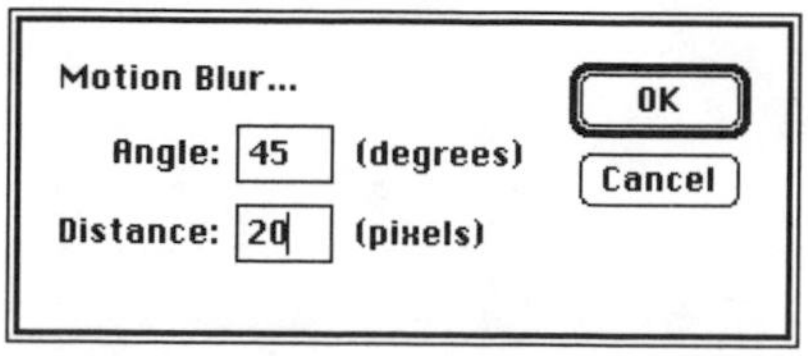

Motion Blur...
Angle: 45 (degrees)
Distance: 20 (pixels)
OK
Cancel

Figure 11–21   Motion Blur dialog

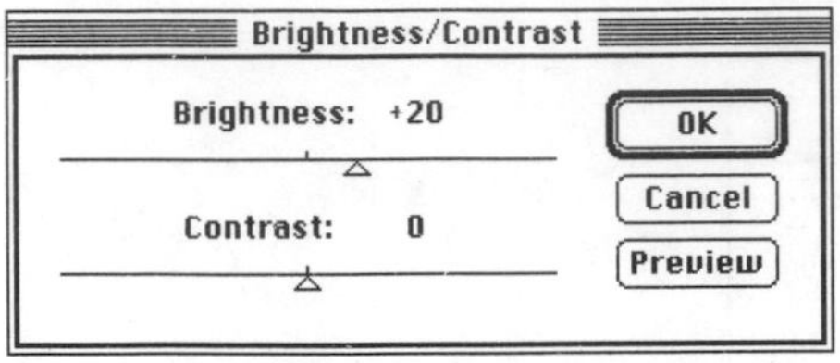

Brightness/Contrast

Brightness: +20   OK

Contrast: 0   Cancel

Preview

Figure 11–22   Brightness/Contrast dialog

The file for the top left was next to be modified.

- Going to the filters again, we used time a Gaussian Blur (Figure 11–23).

- In the dialog, we set the radius to 4. We clicked OK.

- We again invoked the Brightness/Contrast from under Adjust in the Image Menu (Figure 11–24).

- We decreased the brightness, this time to darken the texture.

It was time to bring all the textures together.

- Using the Lasso to make up the image, we selected the upper right-hand side.

- Starting the selection from the upper left-hand corner, we dragged it across the top to the right, down the right side, then

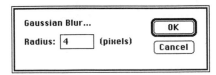

Gaussian Blur...

Radius: 4   (pixels)   OK

Cancel

Figure 11–23   Gaussian Blur dialog

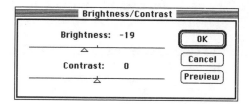

Figure 11–24 Brightness/Contrast dialog

released it. The Lasso selection automatically closed itself, forming a straight line from starting to ending points.

- Under the Selection menu, we selected Feather (Figure 11–25).

- We entered a feather of 1.

- We then copied the selection to the clipboard.

- We activated File 2, the upper left part of the image.

- We selected a paste.

- This positioned the imported image in the upper right area of the image.

- We activated the file with the original gray texture scan.

- We selected it using the Lasso.

- The selection was started from the upper right corner, dragged down the right side, along the bottom to the left, and released.

As before, the Lasso closed the selection with a straight line.

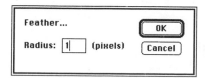

Figure 11–25 Feather dialog box

- We applied a feather of 1, as before, and copied it to the clipboard.

- We activated the file with the two green textures, and the gray was pasted to the lower half.

Next, we activated the file with the airbrush.

- With the Magic Wand, we selected the white of the background.

- Under the Selection menu, we selected Inverse.

Inverse will select everything other than what was selected, thus selecting the entire brush without the background.

- We copied to the clipboard.

- We activated the background file and pasted.

- We positioned the airbrush where we wanted it.

- We did not deselect.

- We selected Inverse once again from the Selection menu.

This time the background was selected, leaving the airbrush masked.

- With a black airbrush, we added the shadows.

We were finished. The end result can be seen in the Gallery color pages—"Brush on Ledge."

Case Study 4: Using 3–D Programs to Create Shapes

This case study goes further than the others by highlighting the techniques in the first two exercises, the scans of the third, and a 3-D program. The illustration was that of a space station revolving in an orbit somewhere between the earth and the moon. (See color pages—"Case Study 4, Chapter 11.")

Using a 3-D program, we created the basic shape of the space station. The model was given its detail in Photoshop. This is a situation which can come up quite often. Perhaps you have to do an illustration of a car or a building. The 3-D object acts like your sketch pad. The object can be viewed at different angles until you have the right angle to achieve the drama or impact that the illustration requires.

It is preferable to have the 3-D model as a wire frame without shading or texture, since those will be added in Photoshop.

- Once we had the best angle, we made a screen dump (Figure 11-26).

- We then switched to Adobe Illustrator.

Figure 11-26 Screen dump from 3-D program

▼ **Tip:** If the 3-D model is clean enough, it can be opened directly in Photoshop. In this case, the image was so complex that removing all the wire frames would take more time than simply making a new outline in Illustrator.

- We opened the screen dump as a template.
- We outlined the basic shape.
- We made a screen dump of the Illustrator file (Figure 11-27).

It was ready to be rendered in Photoshop.

- In Photoshop, we opened the screen dump.
- We created a foreground color of black and a background color of gray.
- With the Magic Wand, we selected each section of the station.

Figure 11-27 Screen dump from Illustrator

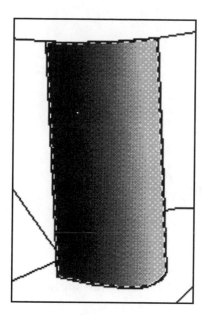

Figure 11–28 Tone added to shaft of space station

- With the Blend tool, we added the tone (Figure 11–28).

▼ **Tip:** It is essential to establish a light source for the casting of shadows. In this case, the sun provided a single light source that will cast strong shadows. Multiple light sources create shadows that darken further where they cross over each other. Colored light sources cast shadows that alter the color of the surface on which the shadow is cast. Simple observation will be the best teacher on the effects of lighting on objects.

Figure 11–29   Shadows cast by sections of the space station

- Additional shadows had to be cast from a section of the space station which obstructed the light from other sections (Figure 11–29).

- While the particular section on which the shadow was cast was still selected, we rendered the additional shadow with either the Paintbrush or the Airbrush.

- We used lights to add life to the station.

- We chose various bright colors.

- With the second smallest Paintbrush, we applied strokes of color (Figure 11–30).

- We produced a glow in the very dark areas of the station by clicking over the paint stroke with a small airbrush of the same color as the light. This added more realism.

We created every pin spot of light with the second smallest paintbrush. If the pencil is used, you get a solid pixel. With the brush, you get a solid central pixel with four lighter ones around it. This adds the glow necessary to get the effect of a light source (Figure 11–31).

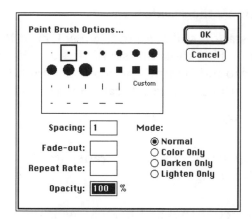

Figure 11–30   Paintbrush Options dialog

With all the details added, we next had to put the space station in place.

- With the Magic Wand, we selected the white background.
- We chose invert from the Map submenu under the Image menu. This turned the background into the black of space. We did not deselect.
- We made scans of the earth and the moon.
- We opened the scan of the earth.
- We selected All from the Selection menu.
- We copied the earth into the clipboard.

Figure 11–31   Pin spot of light

- We reactivated the station's file window.

- With space behind the station still selected, we selected Paste Into from the Edit menu. This took the scan of the earth and pasted it into the background behind the station. Once in, it could be repositioned until the desired location was found.

- With the earth in place, we deselected.

Since the domes of the space station were transparent, it was necessary to show the earth through them.

- With the wand, we selected the dome area over the earth (Figure 11–32).

- The earth was still in the clipboard, so we used Paste Into once again. This time it appeared within the dome.

- We repositioned the earth within the dome to line up with the earth in back. We did not deselect.

Since the earth was being viewed through glass, we had to give it a different tonal value.

- We invoked the Brightness/Contrast dialog from the submenu of Adjust under the Image menu.

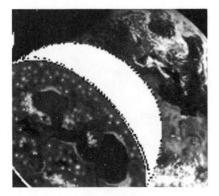

Figure 11–32   Dome selected

- We then lightened the section of the earth just enough to give the illusion of its being viewed through glass.

- We followed the same steps for the moon on the other side of the space station.

The final result can be seen in the color pages—"Case Study 4, Chapter 11."

These tips and whichever ones you come up with can be applied to your own subjects. Considering all the power of Photoshop, the next few years should provide the world with a vast new supply of imagery to boggle the imagination.

Graphics Formats

In our experiences with Photoshop, we've come to refer to it as the "Universal Can Opener": It can open and save in more graphics formats than any other Macintosh graphics program we've seen. Most Mac people will be familiar with many of the formats found in the hierarchical format menu in the Save and Save as dialogs, but some of them won't be familiar to many. Each format has specific uses, as follows:

Photoshop

Photoshop's native file format is extremely powerful and flexible: PS files open and save extremely fast, are very memory-efficient, and can include masks and other channels of information. Whenever you save a file from within Photoshop while working in RGB mode, you will be saving a Photoshop file. They are always full 24-bit color.

At this point it's important to clear up a confusing mistake most people make when talking about "32"-bit color: There are only 24 bits of data dedicated to the color information found in an image (this 24 bits makes it possible to display anywhere up to 16,777,216 colors simultaneously; but remember, not many color monitors in the world have that many pixels on the screen). The other eight bits are dedicated to an alpha channel, which, unfortunately, isn't currently supported by Apple. Photoshop is an exception to this rule—it implements its own alpha channel mechanism, resulting in the ability to have multiple 8-bit alpha channels assigned to each file. Because of this ability, it wouldn't be accurate to call a Photoshop file a "32"-bit file. It can have more bits.

TIFF

TIFF stands for Tag Image File Format—developed by Aldus to allow page layout programs to import and print continuous tone images (scanned grayscale graphics) as screen halftoned images. Aldus originally developed the format for their own PageMaker software, and then made the format specifications available for other software companies to incorporate into their software. In doing so, Aldus was able to establish a format that continues to be the standard for moving scanned images around between different Macintosh software, and between multiple computers. TIFF is readily supported by Intel/IBM PC-type machines, and other computers, such as the NeXT system.

TIFF was optimized specifically for scanned images—it's not a very efficient format for vector or line graphics (that's where EPS comes into the picture). While most people think that there is only one type of TIFF file format, in actuality there are a variety of TIFF subformats and variations; most are supported by current scanner software. For example, one variant of the TIFF format involves a built–in level of Lossless File Compression (LZW encoding) which some scanner software can output, but many page layout programs don't support. Photoshop can import some types of LZW compressed scanned images, and can save images with LZW compression. If you want to export LZW TIFF images from Photoshop, make sure that your page layout program will support compressed TIFF files.

TIFF exists on both Mac and PC formats. When doing save from Photoshop, user has option to select for Motorola/Intel CPU formats. You can use one of the many available file translation utilities to move Photoshop-manipulated images from the Macintosh to a page layout program on the IBM PC; this is made easier if the Macs and PCs are networked together with a networking scheme such as TOPS.

PICT

PICT is probably the principal general-purpose file format for graphics on the Macintosh. There are two different types of PICT files—PICT I and PICT II. PICT I was the original format for object-oriented graphics programs (such as MacDraw). PICT II came out at the same time that the Macintosh II was introduced: it was made to support complex object files and color bitmapped images (of up to 24 bits of color depth). PICT II files are supported by many color bitmap programs such as PixelPaint 2.0, Pixelpaint Professional, Studio/8 and Studio/32 (PICT is the native file format for the Studio programs). When opening a PICT file into Photoshop, load times are usually much longer than when loading a comparable Photoshop image file. This isn't a bug—but it does indicate how efficient Photoshop is when dealing with its own native file format.

If you import an object-oriented PICT file into Photoshop, it will automatically get converted into a 72 DPI bitmap. In order to get the best results, you might want to try enlarging your original image in the source program, and then reduce it in Photoshop. For example, if you're starting with a design in MacDraw, double the image's size in MacDraw, import the image into Photoshop, and then reduce the entire document by 50%.

For the most part, the current Macintosh operating system only supports 72 DPI resolution when moving selections through clipboard—System 7.0 reportedly has the ability to support clipboard resolutions up to 300 DPI, but we haven't had a chance to extensively test this yet. Photoshop's own internal clipboard knows about multiple resolutions, but when you open a desk accessory or export an image through the clipboard, the image resolution is limited to 72 DPI (multiple bit depths are supported by the current Macintosh operating system, and you can specify the normal clipboard bit depth up to 32 bits in Photoshop's Preferences dialog).

MacPaint

MacPaint is the original Mac bitmapped format. Seventy-two DPI fixed resolution, standard format for built-in Mac screen dumps. Supported by most programs because it's easy. Good for Image-

Writers, importing files into HyperCard, and when you absolutely want that crude neomodern digital look.

EPS

Developed by Alsys as a generic PostScript format. Supported by most PostScript Illustration programs as primary output format for page layout systems, it's primarily meant for object-oriented PostScript graphics. Its most useful aspect, in terms of using Photoshop, is that you will export separated images as EPS files for importation and integrated color separation into programs such as Quark XPress.

An EPS file, like everything in the Macintosh universe, is made up of two "forks"—or different types—of information. In the case of an EPS file, the Data fork holds the actual PostScript code portion of a graphic image, while the Resource fork contains the QuickDraw code for Macintosh screen representation. When printed to a Post-Script printer, only the image's data fork/PostScript is sent to the output device.

When importing EPS files into Photoshop, only the QuickDraw portion (resource fork) of the file will be read in, as a 72 DPI bitmap. If the original PostScript image had colors, the imported PICT resource will have the corresponding colors also.

At the time of this writing, Illustrator 88 and 3.0 support 24-bit screen representations of previewed graphics on a system using a 24-bit video card; page layout programs typically display color or grayscale EPS images as dithered 8-bit system palette images, regardless of the video card. We would expect/hope that 24-bit screen preview support for most of the popular page layout programs will be addressed in the near future.

GIF

The CompuServe GIF format is a raster file format that allows color bitmapped images to be moved around multiple computer plat-forms. It was developed in order to allow CompuServe users with different computers to exchange bitmapped and scanned artwork.

The GIF file format is indexed: Image documents contain a color map that is used to maintain optimal colors for the translated image.

Amiga

The Amiga Interchange File Format (IFF)/ Interleaved Bitmap (ILBM) File Format is the standard raster file format for the Commodore Amiga. The IFF file format supports numerous modes. The modes are separated into three types:

1. The first type of mode sets the resolution or number of pixels for both the vertical and horizontal directions. The possible resolution modes are:

   - 320 x 200 pixels (low res)
   - 320 x 400 pixels
   - 640 x 200 pixels (high res)
   - 640 x 400 pixels

2. The second type is the color modes. The possible color modes are:

   - Normal (32 colors)
   - HalfBrite (64 colors)
   - Hold–and–Modify (4,096 colors)

3. The third type is the special modes, which include:

   - Dual Playfield
   - Double Buffering

Targa

The Targa format is the most common format found in higher-end PC-based paint systems. We've decided to share a written description of the Targa format and file transporting written by John Simon, manager of the MFA Computer lab at the School of Visual Arts in Manhattan. Play it, John.

"The graduate computer lab at the School of Visual Arts (SVA) in Manhattan has numerous Macintosh and AT-PC systems. All

PC systems are equipped with Targa32 frame buffers. The addition of a NuVista card for the Macintosh made PC to Mac file sharing at 32–bit color resolution a reality. Users now have the ability to move an image to either Mac or PC paint systems, distributing the work load to more machines and allowing a greater number of output options to be explored. The lab uses a Sun Microsystems 3/260 as a file server. PC's use PC/NFS to remotely mount a directory on the Sun as an additional drive in DOS. Files to be transferred to Macs are copied to this drive. The Macintoshes talk to the Sun with Tops. A directory on the Sun is mounted with the Tops DA and appears as an additional storage device icon on the right side of the Mac screen. Files copied to the shared directory from DOS appear as generic file icons on the Mac. Students may upload files to the Sun from any PC and store the files there until time is available on a Macintosh to work with them.

"Our first file transfers required Apple File Exchange filters to convert the TGA format to PICT. This was time-consuming, forcing students to transfer multiple files in batches. Files are not converted in place; new files are created, filling up disk space and requiring the removal of the original files. Furthermore, the process has to be entirely repeated if files needed to be moved back to PC's. Adobe Photoshop has been used to facilitate the sharing of files among different systems. While in Photoshop, the user chooses the "Open As..." option in the File menu. He selects the file and then uses the file type pop-up menu to select TGA as the desired format. Because Tops functions as a DA, the user may mount the network directories from within Photoshop. If the file has just been copied to the network from a PC, Photoshop will not recognize it when using the "Open" option in the File menu. However, after saving in TGA format from within Photoshop, the file will be recognized. (I assume this is because Photoshop stores things like the file type code and the file size in the resource fork and newly ported files don't have anything important in the resource fork.)

"The ability to read and write TGA format files from within Photoshop has particular advantages to our lab configuration. The Sun may be used as a common space from which to work with files on any system. Many filters are available on our Sun that work with TGA formats. Files may be filtered on the Sun and retouched on the Mac without ever moving, renaming, or converting the files. It is interesting to note that the data is processed on the Macintosh but the file resides on the Sun system. Photoshop eliminates the necessity of downloading and converting files, which results in a significant savings in time. We use Tips for creation of artwork on the Targa boards; files from DGS and Alias animation software are output in TGA format. We have been completely successful in bringing files from all of these sources into Photoshop. We have brought compressed and uncompressed picture (.tga) and window (.win) files of various sizes into the program with no error. Additionally, all TGA files that have been written by Photoshop have been successfully read into both 32-bit and 16-bit versions of Tips. The TGA file routines seem quite robust and complete. Indeed, the input and output to these files is quite a bit faster than Apple File Exchange. We see Photoshop as an important tool in the integration of our lab systems."

Thanks, John.

TGA files can have 8, 16, or 32 bits/pixel. A full screen targa image is 512 x 482. Targa files normally have a 512-byte header—the rest of the image document is either compressed or uncompressed. Eight and 16-bit files are indexed, with the color tables stored in the header. Thirty-two bit images also have index in headers, in the event that file looks proper when displayed on lower bitplane boards.

Scitex

Scitex CT (Continuous Tone) is a high-resolution raster file format developed for representation of scanned images for placement and color separation for the Scitex Prepress system. In order to move Scitext CT images from Photoshop to a Scitex machine, you'll have to use a third-party package, such as Visionary (the Quark XPress–Scitex hardware/software link) to move files around. Scitex scans are saved as the separate CMYK overlays. When imported into Photoshop, a Scitex CT image automatically opens into CMYK mode.

Photoshop Peripherals

Software

No software is an island—one of the great things about using the Mac is that you can use many programs together to do things that no one program can do on its own. We've found that there are some utilities that are great companions for Photoshop, and dramatically extend the program's usefulness. We'd like to share some of our favorites with you.

Adobe Type Manager (ATM)

Adobe Type Manager is software that allows you to use Type 1 font outlines to generate unlimited screen sizes of a font, as well as permit you to create anti-aliased type in Photoshop. See the discussion on type handling in Photoshop for more details on using ATM. If you get Photoshop, get ATM—you'll end up wanting it unless you never work with type.

WindowShade

WindowShade is a wonderfully simple shareware INIT/CDEV that changes the way that windows operate: By clicking on the titlebar of an open document window (with a programmable variety of mouse clicks and/or modifier keys), you can close the main window area, leaving only the titlebar floating onscreen (while the document is still actually open and available) (Figure B1). While this is

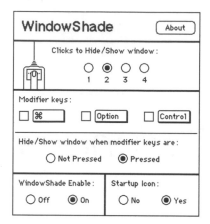

Figure B-1   The WindowShade CDEV

just generally nice for working with multiple documents, it's extremely important in Photoshop—If you are working with multiple large files, Photoshop is constantly redrawing the background windows after certain operations to the foreground window. By using WindowShade, you can keep documents open, but Photoshop doesn't have to go through the window redraw operation, speeding up overall performance quite noticeably. This is an essential utility for Photoshop users.

SmartScrap and Curator

While every Macintosh comes with a Scrapbook desk accessory, SmartScrap is a smart, useful replacement scrapbook that has replaced our standard Scrapbook since its release. Using Smart-Scrap, you can easily maintain multiple scrapbook files (without cumbersome renaming), view thumbnails of the contents of an active scrapbook, and copy only selected portions of a scrapbook entry.

SmartScrap is essential if you plan on creating Director animations with images processed through Photoshop: You create separate scrapbook files of sequences of images processed through Photoshop's image-processing effects, and import the scrapbooks directly into Director. While there are many freeware and shareware scrapbook replacements available for less money, we strongly suggest that you consider purchasing SmartScrap for moving images between these two programs, and as a Scrapbook replacement in general.

Curator is a combination standalone program and desk accessory that allows you to create image databases from many different types of graphics files (1-,4-, 8-, and 24-bit grayscale, color, and object PICTs; TIFF; bitmaps—just about everything except native Photoshop format, unfortunately). You can search for a specific image based on keywords, and convert between various image formats (somewhat overlapping similar functionality found in Photoshop). If Curator supported the native Photoshop file format, it would be the perfect image database for everyday use. As it is, if you're exporting TIFF or PICT images from Photoshop for inclusion in other programs, you'll probably want to look at Curator.

If you're using a 24-bit system, make sure that 24-bit clipboard support is switched on in Photoshop's Preferences dialog. If you don't, you might unknowingly copy 8-bit versions of your 24-bit images into the clipboard.

ScrapSaver

ScrapSaver is a public domain utility that permanently saves the contents of the clipboard; normally, when you restart your Mac, the last item on the clipboard is flushed. With ScrapSaver, the clipboard is saved between restarts and work sessions. Simple but indispensable.

Screen Flipper

Screen Flipper is an INIT that puts a pop-up menu on the Macintosh screen which allows you to instantly select different screen display depths. It automatically detects the number of screen depth supported by your video card, and puts those options in the pop-up menu; you can also specify which modifier keys are used in order to summon the pop-up menu. Normally, you would use the Monitors control to change the screen depth, but depending on

---

NOTE: Since this writing, a new, similar utility, Depthgauge, has appeared, replacing our Screen Flipper forever.

your Mac and system configuration, this can take more than just a couple of seconds. While there are other utilities that offer similar functionality (such as Switch-A-Roo), Screen Flipper is the best in its category.

DiskTop

DiskTop is a popular utility for managing files from within any program: You can create new folders, copy, rename, move and delete files, find files based on a large number of search criteria, and more.

While there are other utilities that offer similar functionality, DiskTop offers one feature that we can't live without: You can create notes for files in the DiskTop Get Info window, and unlike the comments that you enter in a File's Get Info window in the Finder, DiskTop's comments aren't lost when you rebuild the disktop.

QuickKeys

QuickKeys is one of the most useful utilities that you can buy for your Macintosh: It allows you to customize your software in ways that are truly useful. We sometimes wonder why Apple didn't license QuickKeys and make it standard system software, instead of the limited Macromaker software which is bundled with the Macintosh (we obviously aren't Macromaker fans).

QuickKeys is essentially a macro utility: You can assign any command or sequence of commands to keyboard shortcuts, or the unused function keys on the Apple extended keyboard (in fact, QuickKeys is a great reason to get the extended keyboard). You can use QuickKeys with Photoshop in order to

- Make keyboard equivalants for your most used Photoshop commands and menu items.

- Automate many production processes.

Some of the first QuickKeys we cooked up were to select the Selection→Alpha and Alpha→Selection menu commands and keys to switch display modes, as well as sequences to

- Automatically load custom color palette documents upon launching the Photoshop.

- Open the Preferences dialog and click on the Separation Setup button.

- Open the Page Setup dialog and click on the Rulers Size button.

It's also useful to use QuickKey's built-in "Mousie" commands for selecting through layers of overlapping windows if you plan on working with multiple documents simultaneously; this is particularly true for animation production work. When creating some of the animation techniques described in Chapter 9, we stacked up multiple document windows in a specific order in order to be able to do everything from the keyboard in proper sequence.

As we were finishing this book, CE Software released QuickKeys 2, a much-enhanced version of the original software. We didn't have a chance to work with the new version extensively, but it appears to be even better than we hoped. As we've stated, this is essential system software for any serious Macintosh and Photoshop user.

Hardware/Input Devices

There are a variety of input devices that are useful for getting images into a Mac:

- Scanners

- Digitizers/Framegrabbers

- Graphics Tablets

Just about everyone using Photoshop will eventually require one or more of the above-mentioned input devices, depending on the type of work they are doing and the types of image sources they have access to. Following is a discussion of some of the essential criteria for selecting the right type of input device.

Scanners

It's been said that the "eyes are the windows of the soul." These words also apply to the relationship between computers and optical scanners: Scanners open the eyes of the computer to a virtually unlimited world of "analog" artwork. The scanner market is now flooded with a wide range of offerings (in terms of both capability and price), which can be confusing to the prospective buyer.

Photoshop is the ultimate scanned-image processor, and everyone from the fine artist to the corporate publisher will probably end up using a scanner in conjunction with Photoshop. There are some basic issues in selecting a scanner, based on final output requirements and budget factors.

Bit depth/Resolution

The amount of information that a scanner can absorb is expressed as its bit depth and resolution. Most desktop units work with variable resolutions between 72 and 300 (and in some cases, 400) DPI, with anywhere from 4 to 24 bits of color/grayscale information. If you plan on doing grayscale scanning exclusively, then 8 bits is all you'll need, while most color scanners do 24 bits of color data. You can use Photoshop to strip resolution and color depth away from an image as desired, but keep in mind that while you can downsample an image while retaining image integrity, you'll want to scan at high resolutions versus using Photoshop's resampling command to convert a low-res image into high resolution. Slide scanners typically scan at higher resolutions than desktop flatbed scanners.

Film Scanning

If your original images are photographic film transparencies (anywhere between 4 x 5 to 8 x 10 inches), you'll find that a standard flatbed scanner can't scan the film. Most flatbed scanners are made to handle images or printed matter on opaque paper or stock. Film allows light to shine through, requiring a mirror attatchment of some sort, which shines the light back into the scanner. Some of the more expensive flatbed color scanners offer mirror options, while most of the lower-priced desktop color scanners offer no such option. Most of the grayscale scanners on the market don't have a mirror option either; look for scanners that can handle medical Xrays, as these can inherently handle other types of film as well. A company called XOR makes a $2,000 transparency attatchment for the MicroTek flatbed scanner that can supposedly provide this unit with film scanning capabilities. We have not had an opportunity to test this configuration.

Slide Scanners

If your original artwork exists in 35mm slide format, or if you need to create high–res scans on the desktop, you'll probably end up looking at a slide scanner. Slide scanners are typically in the $6,000–$30,000 price range, depending on the types of film accepted, and the output resolution. Many of the images in this book were scanned with a BarneyScan slide scanner, which provides a medium level of quality. There are other comparable scanners, such as the Nikon, which is considered superior to the BarneyScan. BarneyScan has introduced a high-end slide and transparency scanner, which is in the $25–30K price range. We haven't had a chance to try this unit, but we expect that it yields better results than the lower-end units. Note: Some of you might think that you can scan slides on a cheaper color flatbed scanner with usable results. We'd like to tell you that it doesn't really work. We've tried scanning 35mm slides on our Howtek color flatbed, and the results were awful, distorted blotches of color shmutz.

Grayscale/Color

This choice seems fairly obvious: If you don't use color images, then a grayscale scanner is all you need, while any color scanner can do grayscale (either directly, or by stripping the color out of an image using Photoshop). There are a number of companies releasing reasonably good, low-priced desktop color scanners ($1,200–$2,500). While scanners in this price range can produce very acceptable color images for screen presentation and low-end color separation work, the old computer axiom "GIGO" (Garbage In, Garbage Out) still holds true: If you want to create exacting color separations for magazine or high-end publlishing, you'll probably run into the limitations of the aforementioned desktop units.

Flatbed /Sheetfed

Scanners come in two paper-handling flavors: sheetfed and flatbed. Sheet–fed scanners pass the paper by a stationary scanning element, while the element in a flatbed scanner moves as the paper remains motionless. The flatbed mechanisms work much like a standard photocopier. If you plan on scanning artwork from books or other bound sources, flatbeds allow the artwork to be scanned without cutting or otherwise damaging the originating bound materials. Sheet–fed scanners can handle only single-sheet non-bound art, and tend to be sensitive to heavier paper weights (the maximum paper weight that can be handled on a specific scanner varies from unit to unit).

If you need to use a sheet–fed scanner to input bound artwork, simply create a photocopy from the original artwork, and scan the photocopy. If your photocopier has reduction capabilities, artwork can be scaled before being scanned (which tends to result in sharper images compared to artwork scaled in the scanning process, or in software). This rule also applies to color art that is to be scanned: some of the scanners have slight problems with specific colors (for example, the Thunderscan sometimes has a hard time with certain shades of red). The specific color that presents problems is referred to as the "drop–out" color, and may consist of just one or two shades of a particular color family.

High–End scanners/Integration

One of the realistic limitations of Photoshop is that of the quality of scanned source files. While the desktop scanners are typically useful for a variety of color printing applications, the final reproduction method dictates the use of expensive, professional scanners and output systems.

For critical prepress applications, you'll want to use Photoshop with dedicated prepress systems. The Scitex system is the preferred current gateway for Photoshop images: Photoshop can directly read and Scitex CT images, allowing you to use the powerful scanner portion of the Scitex as an input source. If you are working or planning to work in this capacity, we don't have to remind you that file sizes get quite large (30–75 megabytes is an "acceptable" file size). At this point, Photoshop's performance is limited by the CPU, so expect more frequent coffee breaks during most filtering/correction functions. You'll also realize that optical storage is a viable archival investment. We expect these speed issues to be dealt with at some point in time, but as you might guess, there is always a financial price to pay for high performance.

Dedicated desktop scanner systems, such as the Optronics Color-Getter (a drum-laser scanner) are appearing in the $30,000–$60,000 price range that will deliver prepress quality source scans, and when coupled with a calibrated montitor and well-maintained imagesetter, can be used as the makings of a viable high-end Mac-based color separation system.

Software

While all scanners include some sort of software to drive the scanner, Photoshop users should be inquisitive regarding the availability of aquisition drivers for Photoshop. Adobe isn't and won't be the supplier of these modules: You'll have to inquire about the availability of a driver with the actual scanner manufacturer. While this is the preferred route, any scanner that can provide TIFF or PICT images is by definition compatible with Photoshop. At the time of this writing, a few of the major scanner manufacturers were just coming out with Photoshop drivers, with many other companies promising driver availability RSN (Real Soon Now). We strongly suggest getting in touch with scanner manufacturers directly: If you ask your local dealer whether or not scanner X has a Photoshop driver, chances are that the dealer will say "yes" regardless of the truth in order to make the sale (remember, we live in New York, the world capital of landsharks, so if you have a great relationship with a good local dealer, you might have a better chance of getting the real scoop).

Digitizers/Framegrabbers

Video digitizers were the first input devices to hit the Mac world years ago; while scanners have surpassed digitizers as the preferred method of input, they are still quite popular for situations which specifically warrant their use, such as

- Getting pictures of real world three-dimensional objects into the computer without having to photograph them and then scan photos.
- Grabbing images from video sources, such as videotape, camcorders, or still video cameras.

Digitizers come in two flavors: those that are designed to work with standard Mac line (512, Plus, and SE) and those that are designed specifically for the Mac II (these usually come configured as NUBUS cards).

> The actual difference between a digitizer and a framegrabber is that a typical framegrabber has onboard RAM memory for storing at least one (if not more) digitized images. A digitizer simply allows you to grab a frame of video and bring it into the computer RAM.

In order to grab grayscale or color video, you'll need a Mac II. NUBUS digitizers/framegrabbers are the preferred device for video input, and are typically offered as 8-bit grayscale, 8-bit grayscale/color, 16-bit grayscale/color, and 24-bit grayscale/color. Typically, the software included with these devices offers the ability to save images in either PICT or TIFF format. Check with the board manufacturer for availability of a Photoshop driver.

> Some of these cards double as real-time video playback display cards for the Mac II screen, which can be useful for multimedia applications with video-in-a-window.

Graphics Tablets

Many Mac artists find that the mouse is far from perfect for drawing images freehand. Graphics input tablets are a popular alternative to the mouse. There are many manufacturers of graphics tablets for the Macintosh: companies include Kurta, GTCO, and Wacom. The inherent limitations of tablets include the cord that connects the pen or puck (a puck is a mouse with crosshairs, typically multiple buttons normally used on engineering workstations) to the tablet.

We've found that the Wacom tablet is probably one of the most appropriate tablets for use with Photoshop. This is so due to the fact that the entire Wacom line supports multiple levels of pressure sensitivity with many of the tools, including the

- Airbrush

- Stamp

- Paintbrush

- Pencil

When using the cordless stylus on the Wacom, as you apply downward pressure to the stylus against the tablet, the width of the painting tool brush interactively increases or decreases. Very cool for simulating real paintbrush strokes.

The tablet is available in a variety of sizes, and includes an INIT driver. Photoshop automatically recognizes the presence of the tablet without any additional software. Just plug and play!

Compression

Once in the world of high-res color, compression is a crucial issue. Compression allows you to make optimum use of your hard disk space, both for working with and archiving large images. There are various options for image compression from within Photoshop or with separate standalone software.

JPEG (Joint Photographic Expert Group, the name of the committee developing the format) is a proposed standard method for compressing color bitmapped images; it's based on the "Discrete Cosine Transform" algorithm (DCT), which analyzes 8 x 8 pixel (independent of resolution) areas of an image, and performs a sophisticated "averaging" of the values in the cell. The result of this operation is that the image size is dramatically decreased.

JPEG is known as a "Lossy" compression system. There are both non-Lossy (Lossless) and Lossy compression schemes; Lossy compression sacrifices a level of detail and reproduction quality. The JPEG compression format allows you to specify the compression ratio: the default setting is 25, which results in a compressed image with good reproduction quality. The compression factor can vary between 1 and 250, but it's important to understand that these factors do not represent actual compression ratios—a factor of 25 won't necessarily reduce a 25-megabyte file to one meg in size. The higher the compression factor, the more data is stripped out of the image, resulting in increasingly poorer final image quality.

> The Law of JPEG: Higher compression = lower image quality.

In general, images meant for prepress are candidates for lower compression ratios; high–quality color separations require as much original information as possible. Images meant for video output are candidates for much higher compression ratios. A JPEG factor of

15-25 is recommended for print output documents, while 25-40 can be used for video applications. Of course, these numbers may vary with your particular hardware—if you are lucky enough to be dumping images to a digital video format such as D1, or even HDTV, you'll want to stick to prepress compression ratios. We don't expect that many of you will run into this problem.

> One of the golden rules of Lossy compression: Don't get into the habit of compressing a JPEG image more than once; each time you compress an image, a layer of information is "lost," and if you continually compress a JPEGed image over and over again, you'll eventually end up with a useless blob of pixels.

Most of the early software implementation efforts of companies producing JPEG and compression hardware were based around beta and/or release versions of Photoshop; Micron Technologies, C-Cube, and most of the other compression hardware manufacturers in the Macintosh world directly support image compression and decompression with Photoshop acquisition modules.

> There is a notable practical "catch" using JPEG: Once you compress an image with the JPEG format, you lose a level of image detail, and if you recompress the image with JPEG again, you will lose yet another level of detail. JPEG is meant for saving a file once you've done all of the desired manipulation and wish to save a final compressed version on disk.

The JPEG format relies on a custom chip set. The chip set, which has to be placed on a circuit board with other components, vastly speeds up compression and decompression times, as compared to the software alone. JPEG was designed to run with the chip set. While there is no difference in the resulting image quality when using software exclusively, the speed factor considerable—a 5-megabyte file might take anywhere from 45 minutes to an hour to compress with the software implementation of JPEG on a stock Macintosh II, while the same file would conceivably take no more than a few seconds (or less) on any acceleration board with the JPEG chip set. Companies such as EFI, C-Cube, and Micron Technologies have licensed the chip set and are developing consumer-oriented NUBUS JPEG boards.

Stuffit Deluxe

Stuffit Deluxe is the commercial version of Stuffit, which has been the Macintosh industry standard compression and archiving program for years. Stuffit Deluxe has built-in special external optimizers that have been created specifically for Photoshop files. Ray Lau worked on the Photoshop file compression optimizers while writing Stuffit Deluxe.

In Stuffit Deluxe, Optimizers are special compression routines that can compress certain types of files more efficiently than Stuffit Deluxe's standard built-in compression schemes. Stuffit Deluxe comes with three special Optimizers: one for sound files, one for non-Lossy Photoshop compression, and one for JPEG compression. (Figures B2, B3)

The Lossless Photoshop optimizer achieves better compression than Stuffit Deluxe's standard Fast compression without Lossless selected; and you can stuff, unstuff, and stuff the file as many times as desired without any actual loss of image detail or data.

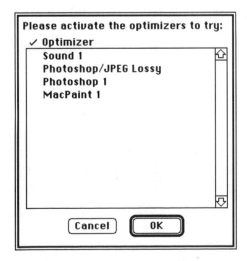

Figure B-2 Optimizer dialog from Stuffit Deluxe

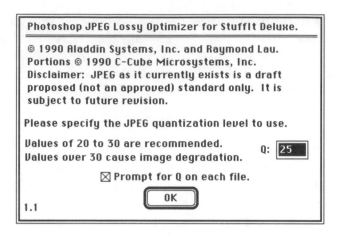

Figure B-3   Stuffit Deluxe's JPEG compression dialog

> Make sure that only one of the two Photoshop compression Optimizers is selected (with a checkmark) in the Optimizer dialog; if both are selected, then Stuffit will default to JPEG.

When the Lossy/JPEG Optimizer is selected in the Optimizer dialog, you'll get the compression factor dialog when stuffing a Photoshop file.

Once you specify a specific compression factor, that factor will be used until you specifically change it before compressing more images.

> You can only use Stuffit Deluxe to decompress images compressed with this technique—the new shareware version of Stuffit (Stuffit Classic) or any other JPEG compression software won't be able to decompress the Stuffit Deluxe JPEG file.

Remember, software-only JPEG is slow. Chant this softly to yourself as the software chugs away.

Appendix C

Photoshop Glossary

Reprinted with permission from Adobe Systems, Inc. © 1990, 1991 Adobe Systems, Inc.

additive primary colors Red, green, and blue, which are the three colors used to create all other colors when direct, or transmitted, light is used (for example, on a computer monitor). They are called additive primaries because when pure red, green, and blue are superimposed on one another, they create white.

alpha channel An 8-bit, gray-scale representation of an image, often used for creating masks to isolate part of an image.

anti-aliasing Smoothing edges created with painting, selection, or type tools.

arbitrary map An option that helps control the amount of black in a color separation by remapping black pixels to white in certain areas of an image, thereby ensuring that cyan, magenta, and yellow will be used in those areas instead of black.

ASCII Acronym for *A*merican *S*tandard *C*ode for *I*nformation *I*nterchange. A standard that assigns a unique binary number to each text character and control character.

aspect ratio The height-to-width ratio of a Marquee selection.

bitmap-type image A single-channel image with 1 bit of color information per pixel, also known as a bitmapped image. The only colors displayed in a bitmap-type image are black and white.

black generation The amount of black generated on the black plate of a color separation.

brightness One of the three dimensions of color; the other two are hue and saturation. The term is used to describe differences in the intensity of light reflected from or transmitted through an image independent of its hue and saturation.

bull's-eyes (registration marks) Marks that appear on a printed image, generally for CMYK color separations, to help you align the various printed plates.

calibration bars The printed 11-step gray-scale wedge that appears on printed output. When you print a CMYK color separation, this step wedge appears only on the black plate. On a color image, this refers to the color swatches printed at the sides of the image.

caption Text that appears below a printed image.

channel Analogous to a plate in the printing process, a channel is the foundation of an image. Some image types have only one channel, whereas other types have several channels. An image can have up to 16 channels.

CMYK Cyan, magenta, yellow, and black, the four process colors.

CMYK image A four-channel image containing cyan, magenta, yellow, and black channels. A CMYK image is generally used to print a color separation.

color correction The changing of the colors of pixels in an image, including adjusting brightness, contrast, mid-level grays, hue, and saturation to achieve optimum printed results.

color separation An image that has been separated into the four process colors of cyan, magenta, yellow, and black (CMYK), and is then printed on four separate plates, each plate representing one of the four process colors.

constrain To restrict the movement of a selection.

continuous-tone image An image containing gradient tones from black to white.

contrast The tonal gradation between the highlights, midtones, and shadows in an image.

crop To select part of an image and discard the unselected areas.

crop marks The marks that are printed near the edges of an image to indicate where the image is to be trimmed.

densitometer An instrument used to measure the density of printed halftones. A densitometer is used to measure the density levels on the printed calibration bars.

density The ability of an object to stop or absorb light. The less the light is reflected or transmitted by an object, the higher its density.

density range The range from the smallest highlight dot the press can print to the largest shadow dot it can print.

dithering The technique of making adjacent pixels different colors to give the illusion of a third color. Dithering can give the effect of shades of gray on a black-and-white display, or more colors on an 8-bit color display.

dot gain A defect in printing that causes dots to print larger than they should, causing darker tones or colors. Dot gain is reflected in an increase in the density of light reflected by an image.

DPI Dots per inch; a measure of resolution.

emulsion The photosensitive layer on a piece of film or paper.

fade-out rate The rate at which the paint brush and airbrush tools fade out as you paint with them to simulate an actual brush stroke.

feather edge The area along the border of a selection that is partially affected by changes you make to the selection.

fill To paint a selected area with a gray shade, a color, or a pattern.

floating selection A selection that has been moved or pasted on an image. It floats above the pixels in the underlying image until it is deselected.

fringe The pixels along the edge of a selection. The fringe pixels contain a mixture of the colors in the selection and the background color(s) around the selection.

fuzziness A parameter that controls how much anti-aliasing is applied to the edges of a selection.

gamma A measure of contrast that affects the mid-level grays (midtones) of an image.

gradient fill A fill that displays a gradual transition from the foreground to the background color. Gradient fills are made with the blend tool.

gray-scale image A single-channel image that consists of up to 256 levels of gray, with 8 bits of color information per pixel.

gray-component replacement (GCR) The removal of a mixture of cyan, magenta, and yellow, and replacement of them with black.

halftone The reproduction of a continuous-tone image, made by using a screen that breaks the image into various size dots.

highlight The lightest part of an image, represented in a halftone by the smallest dots, or the absence of dots.

histogram A graphic representation of the number of pixels with given color values. A histogram shows the breakdown of colors in an image.

HSB image An RGB image that is displayed in three channels: hue, saturation, and brightness. Only one channel is displayed at a time.

HSL image An RGB image that is displayed in three channels: hue, saturation, and luminance. Only one channel is displayed at a time.

hue Color; the main attribute of a color that distinguishes it from other colors.

indexed color image A single-channel image, with 8 bits of color information per pixel. The index is a color lookup table containing up to 256 colors.

kern To adjust the character spacing in type.

labels A printing option that prints the document and channel name on the image.

leading The line spacing for type measured from baseline to baseline of the lines of text.

linear fill A fill that is projected from one point to another in a straight line.

lpi Lines per inch; a measure of resolution.

luminance Lightness; the highest of the individual RGB values plus the lowest of the individual RGB values, divided by two; a component of an HSL image.

luminosity A color parameter that measures the brightness of color.

Luminosity is expressed as a value computed as the weighted average of the pixel's individual RGB values, expressed as a percentage (.30 x red + .59 x green + .11 x blue).

midtone Tonal value of a dot; located approximately halfway between the highlight value and the shadow value.

moire pattern An undesirable pattern in color printing, resulting from incorrect screen angles of overprinting halftones. Moire patterns can be minimized with the use of proper screen angles.

multichannel image Any image that has more than one channel.

noise In an image, pixels with randomly distributed color values.

pattern A selection that repeats in tiles to form a regular design.

pixel A single dot on a computer display or in a digital image.

plug-in module Software developed by a third-party vendor in conjunction with Adobe Systems that lets you use a function that is not available in the standard Adobe Photoshop application.

process color The four color pigments—cyan, magenta, yellow, and black—used in color printing.

1/4 tone Tonal value of a dot, located approximately halfway between highlight and midtone.

radial fill A fill that is projected from a center point outward in all directions.

random access memory (RAM) The part of the computer's memory that stores information temporarily while you're working on it.

registration marks (bull's-eyes) Marks that appear on a printed image, generally for CMYK color separations, to help you align the various printed plates.

repeat rate The rate at which paint is deposited on an image by the painting and editing tools when the mouse is stationary.

resample To change the resolution of an image. Resampling down discards pixel information in an image; resampling up adds pixel information through interpolation.

resize To change an image's size while maintaining its resolution.

resolution The number of pixels per inch in an image, or the number of dots per inch used by an output device. Resolution can also refer to the number of bits per pixel.

RGB image A three-channel image containing a red, green, and blue channel.

saturation The amount of gray in a color. More gray in a color means lower saturation; less gray in a color means higher saturation.

scanned image The image that results when a photograph, slide, paper image, or other two- or three-dimensional image is converted into a digital image.

scanner An electronic device that digitizes and converts photographs, slides, paper images, or other two-dimensional images into bitmapped images. A video camera is a scanner that converts three-dimensional objects into digital, bitmapped images.

screen angles The angles at which the halftone screens are placed in relation to one another.

screen frequency The density of dots on the halftone screen, commonly measured in lines per inch.

shadow The darkest part of an image, represented in a halftone by the largest dots.

spacing The distance between the pixels that are affected by each painting and editing tool.

star targets The printed pinwheels, used primarily in printing color separations, to align the different plates, and measure dot doubling, grain, and slurring during printing.

3/4 tone Tonal value of a dot, located approximately halfway between midtone and shadow.

tolerance A parameter of the magic wand and paint bucket tools that specifies the color range of the pixels to be selected.

toolbox The set of tools normally displayed to the left of an image. The toolbox is a floating palette that you can move or hide.

trap An overlap that prevents gaps from appearing along the edges of an object in a separated image, due to slight misalignment or movement of the separations on-press.

undercolor removal (UCR) The technique of reducing the cyan, magenta, and yellow inks from the darkest neutral shadow areas in an image, and replacing them with black.

virtual memory The memory space that is separate from the main memory (physical random access memory), such as hard disk space. Virtual memory allows you to work on large documents without requiring you to have large amounts of RAM.

zoom To magnify or reduce your view of the current document.

Index

B

D

N

O

U